John
Steinbeck's
Fiction

John Steinbeck's Fiction

THE AESTHETICS OF THE ROAD TAKEN

by John H. Timmerman

UNIVERSITY OF OKLAHOMA PRESS : NORMAN AND LONDON

Library of Congress Cataloging-in-Publication Data

Timmerman, John H.
  John Steinbeck's fiction.

  Bibliography: p. 297
  Includes index.
  1. Steinbeck, John, 1902–1968—Criticism and interpretation.
I. Title
PS3537.T3234Z928   1986   813'.52   86–40084
ISBN 0–8061–1998–5 (alk. paper)

To John J. and Carolyn Jane Timmerman

Contents

Preface

I shall be telling this with a sigh
Somewhere ages and ages hence:
Two roads diverged in a wood, and I—
I took the one less travelled by,
And that has made all the difference.

—Robert Frost

FROM THE START, whether that start is dated from the stories he wrote in high school and sent out to magazines under a false name and without a return address, or from pieces scratched out in his room at Stanford in lieu of attending classes, John Steinbeck had a clear vision of the literary road he wanted to take. Although it had curious dog-legs, detours, and potholes over the course of his career, he followed it with singular determination. He experienced many distractions, as if lured here and there by artistic experiments and innovations. Yet there remains a hard core of purpose and direction in his writing; certain fundamental artistic beliefs and techniques undergird everything he wrote.

The aim of this book is twofold: first, to consider Steinbeck's artistic premises and guiding beliefs, and, second, to appraise the artistic product in the light of those beliefs and according to aesthetic standards for excellence.

Along his own personal road Steinbeck had close friends who affected him profoundly, and whose friendship he acknowledged with gratitude. It would be remiss for me to do less in this work. To Cheryl Heideman, Alma Walhout, and Barb De Vos, whose skills with typewriters, word processors, and other electronic mysteries are beyond me, go my thanks. To James Vanden Bosch and Gorden Bordewyk for reading portions of this manuscript, I give much deserved credit. To Edward E. Ericson, whose scholarship I prize as much as his friendship, I give thanks for his unfailing support. To Calvin College for a generous sabbatical, to the Calvin Alumni Association for a research grant, and to Stanford University Libraries for their expert assistance and priceless resources, all things without which scholarship would not exist, go my thanks. And finally, to John J. and Carolyn Jane Timmerman, to whom this book is dedicated, thanks again.

JOHN H. TIMMERMAN

Grand Rapids, Michigan

Acknowledgments

In the writing of this book, I had occasion to meet and correspond with many Steinbeck scholars. It has been a pleasure to make their acquaintance, and a general note of gratitude is extended to all those to whom I wrote and who, without exception, extended ideas and encouragement beyond my expectation. A special notes goes to Tetsumaro Hayashi and Jackson J. Benson. In the footnotes and bibliography traditional acknowledgment is given for scholarly resources. If I have overlooked some there or in the preface, I ask forgiveness. Special permissions requested and received to quote passages from works by and about Steinbeck include the following:

From unpublished letters of John Steinbeck. Copyright © 1986 by Elaine A. Steinbeck. By permission of McIntosh and Otis, Inc.

From *Cup of Gold*, by John Steinbeck. Copyright 1929, renewed © 1957 by John Steinbeck.*

From *The Pastures of Heaven*, by John Steinbeck. Copyright 1932, renewed © 1960 by John Steinbeck.

From *To A God Unknown*, by John Steinbeck. Copyright 1933, renewed © 1961 by John Steinbeck.*

From *Tortilla Flat*, by John Steinbeck. Copyright 1947 by John Steinbeck, renewed © 1973 by Elaine Steinbeck, John Steinbeck IV, and Thom Steinbeck.*

From *Cannery Row*, by John Steinbeck. Copyright 1945 by John Steinbeck, renewed © 1973 by Elaine Steinbeck, John Steinbeck IV, and Thom Steinbeck.*

From *Sweet Thursday*, by John Steinbeck. Copyright 1954, renewed © 1982 by Elaine Steinbeck, John Steinbeck IV, and Thom Steinbeck.*

From *Of Mice and Men*, by John Steinbeck. Copyright 1937, renewed © 1965 by John Steinbeck.*

From *In Dubious Battle*, by John Steinbeck. Copyright 1936, renewed © 1964 by John Steinbeck.*

From *The Wide World of John Steinbeck*, by Peter Lisca. Copyright © 1958 by Rutgers, The State University.

From "John Steinbeck and Farm Labor Unionization: The Background of *In Dubious Battle*," Benson, Jackson J. and Anne Loftis, in *American Literature* 52 (May 1980), pp. 194–223. Copyright © 1980 Duke University Press.

From *The True Adventures of John Steinbeck, Writer*, by Jackson J. Benson. Copyright © 1984 by Jackson J. Benson.*

*Reprinted by permission of Viking Penguin, Inc.

Abbreviations

FOR THE READER'S EASE of reference, all quotations from the primary sources of Steinbeck's work are noted with page numbers parenthetically or in brackets in the text. If the preferred first edition is readily available, I have used that edition. In some instances, however, the first editions are so rare that it is more reasonable to use the far more accessible Penguin editions. Listed in chronological order of original publication and with abbreviations used in the text, editions used for this study are as follows:

COG   *Cup of Gold* (New York: Penguin Books, 1976).

PH   *The Pastures of Heaven* (New York: Penguin Books, 1982).

TGU   *To a God Unknown* (New York: Penguin Books, 1976).

TF   *Tortilla Flat* (New York: Covici-Friede, 1935; the later Random House-Modern Library edition retains the same pagination).

IDB   *In Dubious Battle* (New York: Penguin Books, 1979).

OMM   *Of Mice and Men* (New York: Covici-Friede, 1937).

TRP   *The Red Pony* (New York: Viking Press, 1959; reissue of the 1945 illustrated edition).

LV   *The Long Valley* (New York: P. F. Collier & Son, 1938; the 1956 Viking Press-Compass edition retains the same pagination).

TGOW   *The Grapes of Wrath* (New York: Viking Press, 1939; the later Viking Critical Edition, ed. Peter Lisca, retains the same pagination).

TMID *The Moon Is Down* (New York: Viking Press, 1942).

CR *Cannery Row* (New York: Viking Press, 1945).

TWB *The Wayward Bus* (New York: Viking Press, 1947).

TP *The Pearl* (New York: Viking Press, 1957).

BB *Burning Bright* (New York: Viking Press, 1950).

LSC *The Log from the Sea of Cortez* (New York: Viking Press, 1951; contains the profile "About Ed Ricketts").

EOE *East of Eden* (New York: Viking Press, 1952).

ST *Sweet Thursday* (New York: Viking Press, 1954).

The Short Reign of Pippin IV: A Fabrication (New York: Viking Press, 1957).

WOD *The Winter of Our Discontent* (New York: Viking Press, 1961).

TWC *Travels with Charley in Search of America* (New York: Viking Press, 1962).

JN *Journal of a Novel: The* East of Eden *Letters* (New York: Viking Press, 1969).

LL *Steinbeck: A Life in Letters,* ed. Elaine Steinbeck and Robert Wallsten (New York: Viking Press, 1975).

John
Steinbeck's
Fiction

1

Steinbeck as Literary Artist

WHILE WORKING ON one of the several versions of *To a God Unknown* in late 1929, John Steinbeck wrote in a letter to A. Grove Day: "It is an awful lot of work to write a novel. . . . I have been working on the present one nearly a year and have not completed it" (*LL*, p. 15). A prolific and remarkably candid letter writer all of his life, Steinbeck also noted that he and Carl Wilhelmson, with whom he was living in San Francisco, "take our efforts to write with great seriousness" (*LL*, p. 15).[1] Although he was to gain a sure control over his fictional craft during a career of nearly forty years, these two statements charted a course for Steinbeck's literary career: writing is work, and work to be taken most seriously.

One might trace the origins of Steinbeck's career to his creating of stories for his sister Mary during their childhood, to his reading of Malory at age nine and his lifelong fascination with the *Morte D'Arthur*, to his telling ghost stories to gain some popularity with and acceptance by his boyhood companions, or to his singularly erratic career at Stanford University, where he studiously ignored academic work in favor of learning the craft of a writer. Whatever the sources, the urge was there, directing, goading, inciting. Years later Frank Fenton recalled the young Steinbeck: "In all my life," said Fenton, "I've never known anyone else to concentrate so deeply on writing or work so hard at writing as John. But writing was an instinct with him, like breathing."[2]

Fenton uses the appropriate word: *instinct*. Writing somehow lived in Steinbeck; it was his essential nature to

3

be a storyteller. It is difficult, and more than a bit dangerous, to try to neatly categorize Steinbeck's writing beliefs
because, in a very real sense, he had few carefully articulated beliefs. He wrote hard and carefully, and he seldom
bothered to explain the why and how of his writing. "Read
the work," he might have said; "let that suffice." Yet it is
clear that certain principles guided Steinbeck's artistry and
that the variations in different works were more resonances
of a basic aim than dramatically different beliefs. The danger seems to be one of artificially imposing some aesthetic
grid on Steinbeck. Despite the risk, however, it is possible
to come to a clear understanding of the essential artistic beliefs that guided his work.

The manifold intention of this study is to recognize the
essential artistic views of the author, his developing conception of humankind in the work, and his aesthetic use of
biblical allusion. With those premises established, one may
better understand the major themes and structures of the
fiction and how they develop from work to work. These
themes are remarkably unified over the course of Steinbeck's career. In the earlier work he establishes a major dialectic between individual dreams and the pressures of society to conform those dreams to the group organism. This
tension between the individual and the group never relaxes. But in the later fiction the tension is complicated by
Steinbeck's growing moral vision as he ponders whether
the individual can not only survive social pressure to conform, not only retain individual dreams and the free search
for their fulfillment, but actually transform society in the
process.

THE ARTIST'S CRAFT

With the exception of his clear and forthright Nobel Prize
Address, which Steinbeck claimed to have rewritten at
least twenty times, one must rely on extrapolation from
letters and random statements in fictional works to reconstruct Steinbeck's artistic beliefs. While each of these will

be developed further in analysis of the major works, three essential artistic premises that govern the making of the work warrant attention here: storytelling, realism, and "hooptedoodle."

Steinbeck was not unlike many modern authors in his disdain for criticism. His letters are punctuated with it, like hard exclamation marks. In his early career this seemed to stem from his own general depression over his work; indeed, the letters of the late twenties and early thirties form a litany of despair but also convey the realistic belief that he was serving his apprenticeship and that on about the fifth novel, as was the case, he would hit his stride as a literary craftsman. Many of his views on criticism can be summarized in his witty article in the *Saturday Review*, "Critics—from a Writer's Viewpoint,"[3] but they are even more pointed in his letter to Pascal Covici in January, 1945: "It is interesting to me, Pat, that no critic has discovered the reason for these little chapters in C. R. You would have known. Nearly all lay readers know. Only critics don't. Are they somehow the lowest common denominator? . . . Far from being the sharpest readers, they are the dullest."[4] The irritation remained in his Nobel Prize Acceptance Speech: "Literature was not promulgated by a pale and emasculated critical priesthood singing their litanies in empty churches—nor is it a game for the cloistered elect, the tinhorn mendicants of low-calorie despair." As one who was burned often by the critics' ire, Steinbeck was never reluctant to point out that critics were the priesthood to the fiction writer's divinity. But what constitutes the fiction writer's divinity? What sets him apart from the critics? For Steinbeck it is the writer's ability to tell a story.

The primary impetus of Steinbeck's fiction was always to tell the story—before the crafting, before the technique, form, or rhythm of the artistry. A born storyteller with an intuitive sense of character and plot, Steinbeck would often experience difficulties in writing when his primary effort became one of discoursing philosophically rather than allowing the philosophical or religious views to emerge naturally through story or plot. Thomas Kiernan provides an accurate assessment of this difficulty in an early stage of Steinbeck's career:

"Contrive" is the operative word for Steinbeck's conceptual approach to writing during this period. To be sure, he felt very strongly the storytelling impulse in himself. This impulse, plus the potential for ego gratification he saw in being a writer, were clearly the origins of his literary ambition. But Steinbeck at this time was also a budding philosopher, a thinker. Impelled by the religious conflict that simmered in his mind, the residue of his early religious upbringing versus his later independent perceptions of divinity, and by the countless moral and social paradoxes he observed in life, he was in the midst of making a number of important philosophical self-discoveries that would eventually become the dynamo of his artistic energy and the benchmark of his literary vision. His primary intellectual conception of writing, then—as opposed to his emotional and intuitive conception of it—was as a vehicle to advance the philosophical "truths" he was in the process of discovering. To use storytelling or the device of fiction to advance his views meant in his inexperienced mind the contriving of stories to serve the larger purpose of his philosophical insights. The situations and characters he tried to invent in his ongoing writing efforts were meant to serve mainly, if not exclusively, as frames for his philosophical canvases. It had not yet occurred to him that whatever philosophical truths he had to impart would be better served by allowing them to filter through his fictional situations and characters.[5]

At his best Steinbeck seemed to sense the story emerging from some primitive source within him, almost as if the story took control over him. As he plotted his trip in Rocinante for what would become *Travels with Charley*, Steinbeck wrote Pascal Covici, "I nearly always write—just as I nearly always breathe," playfully adding, "I haven't written because I have been writing. Now there's a sentence that could only be said in English" (*LL*, pp. 671–72).

In a sense Steinbeck did very much perceive himself as akin to the Platonic scribe possessed by a divine mania, except that in his case the mania was the telling of a story and not, as Plato believed, the inculcating of moral truths at the behest of the gods. Stories welled up in Steinbeck's mind, and his task as a writer was to transcribe and record them. Steinbeck, however, was much more than Plato's severely limited scribe. He believed that his stories had to be arranged in such a way as to provide a permanent record and to live on in the reader's mind.

Steinbeck's short narrative "The Snake" is a fascinating testament to this. Based on an actual event at Ed Ricketts' lab, the incident is recorded in journalistic form in Steinbeck's memoir, "About Ed Ricketts," written after Ricketts' death in 1948 and appearing as a preface to *The Log from the Sea of Cortez* in the 1951 edition. In "About Ed Ricketts," Steinbeck records the incident tersely and objectively: "Ed put the rat in the cage. The snake struck and killed it and then unhinged its jaws preparatory to swallowing it. The frightening thing was that the woman, who had watched the process closely, moved her jaws and stretched her mouth just as the snake was doing" (*LSC*, p. xxiii). Here the recorder "sees" and reports the action of the woman.

In Steinbeck's story, however, the focus is on the character of Dr. Phillips and his reaction to the woman. As the story develops, the reader perceives Dr. Phillips becoming increasingly unnerved by the woman's demands; Phillips wonders, as does the reader, how much of a kinship exists between the woman and the snake. Instead of documentary, we have questioning. When it comes time for the crucial event of the feeding, we find this: "Dr. Phillips put his will against his head to keep it from turning toward the woman. He thought, 'If she's opening her mouth, I'll be sick. I'll be afraid.' He succeeded in keeping his eyes away" (*LV*, pp. 84–85). The crucial scene is handled by implication, the effect of which is to let the reader imagine and decide. This example reflects one of Steinbeck's key intentions—the attempt to involve the reader in the story and to make the story live in the reader.

In several letters Steinbeck overtly stated this intention. While writing *The Red Pony,* which he described as "a very simple story about a boy who gets a colt pony and the pony gets distemper," Steinbeck emphasized that "the whole thing is as simply told as though it came out of the boy's mind although there is no going into the boy's mind. It is an attempt to make the reader create the boy's mind for himself" (*LL,* p. 71).[6] Steinbeck believed, as Thomas Kiernan paraphrases him, that "people only learn about themselves by experiencing themselves. The only effective revelation was self-revelation. Great fiction provided people with the opportunity to experience themselves through their identification with characters and events."[7]

On January 28, 1963, Steinbeck wrote a long, probing letter to Pascal Covici in which, more thoroughly than anywhere else, he set forth his beliefs about fiction, for both his own work and that of his contemporaries. One of his irritations with modern fiction was its tendency to project hard, objective surfaces of events that allow the reader little room for penetration and living in the work. An opponent of journalistic realism, the mere reporting of events, Steinbeck insisted that invitations be extended to the reader through implication, suggestion, symbolism. "Ideally," he wrote, "fiction takes on a greater reality in [the] mind of the reader than nonfiction. Participation in Crime and Punishment has a greater reality to most people than anything that has or is likely to happen to them."[8]

The fictional world, Steinbeck claims, can have a greater reality for the reader than anything he might experience in his own world. In a sense this is puzzling, for Steinbeck has been commonly considered a "realist." In fact, some criticism slights him as being little more than a voluminous journalist.[9] Thus an understanding of Steinbeck's realism is crucial. While it is true that much of Steinbeck's fiction was nurtured by firsthand experience, that experience is transmuted by the artist into a thematic or spiritual experience common to humankind. Realistic in origin, by artistry Steinbeck's storytelling approaches the realism of the human spirit in much the same way, for example, that Faulkner's fiction does—by exploring the enduring questions of the nature of humanity, of good and evil, of tragedy and triumph. "A novelist," Steinbeck wrote to Elizabeth Otis and Chase Horton, "not only puts down a story but he is the story. He is each one of the characters in a greater or a less degree. And because he is usually a moral man in intention and honest in his approach, he sets things down as truly as he can" (*LL*, pp. 552–53). The novelist begins with the real event but arranges that event: "Sometimes there is a flash of fire, sometimes a moody dream, sometimes an anger. For a novelist is a rearranger of nature so that it makes an understandable pattern, and a novelist is also a teacher, but a novelist is primarily a man and subject to all of man's faults and virtues, fears and braveries" (*LL*, p. 554).[10]

In a discussion of Ed Ricketts' scientific view of life, Thomas Kiernan extrapolates from Ricketts' view of fiction—a view which one must assume influenced Steinbeck: "A good writer must tell lies, Ricketts concluded, but only to gain his reader's attention. Once he had his attention, he must then put together the evidence—through the untainted thoughts and actions of his characters—that will lead the reader to accept the inescapable truths of the human condition, and thus the truth about himself. The good writer must be 'a scientist of the imagination.'"[11] The goal of this "science of the imagination" is to open doors of discovery in the reader's mind. "It is the duty of the writer," Steinbeck wrote while working on *East of Eden*, "to lift up, to extend, to encourage" (*JN*, p. 115). It is fair to call Steinbeck a realist, but he is a realist of the human spirit, fully and convincingly disclosing to readers their own essential nature.

Steinbeck believed, moreover, that prose should be rendered with accuracy, vitality, and interest. A reflection in *The Log from the Sea of Cortez* applies to fiction as well as to scientific prose:

There is a curious idea among unscientific men that in scientific writing there is a common plateau of perfectionism. Nothing could be more untrue. . . . In some reports it is impossible, because of inept expression, to relate the descriptions to the living animals. . . . It is usually found that only the little stuffy men object to what is called "popularization," by which they mean writing with a clarity understandable to one not familiar with the tricks and codes of the cult. We have not known a single great scientist who could not discourse freely and interestingly with a child. Can it be that the haters of clarity have nothing to say, have observed nothing, have no clear picture of even their own fields? A dull man seems to be a dull man no matter what his field, and of course it is the right of a dull scientist to protect himself with feathers and robes, emblems and degrees, as do other dull men who are potentates and grand imperial rulers of lodges of dull men. [P. 73]

Surprisingly, while Steinbeck's work has attracted considerable structural analysis, little sustained scrutiny has been given to his rhetorical technique, a study as rich and revealing as any other for unlocking the author's method and meaning. Such study as there is has focused largely on *The Grapes of Wrath*, a novel so rich, startling, and new on the American literary scene of the thirties and forties as to attract the attention of nearly everyone.[12] In a brief discussion of *The Pearl*, however, John M. Nagle suggests that such rhetorical analysis can be productively applied to other works as well. Nagle considers particularly the rhetoric of the scene where Coyotito is bitten by the scorpion. After an analysis of Steinbeck's use of the expletive phrase "it was" to attract and direct the reader's attention, Nagle continues:

Steinbeck is then ready to introduce the dreadful scorpion which will strike Kino's son, and, as an author who is extremely sensitive to the effects of language, he does so in a masterful sentence. Kino and Juana freeze in their positions, and Steinbeck writes: "Down the rope that hung the baby's box from the roof support a scorpion moved slowly." Because unpunctuated, the sentence reads smoothly from beginning to end. Suspense is created, for Steinbeck saves the scorpion for the end of the sentence. The alliterative *s* sounds near the end of the sentence echo and draw out the continuous movement of the scorpion, and beginning the sentence with the adverb *down* creates an inescapable sense of downness. Finally, because of Steinbeck's deliberate word order, the sentence has a rhythm which requires the reader to move just as *slowly* through the sentence as does the scorpion down the rope.[13]

The value of Nagle's brief study lies in his demonstration that, while Steinbeck's excellence as storyteller has been generally noted, insufficient attention has been paid to the way he gets the words out to tell the story.

In his own stylistic technique Steinbeck strove for a clipped, accurate prose. Like Ernest Hemingway (whom Steinbeck professed to have read little and comparisons with whom he disliked) Steinbeck believed that fictional prose should not be a course in "interior decoration." His own prose is generally marked by a spare, yeomanlike rhetoric that relies on active verbs and imagery rather than ornamentation in the pattern of James, for example.

Steinbeck's beliefs about style were remarkably consistent throughout his career. In a letter to A. Grove Day dated December, 1929, Steinbeck distinguished between the manners of the literary marketplace and the prose that he wanted to write: "I have not lost the love for sound nor for pictures. Only I have tried to throw out the words that do not say anything" (*LL*, p. 19). More than twenty years later, while preparing to write *East of Eden*, he made note of his method and seemed to echo the earlier letter: "The form will not be startling, the writing will be spare and lean" (*JN*, p. 3). And in the process of writing the novel, he frequently reminded himself of his rule: "Oh! but watch for terseness. Don't let it ever be adjectivally descriptive. I must hold description to an absolute minimum, must hold my story and all of its strands together" (*JN*, p. 4). The general portrait that emerges is one of a writer who was conscientious and remarkably consistent in exercising his craft. As he plotted Adam's move to Salinas and Moss Landing in *East of Eden*, Steinbeck wrote to Covici: "I don't know why writers are never given credit for knowing their craft. Years after I have finished a book, someone discovers my design and ascribes it either to a theft or an accident" (*JN*, p. 134).

Steinbeck's essentially forthright style is frequently modulated by passages of startling individual beauty and lyricism. "I like a chapter to have design of tone," Steinbeck wrote, "as well as of form" (*JN*, p. 25). Such "tone pieces" are best described by the self-appointed critic of Steinbeck's work, the irrepressible Mack of *Sweet Thursday*, who, in a moment of candor, confesses with appropriate self-derogation, "I guess I'm just a critic." What he says as critic in the prologue to *Sweet Thursday* is, however, vintage Steinbeck: such advice as giving titles to chapters since "sometimes maybe I want to go back, and chapter five don't mean nothing to me"; using a substantial amount of dialogue in a book; and giving attention to such physical details as "how it smells and maybe how it looks, and maybe how a guy feels about it—but not too much of that."

As Whitey No. 2 compliments Mack, "You sure are a critic. . . . I never give you credit before," Mack concludes: "Sometimes I want a book to break loose with a bunch of hooptedoodle. The guy's writing it, give him a chance to do a little hooptedoodle. Spin up some pretty words maybe, or sing a little song with language. That's nice. But I wish it was set aside so I don't have to read it. I don't want hooptedoodle to get mixed up in the story." Hooptedoodle retains a significant place in Steinbeck's writing, providing a break from realistic narrative so that the author may indulge in rhetorical whimsy. Hooptedoodle may contribute to a symbolic pattern that enriches the narrative, as, for example, in the intercalary chapters of *The Grapes of Wrath*. These interchapters are the clearest example of hooptedoodle; with their aesthetic richness they provide a significant pattern corresponding to the narrative unfolding of the plot. *East of Eden* has similarly crafted interchapters that provide historical background or physical description. Either work would survive without hooptedoodle; both are richer by virtue of having it.

In some instances, however, hooptedoodle is simply indulgence of the author's fancy and has virtually nothing to do with the plot, as in the magnificent butterfly story recorded in chapter 38 of *Sweet Thursday*, "Hooptedoodle (2), or The Pacific Grove Butterfly Festival." While working on *East of Eden*, Steinbeck recognized his tendency toward stylistic exuberance in a letter to Covici: "Since you told me what the girl said about wanting to get on with the story and not stop for comment, I have thought a good deal about that. It is going to be one of the most constant criticisms of this book" (*JN*, p. 65).

It is an error, however, to make as narrow a distinction as Mack does; Steinbeck's prose is not simply straightforward telling interspersed here and there with lyrical passages. The prose abounds with literary devices. While the personification and metonymy of the tractor in *The Grapes of Wrath* may attract notice by its deliberate isolation, patterns of imagery interweave through all of Steinbeck's works so subtly as to escape casual notice. For example, Steinbeck uses imagery reminiscent of Flannery O'Connor to set the character of Jim Casy in *The Grapes of Wrath:* "It was a long head, bony, tight of skin, and set on a neck as stringy and muscular as a celery stalk." Steinbeck particularly uses earth, animal, and vegetable imagery to identify his characters, either as complementary to or ironically contrasting with the nature of the character. For example, physically, Samuel Hamilton seems of a piece with his sprawling, arid land, but his human spirit is a well of living water that refreshes others. Cathy Ames, on the other hand, is every bit the vicious, predatory animal that her descriptive imagery suggests.

Another notable stylistic trait is the adapting of rhetorical pacing to character or event. Perhaps Steinbeck's rhetorical skill is frequently overlooked simply because it is expertly paced to the narrative event. A syntactical analysis of almost any section of prose reveals this skill. Consider, for example, the following passage from *Cannery Row:*

Mack and the boys, too spinning in their orbits. They are the
Virtues, the Graces, the Beauties of the hurried mangled craziness of Monterey and the cosmic Monterey where men in fear
and hunger destroy their stomachs in the fight to secure certain
food, where men hungering for love destroy everything lovable
about them. Mack and the boys are the Beauties, the Virtues,
the Graces. In the world ruled by tigers with ulcers, rutted by
strictured bulls, scavenged by blind jackals, Mack and the boys
dine delicately with the tigers, fondle the frantic heifers, and
wrap up the crumbs to feed the sea gulls of Cannery Row. [*CR*,
pp. 14–15]

This is not, contrary to Mack, simply hooptedoodle; rather,
it defines and controls character, clearly fulfilling Steinbeck's belief that "technique should grow out of theme—
not dictate" (*LL*, p. 521). But observe how this occurs rhetorically. The paragraph begins with a simple fragment that
the rest of the paragraph will elaborate. The second sentence contains an independent clause that is suddenly complicated by a pair of parallel dependent clauses modifying
the compound objects of a prepositional phrase that, in
turn, modifies a prepositional phrase: "of the hurried
mangled craziness of Monterey and the cosmic Monterey."
The first parallel clause contains two parallel prepositional
phrases; the second, two parallel participles. While it takes
many words to describe the rhetorical action, the effect
stylistically is one of mellifluous fluidity appropriate to a
description of "the Virtues, the Graces, the Beauties." The
third sentence is a simple declarative structure. But the
fourth sentence, with its cumulative structure that rhetori-
cian Francis Christensen identifies as one of the most
powerful is complex without the appearance of being so.[14]
In syntactical terms the sentence begins with an adverbial
prepositional phrase whose object is qualified by three parallel participles, thereby accumulating rhetorical force, and
develops three parallel verbs that, in turn, develop the
substantive. By use of parallel subordinate clauses and
phrases, Steinbeck avoids the appearance of excessive

ornamentation while providing fluid syntactical development. The net effect is prose that is lean, hard, and
stripped to the bone, while remaining remarkably graceful
and complex.

Although Steinbeck loved it deeply, writing was nonetheless a "task" for him, a life work and calling. Even in the
simple mechanics of the work he made careful preparations
and expended diligent effort. After experimenting with a
typewriter in the early years, he wrote all his manuscripts
in his tight, even longhand—sometimes in ink, as when
he ran across a bonanza ink sale at Holman's and stocked
enough bottles to last several years—but most often in
pencil; he went through pencils by the gross, sharpening
several dozen in the morning with his electric sharpener.
When he was composing *East of Eden,* he began spraying
the pages with a clear spray so that the writing would not
smudge under Covici's handling. He plotted each day's writing carefully, testing dialogue in his mind before writing it.
His early statement that "three hours of writing require
twenty hours of preparation" (*LL,* p. 64) held true for much
of his life. He was fussy about writing surfaces. When
Covici had a draftsman's desk made for him, he liked the
broad surface but despaired of getting it painted the right
color so that the light would not reflect in his eyes. The
light itself was carefully chosen for its intensity and hue.
The care he took in the mechanics corresponds to the care
he took in the craftsmanship.

THE ARTIST'S VIEW OF HUMANITY: SUPERNATURAL
NATURALISM

"Having taken God-like power," Steinbeck announced in
his Nobel Address, "we must seek in ourselves for the responsibility and the wisdom we once prayed some deity
might have. Man himself has become our greatest hazard
and our only hope." Steinbeck's fictional world is incontro-
vertibly a human-centered world from which God has departed, like the dissipation of other ancient myths. Rem-

nants remain, but the vitality is gone. While he did not deny the existence of God and the psychological profundity of the myth that endures, the deity in Steinbeck's conception is so impossibly remote as to have no practical effect on the affairs of humanity. As an author his concern was always first with those human affairs. Three distinct parts of Steinbeck's thinking about human nature may be observed: the tension between teleological and non-teleological thinking that accounts for individual action, the Group Man theory that accounts for the actions of social units, and the "supernatural naturalism" that accounts for human relation with the divine.

Teleological and Non-Teleological Thinking

An inveterate and restless wanderer all of his life, Steinbeck wrote several books based exclusively on his travel, including *The Sea of Cortez, Travels with Charley,* and *A Russian Journal.* Of them, *The Sea of Cortez* is perhaps the best, although often overlooked and seldom carefully studied in Steinbeck's canon. In tone and style the work possesses an excellence that merits closer critical attention. Paced to the leisurely chug of the *Western Flyer,* pausing often to examine fine details of marine life, opening surprises to the reader through powerful imagery and vigorous rhetoric, *The Sea of Cortez* maintains a steadfast thematic course in its application of lessons from marine biology to life itself. It is a minor classic of travel literature, and one unfortunately neglected.

In a jointly written book like *The Sea of Cortez* there is always some dispute over who wrote what. When Pascal Covici suggested to Steinbeck that he be listed as author of the narrative and Ricketts of the catalogue, Steinbeck, in the words of Jackson J. Benson, "was furious" and forbade the procedure.[15] Steinbeck credited Ricketts with much of the idea for chapter 14, the so-called Easter sermon chapter on non-teleological thinking. Clearly, however, Steinbeck felt no reluctance to claim the ideas as consonant with his own thinking. Since Steinbeck worked with both his own and Ricketts' journals of the trip while writing the book, it is best, as Benson suggests, "to view the collaboration, as Steinbeck originally intended, as seamless."[16] Yet it was not entirely so; Peter Lisca details the way Steinbeck worked with the journals in *John Steinbeck: Nature and Myth* and attributes the whole of the Easter Sunday sermon to an unpublished essay of Ricketts.[17]

The Sea of Cortez bears significance for a critical appreciation of Steinbeck, however, for in it he develops his most consistent and careful statement on the nature of humanity, albeit often stated in short reflections stirred by the day's activities on scientific collections. This pattern, in which science provides a basis for speculation about human nature, is deliberate, for that is also the thematic basis of the speculations: life is very much like the marine specimens observed.

The first lesson, however, has to do with one's approach to marine biology or the scientific method itself, for this too parallels one's view of humankind. Steinbeck laments a scientific approach through isolation and statistics, using as his example one specimen they studied early in the trip:

The Mexican sierra has "XVII-15-IX" spines in the dorsal fin. These can easily be counted. But if the sierra strikes hard on the line so that our hands are burned, if the fish sounds and nearly escapes and finally comes in over the rail, his colors pulsing and his tail beating the air, a whole new relational externality has come into being—an entity which is more than the sum of the fish plus the fisherman. The only way to count the spines of the sierra unaffected by this second relational reality is to sit in a laboratory, open an evil-smelling jar, remove a stiff colorless fish from formalin solution, count the spines, and write the truth "D.XVII-15-IX." There you have recorded a reality which cannot be assailed—probably the least important reality concerning either the fish or yourself. [P. 2]

Steinbeck argues that one must observe the specimen in its living reality, in its relation to other things, and in our rela-

tion to it. Ideally, the observer should become a fish and
enter into the environment. This being impossible, one can
at least be conscious of the fish in its own environment and
observe the totality of its experience: "We could see the
fish alive and swimming, feel it plunge against the lines,
drag it threshing over the rail, and even finally eat it." On
the one hand, Steinbeck notes, there are "the embalmers
of the field, the picklers who see only the preserved form
of life without any of its principle. Out of their own crusted
minds they create a world wrinkled with formaldehyde."
On the other hand, "The true biologist deals with life, with
teeming boisterous life, and learns something from it, learns
that the first rule of life is living" (p. 29).

In one sense this is simply a sophisticated application of
Wordsworth's "The Tables Turned":

> Sweet is the lore which Nature brings;
> Our meddling intellect
> Mis-shapes the beauteous forms of things:—
> We murder to dissect.

Indeed, the Romantic orientation of Steinbeck's early thinking has been carefully argued by Joseph Fontenrose:

> Steinbeck has much in common with the Romantics. He is
> usually classified as a realist or naturalist, but these are mere
> labels, and they hardly suit *To a God Unknown* and *Tortilla
> Flat*. . . . Steinbeck is an heir of the Romantic movement. The
> organic view of the world renews primitive animism at a more
> sophisticated level. To the animist, sky and earth, wind and
> storm, tree and rock are living entities. Out of animism springs
> myth and so Steinbeck's biological interpretation and his mythical
> interpretation of the human condition flow from one and the
> same source.[18]

In a more concrete sense, however, Steinbeck's view also
affected his literary method. "Cannery Row in Monterey in
California is a poem, a stink, a grating noise, a quality of
light, a tone, a habit, a nostalgia, a dream." Thus Steinbeck
begins his famous description of the bleary section of Mon-

terey. Whatever else it is, for Steinbeck it is bursting with
life; like a school of excited fish his characters swirl about
the friendly swells of their environment on the wharves
and flats of Cannery Row.

As the method of the author is linked in part to his biological views, so too is the relationship of humankind itself
to marine biology. The linking is tentative and speculative
early in the text of *The Sea of Cortez*, as if Steinbeck is testing the waters: "If we used the same smug observation on
ourselves that we do on hermit crabs we would be forced to
say, with the information at hand, 'It is one diagnostic trait
of *Homo sapiens* that groups of individuals are periodically
infected with a feverish nervousness which causes the individuals to turn on and destroy, not only his own kind, but
the works of his own kind'" (p. 17). But he goes deeper:
"Perhaps this is the same narrowing we observe in relation
to ourselves and the tide pool—a man looking at reality
brings his own limitations to the world. If he has strength
and energy of mind the tide pool stretches both ways, digs
back to electrons and leaps space into the universe and
fights out of the moment into non-conceptual time. Then
ecology has a synonym which is ALL" (p. 85). Steinbeck
speculates at one point that our sense of memory, of rhythm,
of archetype, is nothing less than the stirrings of ocean
waves and the primordial slime of our evolutionary beginning: "For the ocean, deep and black in the depths, is like
the low dark levels of our minds in which the dream symbols incubate and sometimes rise up to sight like the Old
Man of the Sea" (p. 31).[19] And again: "There is tied up to
the most primitive and powerful racial or collective instinct
a rhythm sense or 'memory' which affects everything and
which in the past was probably more potent than it is now.
It would at least be more plausible to attribute these profound effects to devastating and instinct-searing tidal influences during the formative times of the early race history of
organisms" (p. 34).

With this tenuous link between marine biology and human nature Steinbeck forms his speculation on the distinc-

tion between teleological and non-teleological thinking. This distinction between two human approaches is first suggested in chapter 10, where Steinbeck describes teleological thinking as projection—living beyond the immediate reality in an artificial world of aspirations, goals, and dreams that obscures and ultimately destroys the present moment by an act of displacement. In Steinbeck's view the teleological thinker lives in perpetual discontent in the present and instead "considers changes and cures—what 'should be' in terms of an end pattern." Steinbeck says further about teleological thinking that

it presumes the bettering of conditions, often, unfortunately, without achieving more than a most superficial understanding of those conditions. In their sometimes intolerant refusal to face facts as they are, teleological notions may substitute a fierce but ineffectual attempt to change conditions which are assumed to be undesirable, in place of the understanding—acceptance which would pave the way for a more sensible attempt at any change which might still be indicated. [Pp. 134–35]

Rather than understanding the present reality, then, teleological thinking insists upon seeing it in terms of some ideal and also insists on trying to reshape the present to somehow fit that ideal.

Non-teleological, or "is," thinking focuses on and accepts present reality and does not ask *why* this reality is the way it is or *how* it might be changed or *where* it is going. "Non-teleological thinking concerns itself primarily not with what should be, or could be, or might be, but rather with what actually 'is'—attempting at most to answer the already sufficiently difficult questions *what* or *how*, instead of *why*" (p. 135). Those who think non-teleologically "more than any other seem capable of great tenderness, of an all-embracingness which is rare otherwise" (p. 146). Non-teleological thinking sees life whole, not through narrow spectacles of specialized interest: the whole forms part of the picture only, and the infinite whole is unknowable except by *being* in it, by living into it" (p. 148).

It is easy to be sympathetic toward the heart and aim of Steinbeck's thinking, and the issue at hand never entirely escaped him throughout his long career. Essentially, he believed, humanity has two choices: either the corrosive pursuit of one's own special and egocentric aims that may, in their achievement, destroy all about one, or the effort to live life fully in the present with full appreciation of and concern for others sharing that life. In the former group we have, for example, Cathy Ames; in the latter, Samuel Hamilton. Steinbeck never lost his dislike for those who use other people as rungs on the ladder of their ambition; he never departed from his special affection for those who, like Hazel in *Sweet Thursday*, nearly lay down their lives to raise someone higher. This quality in itself, according to Jackson Benson, gives Steinbeck's fiction much of its enduring appeal:

I would suggest that his work attracts our special attention and affection because he was a lover of life, rather than a hater of life. . . . The sense that Steinbeck is a writer in tune with the rhythms of life is partly due to the fact that he was not a writer obsessed with himself. He sent his feelings outward. There is life in this very act of reaching out, and life in the very fallibility of the act. In an age that often appears to be dominated by writing which is essentially the autobiographical exploration of the writer's own morbid psyche, Steinbeck was exceptionally unautobiographical in his work.[20]

While one may be sympathetic toward Steinbeck's view and its effect on the characters of his fiction, taken on its own terms, however, there are obvious deficiencies in Steinbeck's distinction between teleological and nonteleological thinking. However suitable it may be for daydreaming under a Mexican sun on a white cove, and however well it may in part describe Steinbeck's own attitudes toward humanity, it simply does not stand up to careful philosophical analysis. The chief difficulty with the view lies in its inadequate explanation of the problem of evil. It may be sufficient to say of the sea turtle caught by the crew of the *Western Flyer* that "from gullet to anus the digestive tract was crammed with small bright-red rock-lobsters" (p. 45). For this is the natural course of the sea turtle. That is a non-teleological "is": the nature of the sea turtle is to have its intestines so crammed. But one may extrapolate from the premise. It is sufficient to say that the intestine of this person is stuffed from gullet to anus with spaghetti. But what of the person who stuffs those intestines with sleeping pills? Or injects heroin into his veins? Or cruelly mistreats a child to obtain the heroin? Is this equivalent to the sea turtle's devouring of the rock lobster?

Non-teleological thinking simply will not answer these questions, as Steinbeck clearly recognized by the time of *East of Eden*. His answer there, that Cathy was a monster, is also insufficient. The deficiency becomes clear when one applies a reflection from *The Sea of Cortez*—an example of non-teleological thinking—directly to *East of Eden*. The reflection is this:

The lies we tell about our duty and our purposes, the meaningless words of science and philosophy, are walls that topple before a bewildered little "why." Finally, we learned to know why we did these things. The animals were very beautiful. Here was life from which we borrowed life and excitement. In other words, we did these things because it was pleasant to do them. [P. 209]

We might ask, then, whether Cathy Ames gains pleasure from her malice. Why does she behave as she does? If we say that only good things give pleasure, then we have introduced the essentially teleological question of what is the good. In Steinbeck's own terms, how does he account for what he describes in *The Log* as "the sad trait of self-destruction that is our species" (p. 16)?[21]

If we observe aberration in the animal world, we classify it; if we find it in the human world we ask why. Then we try to find cause and effect and remedy. Why? Because human life has will; the very fact that one wonders about the distinction between teleological or willful thinking and non-teleological or nonwillful thinking presupposes a will capable of choosing one or the other. While it is easy, lying on that sunbaked Mexican shore on an Easter Sunday afternoon, to miss this principle, it does not do very well for dealing with life itself.

It is enlightening but not altogether surprising that Steinbeck, albeit briefly, tosses Emerson into his hodge-podge of non-teleological thinkers. Emerson's "Nature" is similar in its romantic transcendentalism to the non-teleological thinking of Steinbeck. Emerson believed that the modern age had become sterile, had lost meaning. Everything was valued for its usefulness and not for any inherent value or meaning. For Emerson, ultimate meaning is found not in things but in the mind, and "intellectual beauty" occurs best when the mind becomes attuned to the harmony of nature, the great cosmic thing which in "The American Scholar" he calls "the shadow of the soul." But Emerson was no more successful than Steinbeck in accounting for the presence of evil.

Steinbeck postulates a view that sees humanity whole, as it is, and in relation to human environment. Despite its philosophical insufficiency, the theory had a profound effect on Steinbeck's artistry, particularly in the animal and vegetable imagery that roots his characters to the earth. The close linking of humanity to the environment, and metaphorically to marine biology also set up Steinbeck's theory of the Group Man, a theory closely allied with non-teleological thinking.

The Group Man

Perhaps the first articulation of the Group Man philosophy occurs in the June 21, 1933, letter to Steinbeck's Stanford friend and lifelong confidante Carlton ("Dook" or "Duke") Sheffield. Typically, the letter is candid and sprawling, and it contains the proviso that "this is not a letter to read unless you have so much time that you just don't care. I just want to talk and there is no one to talk to" (*LL*, p. 75). In his letter Steinbeck puts forth observations based on notes he had been gathering for three years, here linked, as in *The Sea of Cortez*, to marine biology. He observes that the work of the coral building an atoll is not unlike human groups that have worked to build, for example, a Gothic spire. No one coral can build an atoll; no one person can build a Gothic spire. Steinbeck concludes: "When acting as a group, men do not partake of their ordinary natures at all." Some unique force empowers the group so that it becomes a new living organism which subsumes its "individual parts" (*LL*, p. 76). In a letter written a few days later to George Albee, Steinbeck reiterates the theme, here introducing the term "Phalanx" to describe this group action. Again, the premise is biological:

A further arrangement of cells and a very complex one may make a unit which we call a man. That has been our final unit. But there have been mysterious things which could not be explained if man is the final unit. He also arranges himself into larger units, which I have called the phalanx. The phalanx has its own memory—memory of the great tides when the moon was close, memory of starvations when the food of the world was exhausted. . . . And the phalanx has emotions of which the unit man is incapable. Emotions of destruction, of war, of migration, of hatred of fear. . . . You have heard about the trickiness of the MOB. Mob is simply a phalanx, but if you try to judge a mob nature by the nature of its men units, you will fail as surely as if you tried to understand a man by studying one of his cells. [*LL*, pp. 79–80]

The idea of an evolutionary memory is echoed in *The Log* (pp. 31–34). But this letter also contains the germ of *In Dubious Battle* as Steinbeck describes "the trickiness of the MOB," and, in fact, he concludes the letter by announcing his intention to write a novel with this as its theme. Ed Ricketts, he adds in the letter to Albee, had "dug up all the scientific material." Thus, the trip recorded in *The Sea of Cortez*, taken during March and April, 1940, and *In Dubious Battle*, probably started in late 1933 and published in 1936, share their roots in Steinbeck's work in marine biology and his intimate association with Ricketts.

The Group Man theory is the focus of *In Dubious Battle*, usually under Doc Burton's careful questioning of the radical leader Mac (Ed Ricketts served as prototype for Burton). Doc reflects: "'A man in a group isn't himself at all, he's a cell in an organism that isn't like him any more than the cells in your body are like you' (*IDB*, 144–45). But Doc, whom Mac describes as too far left to be a Communist, remains skeptical of the Group Man. Why? What is left out? Steinbeck himself had discovered the answer in the process of writing *In Dubious Battle*, and it is the same thing that non-teleological thinking, paradoxically, strives for: tenderness and compassion for other individuals. Doc Burton has these qualities; Mac and later Jim Nolan totally lack them. "'We can't think about the hurts of one man. It's necessary, Doc,'" says Mac at one point. Doc replies: "'I wasn't questioning your motives, nor your ends. I was just sorry for the poor old man. His self-respect is down. That's a bitter thing to him, don't you think so, Mac?'" To which Mac replies sharply: "'I can't take time to think about the feelings of one man. I'm too busy with big bunches of men'" (*IDB*, 201).

It is doubtful whether Steinbeck was ever completely satisfied with his Group Man theory. It was an exciting theory, new and challenging, and its analogy to marine biology certainly attracted him. Moreover, it contained a degree of truth—people do act differently in a mob from the way they act individually—that provided a powerful theme for *In Dubious Battle* and *The Grapes of Wrath*. Within each of these novels, however, and in all the later works Steinbeck offers an alternative to the Group Man: the compassionate and creative individual. To John O'Hara he wrote in 1949:

I think I believe one thing powerfully—that the only creative thing our species has is the individual, lonely mind. Two people can create a child but I know of no other thing created by a group. The group ungoverned by individual thinking is a horrible destructive principle. The great change in the last 2,000 years was the Christian idea that the individual soul was very precious.

Unless we can preserve and foster the principle of the precious-
ness of the individual mind, the world of men will either disinte-
grate into a screaming chaos or will go into a grey slavery. And
that fostering and preservation seem to me our greatest job. [*LL*,
pp. 359–60]

And in his memoir of Ed Ricketts, added as a preface to
The Sea of Cortez after Ricketts' death in April, 1948,
Steinbeck reflects on the Group Man theory and finds it
wanting: "The creative principle is a lonely and an individual matter. Groups can correlate, investigate, and build,
but we could not think of any group that has ever created
or invented anything. Indeed, the first impulse of the group
seems to be to destroy the creation and the creator" (p. xiv).
In fact, at the end of *The Sea of Cortez* Steinbeck covers
his philosophical bets with a disclaimer: "The safety-valve
of all speculation is: *It might be so*" (p. 265). It might be so;
there is value in Steinbeck's theory of the group and in its
analogy to marine biology. Finally, however, his emphasis
is on individuals, as they are, in living relationship to their
environment.

Supernatural Naturalism

The large picture of humanity in Steinbeck's fiction remains
a naturalistic one in which people struggle within and
against natural forces and are partly victims of them. As
such, the philosophy of Naturalism [22] constitutes Steinbeck's
essential view of humanity. He operates solidly within
the framework of his literary precursors—among them
Stephen Crane, Bret Harte, Theodore Dreiser—although
it would be erroneous to suggest any of them as direct influences upon Steinbeck. Rather, there exists a tempera-
mental kinship between them. For example, in Crane's
"The Blue Hotel" the naïve Swede is the victim of many
things outside him: the trip he takes, the storm, the people
around him. He is also, however, the victim of forces
within him, those of his own mind. His imagination has

concocted a scenario that he is determined will come true. And it does, at the expense of his life. When he stumbles against the cash register, fatally wounded, all eyes fix on the "dreadful legend" atop the machine: "This registers the amount of your purchase." Precisely. He has brought this upon himself; he has purchased his death. But he has not desired it, nor particularly willed it, nor, possibly, controlled it. Rather he seems a victim of his own incontrollable imagining. Nearly the same sorts of circumstances are present in Steinbeck's haunting story "Flight," in which Pepe's doom is fixed from the earliest lines—in the hot, oppressive coastal environment; in his desire to be a man; but mostly in the subconscious flick of his knife like a serpent's darting tongue. The preponderance of snake imagery in the story is of a piece with the deadly act and the theme. Some ancient darkness shapes and determines the way Pepe will go.

In "John Steinbeck: Naturalism's Priest," Woodburn O. Ross describes the development of Steinbeck's naturalistic views to the date of the article, 1949, but Ross is one of the few to point out that, although Steinbeck's premises are naturalistic, he often violates his own premises: "Steinbeck's naturalistic ideas have clearly done much to determine the character of the fiction which he writes. Yet to describe him as a naturalist is in one sense false. The description is incomplete; for, while never repudiating the points of view which I have just described, he amalgamates them with others which many would consider contradictory."[23]

While Ross's case may only be strengthened by a consideration of the work after 1949, a kind of supranaturalism, or "supernatural naturalism" is solidly evident in all of Steinbeck's work. He simply is not content to leave humankind in a thoroughly naturalistic state. While he says in *The Sea of Cortez*, "There would seem to be only one commandment for living things: 'Survive!'" he also uncomfortably recognizes in the same work that only humans seem capable of dreams, of hopes, of heroic acts that both motivate and transcend their mere effort to survive. While this may seem teleological and contradictory to his premises, it remains, nonetheless, a fact.

In *The Grapes of Wrath*, Jim Casy turns from the "Holy Sperit and the Jesus road" since he figures "there ain't no sin and there ain't no virtue. There's just stuff people do" (p. 32). But in its place he provides for "the human spirit"—"Maybe all men got one big soul ever'body's a part of" (p. 33). Above all, he searches for, and finds, that spirit in acts of human kindness. In his famous breakfast prayer before leaving Oklahoma, Casy reflects: "'I can't say no grace like I use' ta say. I'm glad of the holiness of breakfast. I'm glad there's love here. That's all'" (pp. 110–11). Similarly, opposed to the Group Man theme that threads through the novel, Ma Joad insists on the "fambly of man." Even in the heart of his most naturalistic years and when he was most enamored by the Group Man theory, Steinbeck did not confine his views to that philosophical system.

Ross indicates four ways in which Steinbeck goes beyond simple naturalism. First, Steinbeck's work possesses "a quality which is the result of an emotional bias rather than an intellectual conviction. Steinbeck's writing is outside the strict scientific, naturalistic tradition, in that he is not objective. Steinbeck loves whatever he considers 'natural' and is keenly sensitive to its emotional values."[24] Second, Steinbeck supports an ethical system beyond a simple Malthusian "struggle for survival," one founded on altruism. Only this can explain the actions of Ma Joad, Rose of Sharon, or, for that matter, Doc Burton, Samuel Hamilton, and Mack and the boys. Third, "Steinbeck has developed ideas about the unity of the cosmos which may fairly be called 'mystical,' ideas which, of course, ultimately go considerably beyond what his scientific naturalism would support but which are, I think, connected with his love of the natural."[25]

While Ross finds clear evidence of the writer's affection for characters, of the virtue of altruism, and of a mystical attitude toward the cosmos, he finds the fourth point more difficult to express. "Religious sensibility," however, seems to summarize Ross's final argument. Steinbeck's work is impelled by a sense of divine presence, apparent perhaps in folk beliefs, in overt religious rituals, but also in the larger sense of living in the presence of what Rudolf Otto calls the mysterious "Other." Steinbeck fuses this religious sensibility into his novels with the very real daily life of his characters. Ross suggests that

nineteenth-century fears that the development of naturalism meant the end of reverence, of worship, and of "august sentiments" are not warranted in the case of Steinbeck. He has succeeded in taking the materials which undermined the religious faith of the nineteenth century and fusing them with a religious attitude in the twentieth, though a religious attitude very different from what the orthodox of the nineteenth century would have thought possible.[26]

In the face of such observation, which the work indeed bears out, the term "naturalistic" simply will not do as a final description of Steinbeck's view of humankind. While predicated on scientific principles and an urge to see life in its environment, as it really is, Steinbeck's fiction also suggests a larger mystery that is humankind, that "thing" that sets human beings apart from merely biological mechanism. A more proper term for Steinbeck may be "supernatural naturalist." By the term I do not mean the "natural supernaturalism" of Meyer Abrams in his book by that title, in which he describes a flattening out of the supernatural, a conflation of the supernatural with the natural. Instead, I mean to suggest that Steinbeck finds a supernatural power and presence observable *in* the natural, in the flora and fauna and earth itself, and in humankind.[27] Steinbeck, in fact, structures his symbolism around this belief, a topic examined in the next section. In a letter to Louis Paul, dated 1936, Steinbeck wrote:

You say you are afraid of symbols. But you see in this country the deep symbol of security is rain—water. And the symbol of evil is drought. There isn't any twisting of symbols there. It's a very real

thing. My father lost nearly all his cattle in the year I was writing
about. It's a pretty awful thing to have your herd die of thirst and
starvation. I was simply trying to reduce that pattern to utterance. [*LL*, p. 130]

The earth itself suggests the abstractions for which the novelist finds appropriate "utterance."

Although Steinbeck's view of humankind is ostensibly
rooted in a naturalistic view of life that corresponds to his
literary realism, Steinbeck also probes the supernatural
through typology and symbolism.

ARTIST AS SYMBOLIST: BIBLICAL ALLUSION, SYMBOLISM, TYPOLOGY

If his view of humanity is finally that of the "supernatural
naturalist," the path Steinbeck follows in his literature
winds through the obscure operations of the human spirit.
The quest to discern humanity's personal and moral nature
is always elusive, its obliquities always confounding, its
goal impossible to peg into neat categories, its very ambiguity the thing that compels Steinbeck irresistibly along its
path. He never wearies of pursuing it.

Along the way Steinbeck excavates every nook and cranny
of human nature, including the religious and the moral.
Since this is the case, one should distinguish carefully between Steinbeck's literary exploration of religion and ethics—including his literary use of biblical allusion and symbolism—and his personal beliefs in religious and ethical
matters. Any analysis of biblical allusion in an author's work
invites assumptions about the author's personal religious
belief. That an author uses biblical symbols, themes, or allusions does not imply that the author endorses biblical
ethics and principles.

The evidence, in fact, runs quite to the contrary. As a
young boy Steinbeck was required to attend his parents'
church, where his highest ambition was to wear the white
surplice of a choirboy, although not for any sacerdotalism of

the position but rather for the pure, clowning whimsy of the garb itself. It was, after all, almost medieval, and the Middle Ages was his first love. Although during later years he would occasionally visit a church out of curiosity about traditions and rituals, it was never to nurture any personal spiritual need. He directly stated his personal religious convictions: he had none. His fascination with the Bible was endless; Jesus enters his vocabulary often and not always blasphemously. But Jesus was simply one of the great heroes, on the order of Zeus, for the mythology of Christianity. He once envisioned writing a film script based on the life of Christ, but, whether through busyness, lack of sustained interest, or supersession by other interests, he never attempted it.[28]

Jesus was for Steinbeck a man for all seasons, and little more than similar men who weather those seasons. To Jacqueline Kennedy at the time of the president's assassination, he wrote:

As we all do—I have need, and consider the New Testament many times. And it has seemed to me that Jesus lived a singularly undramatic life—a straight line life without deviation or doubt. And then we come to that heart-breaking moment on the cross when He cried "Lama sabachthani." In that one moment of doubt we are all related to Him. And when you said you had questions to ask, please remember that terrible question Jesus asked: "My Lord, wherefor hast thou forsaken me?" In that moment He was everyone—Everyone! [LL, p. 795][29]

This is a thoroughly humanized view of Jesus, free of the claims of doctrine, free also of Jesus' claims for himself and the claims of the New Testament about him.

Steinbeck's third wife, Elaine, who attended Sunday services regularly, was neither helped nor hindered by her husband in her interest. That was her interest, not his. He wrote:

Yesterday, Easter, we went to services in the Bruton church. I found it nostalgically moving because I knew it all from my childhood, but also I found again that there is nothing in it that I need or want. Elaine both needs and wants it and so she may have it. But I'll take my birds any day and the processional of the sun. [*LL*, p. 623]

On the other hand, one recalls that, in *Travels with Charley*, Steinbeck expresses enthusiasm for a Vermont minister's "glorious sermon, a fire-and-brimstone sermon," in which he "spoke of hell as an expert" (*TWC*, p. 71).

The writer's clearest statement of unbelief occurs in a late (March 5, 1964) letter to Dr. Denton Cox in which Steinbeck becomes more explicit about what he calls his "mortal record called a medical passport." There he states: "Now finally, I am not religious so that I have no apprehension of a hereafter, either a hope of reward or a fear of punishment. It is not a matter of belief. It is what I feel to be true from my experience, observation and simple tissue feeling" (*LL*, p. 57). This is not a view his life led up to, like a conclusion on the basis of evidence experienced; it was one he held all his life. The language in *The Sea of Cortez* is tougher, more acerbic, more truculent, but the idea is the same:

Certain communicants of the neurological conditioning religions practiced by cowardly people who, by narrowing their emotional experience, hope to broaden their lives, lead us to think we would not like this new species. These religionists, being afraid not only of pain and sorrow but even of joy, can so protect themselves that they seem dead to us. The new animal resulting from purification of the species might be one we wouldn't like at all. For it is through struggle and sorrow that people are able to participate in one another—the heartlessness of the healthy, well-fed, and unsorrowful person has in it an infinite smugness. [Pp. 117–18]

While there is a remarkable consistency in his unbelief in traditional religious dogma, there is nonetheless an ever-developing moral concern over the course of his life. One assumes that the young Steinbeck—who turned his back on his parents' religion, including his regular boyhood

attendance at Saint Paul's Episcopal Church (now, ironically, the East of Eden restaurant), catechism sessions, and
youth choir—did not have a particularly religious or even
moral attitude toward life. His lust and capacity for alcohol
were unrivaled among his youthful peers. Perhaps an unpublished letter to Katherine Beswick, written sometime
in August, 1928, best summarizes this view: "As long as you
are not ashamed, then you have not been immoral. And
you know very well that I haven't the least conception of
the word moral."[30]

It is quite commonly assumed that Steinbeck entered a
so-called moral phase in his writing of *East of Eden*.[31] The
transition was not that abrupt. Several other factors contribute to the mature moral vision of *East of Eden*, most
notably the happiness of his marriage to Elaine, which re-
juvenated his will to work. Nonetheless, a statement in a
letter to Adlai Stevenson of November 5, 1959, stands in
marked contrast to his earlier expressions of moral rela-
tivism. After a trip to the presumed site of Camelot, Steinbeck charged that Americans had become greedy, rich, and
soft:

> Back from Camelot, and, reading the papers not at all sure it
> was wise. Two first impressions. First a creeping, all-pervading
> nerve-gas of immorality which starts in the nursery and does not
> stop before it reaches the highest offices, both corporate and gov-
> ernmental. Two, a nervous restlessness, a hunger, a thirst, a
> yearning for something unknown—perhaps morality. . . . Hav-
> ing too many THINGS they spend their hours and money on the
> couch searching for a soul. [*LL*, pp. 651–52][32]

The point here is that Steinbeck's personal spiritual belief, or unbelief, which biographers have largely ignored,
must be separated from his aesthetic use of Scripture and
his artistic techniques of biblical allusion and symbolism. But if one turns to the work itself, a further danger is
posed, namely, the danger of transmuting the literary work
into the biblical pattern itself—that is, the temptation to
reconstruct the literary work into the mold suggested by

the innumerable biblical allusions. A necessary distinction must be made between the artist as craftsman and the artist as believer, and the artistry must be understood first of all on aesthetic terms.

Biblical allusion in a literary work evokes a secondary and anagogic imaginative sphere that is whole in its own right and provides a vantage point from which the reader may view the primary action. When allusions are used with internal consistency yet remain in relationship with the primary narrative, they are said to function as typology. Allusion may be individual, unpatterned, random. Typology assumes a deliberate pattern that is both prefigurative and evocative. It prefigures, that is to say, it contains in a previous action intimations of actions in the primary work, and it evokes from the storehouse of common experience by which we ascertain the actions in the primary work.

Mason I. Lowance's careful study of metaphor and symbol in *The Language of Canaan* is helpful to an understanding of typology in general. The safeguards a critic imposes on typological hermeneutics must be stringent, for the very suggestiveness of typological language contributes to ambiguity. What is at once its pleasure—an invitation to the reader to form insights not wholly dependent on the primary narrative—is also its danger: the risk of reading the work as something wholly other than the primary narrative. Lowance provides guidance by his distinguishing among "types" in literature. The first type, observes Lowance, "is a simple representative figure. In the rhetorical tradition of synechdoche, this type stands for the whole, or for an abstract idea. Thus Adam is a type of mankind, who represents the process through which all men eventually go in falling from divine grace."[33]

This is the most frequent kind of typology in Steinbeck's work, the simple, evocative, representative figure or symbol. It may be distinguished from a second kind of typology, exegetical or biblical typology, which Lowance defines as follows:

Biblical or exegetical typology is derived from the practices of the early fathers and medieval theologians, who attempted to give continuity to the canon of Holy Scripture by demonstrating how the Old Testament prefigured the New through types and figures of which the New Testament persons and events were the antitype, or fulfillment. Thus, the historical Abraham became a type of God the Father in the sacrifice of his only son, Isaac. In contrast to the purely representative type, the exegetical type exists in the historical context of time, and its relation to the substance it represents is that of foreshadowing, or adumbration. The substance foreshadowed is denoted the antitype and it usually exists in time, fulfilling the type.[34]

This second kind of typology, Lowance argues, "is the more important for New England Puritanism," and it does in fact apply more to nineteenth-century New England than to Steinbeck and his contemporaries. This kind of typology may be found, for example, in Herman Melville's novella *Billy Budd*. In Steinbeck it is more often the case that a fictional character may share representative traits with a biblical type, rather than that the character and his actions point to a biblical fulfillment or antitype.

Typology is related to the common critical term "archetype," which figures prominently in *The Winter of Our Discontent*, where Steinbeck works deliberately with Jungian images, and also, perhaps, in *The Red Pony*, where he evokes the "westering" consciousness as background for Jody's maturation. An archetype, however, is not necessarily biblical, or even religious. Maud Bodkin defines archetypes as "themes having a particular form or pattern which persists amid variation from age to age, and which corresponds to a pattern or configuration of emotional tendencies in the minds of those who are stirred by the theme."[35] Similarly, Northrop Frye argues that archetypes are recurring patterns that point to a theme or experience common to humanity.[36] As with typology, however, these are patterns against which we observe the primary action of the work. They are not the determining action itself but the imaginative context, the frame for consideration of the action.

Allusion and symbolism may be considered the suborder, or the tools, of typology, and Steinbeck uses both tools frequently. The simplest distinction between allusion and symbolism (although it involves the intentional fallacy by presuming to know the mind of the author) has to do with deliberation, allusion being a casual thing in the literary work and symbol the deliberate, patterned thing. The distinction lies in degree of specificity. Many of the biblical allusions in Steinbeck's work serve as a "coloring" for the story that establishes tone and context.[37]

In *To a God Unknown*, Steinbeck uses some familiar allusions, such as the naming of the tribe and of individuals such as Joseph and Benjamin to support the theme of a sojourn to a new land and Joseph's discovery of sacredness. There are more specific allusions in the novel, some of which may escape casual notice. For example, when old John Wayne dies, he passes on his benediction to Joseph in the fashion of the Old Testament patriarchs. He says: "'Come to me, Joseph. Put your hand here—no, here. My father did it this way. A custom so old cannot be wrong. Now, leave your hand there!'" (p. 3). The specific biblical allusion here is to the Old Testament oath, one example of which is Abraham's charge to his chief servant in Genesis 24: "Put your hand under my thigh, and I will make you swear."[38] The curious point here is the license Steinbeck takes to link the blessing with the motif of a mystical fertility religion in the novel. The hand under the thigh was used in the Old Testament Hebraic society—as well as in other cultures, including, for example, the American Sioux Indians—to swear an oath. However, it never signified a blessing, which was always accompanied by a laying on of hands as a sign of transferral—not fidelity—by the bestower of the blessing.

While allusion is the casual introduction of biblical items to provide "coloring"—tone, implication, suggestiveness—

symbolism provides a much more rigid structure. Although this claim of discovering such a structure does presume upon the author's intentions, Steinbeck made his intentions regarding symbolism manifestly clear. It is not surprising that his most specific statements occur around the time he was writing *East of Eden*, a work whose symbolism is more carefully sustained than that of any other except *The Pearl* and *The Grapes of Wrath*. In all three books the titles themselves are symbolic and indicate the importance Steinbeck placed on the immediate apprehensibility of a symbol. He believed that a symbol should suggest clearly and directly a spiritual dimension to the work not readily apparent in the narrative alone. Of *The Grapes of Wrath*, H. Kelly Crockett observes:

By the use of symbolism it identifies its elements with human experience and tradition, and by this and other means makes a strong appeal to the reader's imagination, intellect, and emotion. These added significances have been described as further layers or levels of meaning, but a more satisfactory comparison would be to ripples or waves spreading one after another in ever widening circles from the center of action, of character, or locale. Thus, the reader gains as much from reflection upon the novel as he does from reading it, and in later readings will always discover some new element to delight in.[39]

Selection of titles was never easy for Steinbeck, and perhaps because of that it was an important task. Most of the final decisions were fortunate ones: the innocuous "Something That Happened" became the memorable *Of Mice and Men* from Robert Burns's poem; "A Lady in Infra-Red" became *Cup of Gold;* "The Green Lady" became "To the Unknown God," "To an Unknown God," then *To a God Unknown;* "Dissonant Symphony" became *The Pastures of Heaven*.[40] Above all, Steinbeck wanted titles that were both faithful to the narrative account and also suggested its larger significance. Thus the titles should be both descriptive and symbolic. While this art of titling will be examined more closely in the discussion of certain individual books, the titling of *East of Eden*, perhaps the most difficult single work for Steinbeck to name, provides one of the clearest examples.

The difficulty Steinbeck had in titling *East of Eden* is related to the fact that the book is, in part, about naming. In *The Sea of Cortez* Steinbeck remarked that "this name-giving faculty is very highly developed and deeply rooted in our atavistic magics. To name a thing has always been to make it familiar and therefore a little less dangerous to us. 'Tree' the abstract may harbor some evil until it has a name, but once having a name one can cope with it" (p. 54). This is surely the case with *East of Eden*, where the names are heavily freighted with symbolism.

East of Eden is a deliberately symbolic work, one of those that Steinbeck spoke of as having four or five layers of meaning. To peg down those meanings, he relied in part on names. This held true first of all for the title of the book itself. For years Steinbeck speculated on, pondered, projected this work. It was the one, he often said, he had spent all his life preparing to write. During the years of preparation he spoke of it simply as the Salinas Valley novel. The actual writing commenced in late January and early February, 1951. In a letter dated May 10 of that year, Steinbeck notes that at the suggestion of Lawrence Hagy, a relative of Elaine, he had decided on the title "My Valley." Pascal Covici did not like the title, and for a time Steinbeck pondered "Valley to the Sea." On May 22, as he pondered the symbolic structure of the story, Steinbeck reread Genesis and thought of "Cain Sign." But it was not until June 11, after writing the Cain and Abel episode, that he decided on "East of Eden."

The symbolism of the title is internally consistent with the story. The great quest of Adam Trask is not to find an Eden but to learn to live east of it—in a fallen world of mortal evil. So adamant was Steinbeck that to name a thing is to know that thing, that he deliberately wrote the section on regional California place names (chapter 1, section 2), observing to Covici: "I think I had better put down a section on the place names of the Valley because sometimes they seem contrived unless it is known that there are many strange and interesting names in the region. . . . People are interested in names" (*JN*, p. 65). And in the novel itself Sam Hamilton says, "Names are a great mystery. I've never known whether the name is molded by the child or the child changed to fit the name" (p. 263). Early in the novel Steinbeck had struggled with the name Carl Trask, and wrote that "I am forced to change the name of Carl Trask. . . . He has changed his symbolic nature to a certain extent" (*JN*, p. 27).

In the same letter to Covici, Steinbeck added:

Since these people are essentially symbol people, I must make them doubly understandable as people apart from their symbols. A symbol is usually a kind of part of an equation—it is one part or facet chosen to illuminate as well as to illustrate the whole. The symbol is never the whole. It is a kind of psychological sign language. . . . I want to clothe my symbol people in trappings of experience so that the symbol is discernible but not overwhelming. [*JN*, p. 27]

Nowhere is this more important than in our understanding of Cathy Ames, for in a novel that places such significance on naming as knowing, Cathy is as chameleonic a monster as her changing names suggest. She is unknowable. The reader first meets her in chapter 8 as Cathy Ames, but by the next chapter, where she tries to destroy Mr. Edwards, her name has already slid to Catherine Amesbury (the play on having "buried Ames" is obvious). When she arrives at the Trask farm, she is virtually nameless, feigning amnesia and not knowing who she is. As she takes over Faye's whorehouse, after becoming Cathy Trask, she adopts yet another name: Kate Albey. Cathy's names, however, are only a piece of a larger design of names in the novel in which the reader observes all the principal characters, with the exception of Sam Hamilton and Lee, falling into the Abel group—Adam, Aaron (who changes his name

to Aron), Alice Trask, Mr. and Mrs. Ames, Abra Bacon—or
the Cain group: Cyrus, Charles,·Caleb, Cathy. There is an
ironic tension in Cathy's surnames, since they all start with
the letter A.

The symbolism of the novel is of a piece with Steinbeck's
larger view of literary art and suggestiveness. In the early
stages of writing *East of Eden*, he stated that "the craft or
art of writing is the clumsy attempt to find symbols for the
wordlessness. In utter loneliness the writer tries to explain
the inexplicable. . . . A good writer always works at the
impossible" (*JN*, p. 4). In his effort to find "symbols for the
wordlessness," Steinbeck frequently uses familiar symbols
emerging from biblical patterns. But the biblical symbolism
is never used, finally, as a companion or compendium to
holy writ, but is used to evoke a certain consciousness in
the reader, opening a door on the reader's own nature. Midway through the writing of *East of Eden*, Steinbeck himself
made this clear: "I have finally I think found a key to the
story. . . . If this were just a discussion of Biblical lore, I
would throw it out but it is not. It is using the Biblical story
as a measure of ourselves" (*JN*, pp. 104–105). Significantly,
he wrote this while working on chapter 22, which contains
the crucial allusions to Cain and Abel and the naming of
Caleb and Aaron.

While Steinbeck's use of symbolism has attracted great
attention from both specialized critics and general readers,
a preoccupation with that technique alone is dangerous to a
full appreciation of his literary artistry. It is far more profitable to bring the full range of his artistic achievement and
beliefs to bear on an understanding of his fiction, for in so
doing one sees his use of allusion and symbolism as parts of
a larger whole and a remarkably full aesthetic. The specific
principles that are established in this introduction and
will be applied in the discussion of Steinbeck's fiction are
grounded first of all in the author's sense of story and the
power that he gives his story through patterns of rhetoric
and imagery. These patterns, as well as those of allusion
and symbolism, combine to open imaginative insights for

the reader, disclosing Steinbeck's view of human nature to the reader and also something of the reader's own nature to himself.

Because Steinbeck was insistent upon seeing the characters of his stories in their living environment, subsequent chapters in this book pay close attention to Steinbeck's own story in composing each of the works. Clearly, each has such a story, such an environment, behind it. The second effort will be to examine the works in their structural and thematic unity and the particular artistic techniques Steinbeck used to develop those structures and themes.

2

Individual Freedom and Social Constraint: *Cup of Gold*

YOUNG STEINBECK is often depicted as a hard-eyed rebel in contention with his religious ties, his family, and educational and social systems. A certain amount of truth undergirds the portrait, borne out by Steinbeck's own recollections ("I remember this sorrow at not being a part of things from very early in my childhood" [*JN*, p. 53]) and by other records, such as his candid and passionate early letters to Katherine Beswick and the accounts of those who knew him. That young Steinbeck possessed vigorous personal passion and that it was often directed against social institutions of his time no one questions. That passion, however, often overshadows his serious-minded, passionate apprenticeship as a literary craftsman. Although his apprenticeship was often clouded by despair as the rejections flooded in and the manuscripts seemed never to achieve polished form, he was, nonetheless, able to structure his personal rebelliousness into the fiction itself. The conflict between the freedom of the individual and social constraint plays a major role in nearly all his fiction through *The Grapes of Wrath* and finds at least a minor role in much of the fiction thereafter. This conflict, particularly when coupled with the dreams of people gripped in the conflict, creates a natural power in his early fiction that grants it considerable, if sometimes flawed, excellence. An example is *Cup of Gold*.

Cup of Gold remains a neglected work in Steinbeck's canon and, as a first novel in which he was just beginning to explore his artistic and thematic goals, perhaps rightfully so. But precisely for the reason that Steinbeck was developing his artistry in the novel, it merits close attention in this book.

BACKGROUND TO THE NOVEL: THE DEVELOPING ARTIST

Steinbeck himself considered *Cup of Gold* an artistic failure. Before the novel was published, he wrote to Katherine-Beswick:

I have just finished being drunk for three days, a horrible period wherein I hurled dirty taunts at my spirit, called it a literary magpie in peacock tips and a charlatan and a sneak. But I am sober now and the ego reasserts itself. I know that though Cup of Gold is a bad book, yet on its shoulders I shall climb to good books.[1]

Soon after the publication of the novel Steinbeck wrote A. Grove Day:

The book was an immature experiment written for the purpose of getting all the wise cracks (known by sophomores as epigrams) and all the autobiographical material (which hounds us until we get it said) out of my system. And I really did not intend to publish it. The book accomplished its purgative purpose. [*LL*, p. 17]

While Steinbeck often spoke flippantly about this book in which he had invested so many hours, it is probable that he was reacting more to the lack of reception of the book than to the work itself. It is not unusual for a novelist to interpret poor reception as poor artistry. Curiously, although it was almost ignored by reviewers, *Cup of Gold* sold out its 1,500-run edition, which represented better sales than those of his next two books combined. One may wonder what role the stock market crash, which came only months after publication, had in the novel's poor critical reception. When the world seems to be falling down, it is unlikely that one would pay serious notice to a small book by a new author, even if its theme detailed the collapse of greedy and adventurous dreams.

Steinbeck's despairing objections aside, *Cup of Gold* in

many respects is a fine little novel in which the seeds of the author's mature power are clearly in evidence. It remains somewhat puzzling that the work has attracted only scant and superficial attention. It does not make momentous and unfulfilled claims for itself, as does the pretentious myth-making of *To a God Unknown*. It purports to be a romance of Henry Morgan, with "Occasional References to History" but in fact achieves much more than this. Several items in particular are impressive.

The novel has a superbly rich (although sometimes un-controlled) diction and imagery. Beside it, a late novel, *The Winter of our Discontent*, for example, appears thin and forced. The diction and imagery in *Cup of Gold* succeed for several reasons. Although Steinbeck himself believed that the novel suffered from his attempt at colloquial and dialectical speech patterns, particularly the Byrnian, these are not obtrusive and presage his expert use of dialect in *Tortilla Flat* and *The Grapes of Wrath*.[2] Steinbeck pos-sessed the novelist's gift for listening and reconstructing what he heard with natural rhythm, pace, and nuance. While this gift flowers in *The Grapes of Wrath*, it is already evident in *Cup of Gold*. Steinbeck allows speech patterns to form naturally and to shape character. Clearly the power of language is his; control over that language is not yet fully apparent. He had not matured as an artist to the point of learning that he must cut back, especially in those rich pas-sages of seeming overindulgence. Steinbeck could have learned a valuable lesson from Willa Cather, who reflected on her first novels that "too much detail is apt, like any other form of extravagance, to become slightly vulgar."[3] Too often, in *Cup of Gold*, Steinbeck's diction seems merely ex-travagant, there simply for the author's pleasure. While Steinbeck never entirely lost his ability to write a thor-oughly bad line that he might better have cut, such as "Oh, but strawberries will never taste so good again and the thighs of women have lost their clutch!" (*East of Eden*), *Cup of Gold* has more than its share. Too many lines, their syn-tax as scrambled as dice, rattle meaninglessly through the book: "Her mind which had been always a scalpel of reality,

her imagination which dealt purely with the present out-
sides of things, went fondling back to the baby who had
crawled and stumbled and learned to talk" (p. 26). At other
times the language is stilted: "At the end of her speaking,
Ysobel thriftily drew aside the webby lace of her mantilla
that it might not be spotted with blood" (p. 149). Examples
of strong and compelling prose offset these, however, in-
forming us that in the process of rewriting the manuscript
six times Steinbeck was in fact learning a great deal about
the novelistic craft.

Artistic excellence is noticeable particularly in the vigorous imagery, which functions both to describe and to define character. Harry Moore was accurate in his early assessment in *The Novels of John Steinbeck* that "the young
author testing his strength sometimes looked awkward when
he slipped, but when he didn't fail his efforts gave promise
of remarkable power."[4] At times the imagery, like the diction, is overripe and gives a strange effect of incongruity, as
in the following passage, where the Chagres River is described in snake imagery (already a favorite with Steinbeck),
and explodes suddenly and chaotically into other patterns:

And Chagres twisted on ahead in loops and tremendous horse-
shoe turns. The yellow water, like a frightened, leprous woman,
timidly caressed the hulls. . . . It was a sluggish, apathetic river
of many shallows where the bright sand glittered in the sun.
Chagres was a dilettante in the eternal and understood business
of rivers—that of getting to the ocean with as little bother and
effort as possible. [P. 124]

At its best, however, the descriptive imagery expertly locates places, actions, and moods. As Henry Morgan leaves
his Welsh village, he leaves not just a place but a whole,
irrevocable time, which has formed his very being. Steinbeck captures this psychological displacement in an image:
"He had been alone before, but never so thoroughly alone,
among new things, in a place he did not know. The terror
was growing and swelling in his breast. Time had become
an idling worm which crawled ahead the merest trifle,
stopped and waggled its blind head, and crawled again"

(pp. 32–33). Furthermore, Steinbeck reveals a skill in this first novel for short, abrupt images such as in this passage conveying the power and mood of the sea: "The sea rose up and snarled at them, while the ship ran before the crying dogs of the wind like a strong, confident stag; ran bravely under courses and spritsail. The wind howled out of Winter's home in the north, and the *Bristol Girl* mocked it across its face to the southwest" (p. 44). This same power of imagery is evident in purely descriptive passages: "The streets were only narrow alleys lined with dirty wooden houses. And each house had a balcony above the street where people sat and stared at Henry as he passed; stared not with interest, but wearily, as men in sickness watch flies crawling on the ceiling" (p. 78).

In the same fashion that Steinbeck evokes a mood or conveys a descriptive setting, he evidences his lifelong ability to locate and familiarize a minor character in startlingly clear images. The old hag-seer Gwenliana has visions that are at best troubled dreams. She is a relic, living on the shadowy edge of reality: "A long time she sat entranced, and it seemed that her old brain combed out the tangles of the past to make a straight, tellable future. At length she spoke in the low, hoarse, chanting voice that is reserved for dread things" (p. 27). When she delivers herself of a prophecy, tangled and ill-shaped, the Morgans praise her effusively and treasure her childish delight. It is a warm, sympathetic portrait, abetted by skilled imagery. Another minor character who attains artistic eminence is befuddled old James Flower, the man who lived his life in hot pursuit of an idea that always eluded his grasp:

James Flower was not a hard man, and certainly he was not a very brilliant man. His whole life had been a hunger for ideas—any ideas—the creation of them. He wanted to conceive ideas, to warm them to throbbing life, then to hurl them on an astonished world. They would go bounding like stones started down a long hill, awakening an avalanche of admiration. But no ideas came to him. [Pp. 54–55]

Many such passages appear in *Cup of Gold*, and they initiate an enduring excellence of Steinbeck's art; in fact, he is often more skilled at sharply defining minor characters than primary ones. But Henry Morgan's character, given the short space of narrative development in the novel, is amply drawn. His motivation to action is clear, his actions consistent with that motivation, the consequences of those actions in keeping with their nature. He too is often captured in terse portraits charged with potent imagery:

Through all his life his will had been like an iron weathervane, steadfastly pointing, always, but never long in one direction. The Indies and the sea and pillage and glory all seemed to have failed him. He had touched all things and watched them pale and shrivel at his touch. And he was lonely. His men regarded him with respect and sullen awe. They were afraid of him, and this state did not feed his vanity as once it had. [P. 93]

Cup of Gold is marked by varying degrees of excellence in diction and imagery, often offset by marred passages to be sure, but sustained by a carefully worked out narrative technique. For the first time we see Steinbeck using the narrative "overvoice," the technique that sprang into full power in the intercalary chapters of *The Grapes of Wrath* and reappeared in many later works. *Cup of Gold* itself is divided into five parts as follows:

Part I (seven chapters): Henry's life in Wales.

Part II (seven chapters): His flight from Cardiff and indenture on James Flower's plantation.

Part III (six chapters): The rise of Henry as pirate.

Part IV (eight chapters): The taking of Panama—the physical Cup of Gold, and the forsaking of Ysobel—the symbolic Cup of Gold.

Part V (four chapters): Henry's return to civilization, marriage to Elizabeth, and death in Jamaica.

While part I begins directly with the biographical narrative of Henry Morgan and part V with the biographical denouement, each of the three inner parts begins with a narrative

overvoice filling in historical, geographical, or social details
that bear on or frame the narrative action and the character
of Henry Morgan. Each of these brief chapters is written in
a lyrical style quite different from that of the narrative and
quite similar to that of the intercalary chapters in *The
Grapes of Wrath*.

This carefully worked out structure, with its rich diction
and imagery, serves notice of some first-rate craftsmanship,
but this is not to suggest that the novel is without flaws beyond those items of syntax and diction already mentioned.
Indeed, the lushness and occasional obscurity of diction
and imagery are but a part of larger flaws that, like the artistic excellences, remained with Steinbeck for much of his
career. For example, while the story of Henry Morgan is in
itself fascinating, Steinbeck visits upon it a grandiosity that
it cannot quite bear.[5] The story sometimes lacks unity of action, and while the overvoice chapters help provide sequence, there remains a feeling of the turgidly episodic.
Most successful is the transition in Morgan from James
Flower's plantation slave to pirate; least successful is the
transition from pirate to lieutenant-governor and judge.
Furthermore, as important as Merlin is to the dream motif
of the story, he fails to achieve an organic part of the story
itself. Henry visits Merlin out of parental duress, and his
meeting with Merlin is a kind of cookies-and-tea chitchat.
Merlin has no actual power and inspires little of the reverence that he commanded in Arthur's kingdom. In the
anachronistic setting of the seventeenth century it is likely
that Merlin simply represents for Steinbeck a font of traditional folk wisdom against which the young Henry rebels,
but Merlin's character here is too enigmatic and vacuous for
the importance Steinbeck places on his words.

In the tradition of romance, moreover, all major characters have a hard time dying, and the reader comes to expect
long deathbed soliloquies as the nearly deceased hang on to
impart final words of wisdom. In the hard and bloody realism that Steinbeck has made here of the romance, the
lengthy death scenes seem almost a page from comedy.

Surely that is the case with Sir Edward's wondering if he might at least groan:

"I have heard that you can tell a gentleman by the way he dies—but I should like to groan. Robert would have groaned if he had wished. Of course, Robert was queer—but then—he was my own brother—he would have shrieked if he had felt like it. Elizabeth, will you—please—leave the room. I am sorry—but I must groan. Never speak of it—Elizabeth—you promise— never—never to speak of it?" [P. 104]

Much to the horror of others, the secret leaks out that Sir Edward did in fact groan. Similarly, Coeur de Gris's macabre death at Henry's hand is so bizarre as to elicit a nervous chuckle rather than pathos:

Coeur de Gris went slowly to his knees. He steadied himself with his knuckles on the floor. "It is my knees, sir; they will not bear me any more," he apologized. He seemed to be listening for the throbbing sound again. Suddenly his voice rose in bitter complaint. [P. 153]

No better handled is Henry's own death: the narrator suddenly attains the omniscience of God himself and follows Henry beyond death to watch him confront his sins and wander in a black night.

As artistry, then, *Cup of Gold* shows at once sufficient promise to warrant attention and sufficient flaws to place it as a splendid failure. The consensus seems to be that the work merits little attention. Such is the opinion, for example, of Warren French, who, as a generally sympathetic reader of Steinbeck, is surprisingly negative in his assessment:

If Steinbeck later had not written better novels, *Cup of Gold*, his first published book, would surely be as deservedly forgotten as most of the 10,186 others Lewis Gannett says were published in the same end-of-the-boom year of 1929. It is difficult to speak well of the novel. The dialogue is stilted; the characters, two-dimensional; the plot, awkwardly managed; the theme, confused.

Yet one cannot ignore it since it is important both as a symbol of its era and as a portent of the author's future. Steinbeck struggled in it with ideas he was later to treat masterfully.[6]

The key to French's statement lies in the last sentence quoted. French specifically identifies these "ideas he was later to treat masterfully" as an "anti-Arthurian" Grail quest—the elusive Cup of Gold Henry seeks—and also, like Fitzgerald's *The Great Gatsby*, the detailing of one of "the lost generation."

The Elusive Dream

The thematic heart of *Cup of Gold*, however, lies in the conflict between Henry Morgan's freedom to pursue his dream and the constraints society places on him and his dream. Robert Morgan recognizes the dream incipient in his son, and in a sense his own dreamless life stands against it: "For whereas he runs about sticking his finger into pot after pot of cold porridge, grandly confident that each one will prove the pottage of his dreaming, I may not open any kettle, for I believe all porridge to be cold. . . . He tests his dreams, Mother, and I—God help me!—am afraid to" (p. 12). Robert has been domesticated by society, content to practice such little dreams as he has in his rose garden, which represents his own little civilized "cup of gold" and forms a careful substructure in the novel, a place where Robert picks rose petals and showers them in the air while his neighbors wonder about his sanity. At the same time his son will ravage the gardens of the Caribbean, tossing petals of people's lives in the air, while others proclaim his greatness.

Henry's dream appears to him first as a kind of inchoate, primitive urge that will eventually rip him from his family and homeland: "There was no desire in him for a state or condition, no picture in his mind of the thing to be when he had followed his longing; but only a burning and a will overpowering to journey outward and outward after the earliest risen star" (p. 16). But before he leaves civilization for the freedom to pursue his dream, Henry agrees to a meeting with Merlin. The topic of discussion is the mystery of one's own place, symbolized by Merlin's analogy of the moon and the firefly:

You are a little boy. You want the moon to drink from as a golden cup; and so, it is very likely that you will become a great man—if only you remain a little child. All the world's great have been little boys who wanted the moon; running and climbing, they sometimes caught a firefly. But if one grows to a man's mind, that mind must see that it cannot have the moon and would not want it if it could—and so, it catches no fireflies. [P. 19]

Juxtaposed here are two kinds of people. The first always has the child's heart for freedom, the challenge of the moon, and is self-destructive like the moth and the flame. The second domesticates and civilizes this freedom and thereby survives. Henry asks Merlin if he ever wanted the moon, to which the seer—the first of many in Steinbeck's fiction—replies:

I wanted it. Above all desires I wanted it. I reached for it and then—then I grew to be a man, and a failure. But there is this gift for the failure; folk know he has failed, and they are sorry and kindly and gentle. He has the whole world with him; a bridge of contact with his own people; the cloth of mediocrity. But he who shields a firefly in his hands, caught in reaching for the moon, is doubly alone; he only can realize his true failure, can realize his meanness and fears and evasions. [Pp. 19–20]

The one who reaches for the cup of gold will finally hold only one's own loneliness. The person who learns to compromise personal freedom and dreams with society will at least have the company and sympathy of others. Merlin leaves Henry with a prophecy—he will achieve greatness and have no friend, for such is the expense of individual greatness. Henry determines to pursue his dream no matter what the cost.

From the start the dream sets Henry apart from human-

kind: "Silly, spineless creatures, he thought them, with no
dream and no will to leave their sodden, dumpy huts"
(p. 31). Others become mere tools or pawns on his path to
the moon. As Henry perceives freedom at this point, he
sees himself as wholly autonomous, a law unto himself, un-
restricted by civilization; and as he enters his buccaneering
career, he becomes more and more the wholly lawless entity, but he also becomes more aware of the hollowness that
grows in the pit of his freedom:

> He had gone out with Grippo in the *Ganymede*, assured that
> when his guns roared into a Spanish hull, when he stood embat-
> tled on a Spanish deck with cries and clash of iron weapons about
> him, there would come that flaming happiness his heart desired.
> These things he had experienced, and there was not even con-
> tent. The nameless craving in him grew and flexed its claws
> against his heart. He had thought the adulation of the Brother-
> hood might salve the wound of his desire; that when the pirates
> saw the results of his planning and marveled at them, he would
> be pleased and flattered. And this thing happened. The men
> fairly fawned on him, and he found that he despised them for it
> and considered them fools to be taken with such simple things.
> [P. 90]

The Red Saint finally becomes the moon for Henry to
grasp, a moon he has set in place of the once attainable
country girl, Elizabeth. For Henry only the unattainable,
the distant, dreamlike moon, can assuage his lonely freedom. While Henry takes Coeur de Gris as his friend and
plots his coup of the Cup of Gold, his father and Merlin
reflect in Henry's forgotten homeland:

> "So," Merlin mused, "he has come to be the great man he
> thought he wanted to be. If this is true, then he is not a man. He
> is still a little boy and wants the moon. I suppose he is rather un-
> happy about it. Those who say children are happy, forget their
> childhood. I wonder how long he can stave off manhood." [P. 108]

Manhood consists in learning to compromise between civilization and individual freedom. But Henry is possessed by
the moon, and he is desperately lonely. That is the price

one pays for absolute freedom: "'But I think there is more than lust. . . . You cannot understand my yearning. It is as though I strove for some undreamed peace. This woman is the harbor of all my questing'" (p. 128).

The woman who will be the final harbor of his questing, the Santa Roja, is indeed the symbol of attainment for him, but she succeeds thoroughly and painfully in disclosing to him the vacuity of his own aspiration. While Henry perceives her as a dream goddess, this is a real woman who faces him, and her words flay him like whips. She brings Henry out of the childlike dream to his recognition of manhood—that one must give up a piece of the dream, a part of freedom, to survive in this world: "'I think I am sorry because of your lost light; because the brave, brutal child in you is dead—the boastful child who mocked and through his mockery shook the throne of God'" (p. 162). And Henry himself confesses when he attempts to reenter society: "'Civilization will split up a character, and he who refuses to split goes under'" (p. 187).

Although Henry's capitulation at the close of the novel may be disappointing in a romance—the genre would suggest that he go out in swashbuckling glory on the high main instead of filling his compromising little position as a judge in Jamaica—it does set a pattern of tension and compromise between the individual and society that we see often in Steinbeck's art. When Henry comes before the king, he is a swaggering braggart bartering stories and money for respectability (the ransom for the Santa Roja grows each time he tells of it), yet, for all that, his dream has carved a legend in time. When the two Burgundians appear in Henry's court, they tell him how his legend has grown into greatness, into myth, where the hero, no matter how humanly despicable, could do no wrong. Even though he should be hated for his treachery of forsaking his men, how can one hate a legend? A legend acts in its own way, not as civilized men would expect. Something of the dream survives, and perhaps one of the stories Merlin the poet sings in Avalon concerns his wayward charge, Henry Morgan.[7]

Apparent everywhere in the novel, finally, is the influ-

ence of the Grail Quest of Malory's *Morte D'Arthur*. The
story functions as a plot motif and a thematic complement
to the individual-social tension in *Cup of Gold*. The Grail
Quest was a significant addition to Malory's Arthurian legend, for prior to that time, in the quasi-historical renditions
of Geoffrey of Monmouth and Wace, the Arthurian story
was a tale of capable defense of the land, the birth and
management of a nation, and the rule of a peerless king. In
early tales Merlin is depicted as a "wizard" whose genius
lay in sage political advice rather than in spiritual intui-
tions. In Malory, the story of Guenevere (whom Merlin advises Arthur not to marry) and the sacred grail gain preemi-
nence as spiritual pivots for the fortunes of the kingdom.
The two, Guenevere and the grail, both contain the possibility of Arthur and his knights setting aside social respon-
sibilities to pursue the dream. Both are ultimately destructive to the kingdom. In the case of the grail, the knights are
encouraged *not* to seek it unless specifically directed to do
so by the Holy Spirit. The great heroes of the Round Table
are disqualified from pursuing it, and when Lancelot un-
dertakes the quest, he is led to madness in its pursuit. The
Grail Quest is reserved for those specially marked by God
for its pursuit; to others is given the task of maintaining
order in the kingdom. Some equilibrium must be established between the dream and the kingdom.

In *Cup of Gold* the beautiful lady and the grail theme
mesh at the beginning of the novel when Henry forsakes
the attainable lady, Elizabeth, for his idealized cup of gold,
the Santa Roja. The two women, the lost Elizabeth and the
unattainable Santa Roja, linguistically merge. The woman
known as the Santa Roja is actually named Ysobel, the
Spanish form of Elizabeth. In his pursuit of Ysobel, Henry
displaces his attainable reality of the Welsh Elizabeth with
a dream goddess who proves unattainable. Elizabeth is a
poor Welshman's daughter, whom Merlin advises Henry to
see before he leaves, perhaps in a last, futile attempt to
ground his dream in attainable reality. But Henry cannot
even bear to say farewell to her because he has already

dreamed her into something she is not. Through the years
the dream picture grows. To Tim the sailor he tells of a
touching farewell that never occurred; to Paulette, his
slave-lover, Elizabeth is the daughter of a squire; to Coeur
de Gris she is the daughter of an earl; to the king, near the
end of the novel, she is a princess of France imagined
as Psyche herself whom he, like Tiresias, had discovered
bathing naked in a river.

As Elizabeth becomes increasingly abstracted to the
point of a dream myth, she is transformed for Henry into
the Cup of Gold, the delusive grail of Ysobel. When he
goes to take Panama, the geographical Cup of Gold, he
really thinks of the Santa Roja as "the harbor of all my
questing." Cuplike and golden imagery dominate all his
imaginings of her. Peter Lisca provides an analysis of just
one of these cup symbols:

After his disappointment with Ysobel, Morgan finds among the
loot taken in Panama an actual cup of gold, very curiously in-
scribed. Around the outside is a frieze of "four grotesque lambs."
Inside, however, on the bottom, "a naked girl lifted her arms in
sensual ecstasy." Captain Morgan perceives that the contrast between the exterior and interior of the cup symbolizes precisely
the contrast between his own naïve dreams and the reality which
he has been made to face. He violently throws the cup across the
room.[8]

When Ysobel finally scorns him and belittles his marriage
proposal with hard-eyed cynicism, Henry's world of dreams
crashes like the pillaged city. He barters his captive Ysobel
for 20,000 pieces of eight and sails back to England to work
his way into the King's favor and to marry still another Elizabeth, a manipulative, domineering creature who clearly is
not the Elizabeth of his boyhood dreams. This Elizabeth
domesticates his dream by bringing it into social conformity.

Steinbeck does not directly offer a neat compromise to
the tension between social structures and individual freedom in *Cup of Gold*. Implicit is the notion that people will
dream and must be free to dream to find self-worth and

order. Also implicit, however, is the idea that the dream it-self can possess a person and must be ordered according to some social framework. Henry Morgan is hurled to terrible extremes: in the first he is consumed by the dream; in the second he is consumed by civilization. This tension pro-vides a recurring framework for Steinbeck throughout his early work, perhaps dominant in *Of Mice and Men,* and controlled finally in *The Grapes of Wrath.* It always is close at hand in his fiction, however, and can be traced down the many pages through *The Winter of Our Discontent.*

Cup of Gold was a notable experiment and announced several of Steinbeck's primary artistic themes, although they were not clearly articulated. Flawed in composition, it nonetheless tells a captivating story with energy and force, and is certainly superior to the murkiness of his third book, *To a God Unknown,* which fails primarily because Stein-beck was using a rather thin story line as a vehicle to probe some peculiar mysticism. In a letter to Carlton Sheffield, Steinbeck expressed his intention in *To a God Unknown:* "The story is a parable, Duke. The story of a race, growth and death. Each figure is a population, and the stones, the trees, the muscled mountains are the world—but not the world apart from man—the world *and* man—the one in-separable unit man plus his environment."[9] This aim—to have each element of the story point toward parable—fi-nally diminishes the telling of the story itself. Steinbeck had not yet learned the lesson he later mastered in *The Pearl:* to let the parable arise naturally from the narrative. When Joseph Wayne says, for example, "'They might say I feel like the bull. Well I do, Burton. And if I could mount a cow and fertilize it, do you think I'd hesitate?'" (*TGU,* p. 23), one would expect the man to be a bit concerned, at least, for the details of his farming. But Wayne is more in tune with a kind of orgiastic religion of fertility than with fertility itself. His lands and flocks multiply almost in spite of him, and they deteriorate, Steinbeck would have us be-lieve, because of him. Joseph is given too often to melo-dramatic stage speeches, while he seems physically incapable of much more than lying with his brother's wife or slitting his wrists atop the mossy rock. His own thinness as a character finally calls into question the whole mystical attitude Steinbeck advances in the novel. Howard Levant suggests that "the authorial indecision that presents Joseph, until the last possible moment, as a confused mystic rather than a convinced priest or god profoundly affects the credible presentation of nature worship."[10] One recalls Byron's lament in canto 1 of *Don Juan:*

I want a hero: an uncommon want,
    When every year and month sends forth a new one,
Til, after cloying the gazettes with cant,
    The age discovers he is not the true one.[11]

Steinbeck, too, wanted a hero but cast Joseph Wayne in such tattered rags of mysticism that he was unrecognizable as such. What Steinbeck needed, as he discovered soon after his apprenticeship with *Cup of Gold* and *To a God Unknown*, was a hero with dirt on his feet, human tears in his eyes, perhaps a small smile in his heart—one of the real people of the earth that he would find through his short stories of this period.

3

Dreams and Dreamers: The Short Stories

IN *Cup of Gold*, Steinbeck began to realize the importance of locating a physical, geographical place for his characters, of seeing them in a living environment, as he later made clear in *The Sea of Cortez*. Many of the flaws in *Cup of Gold* and *To a God Unknown* are attributable to his inability at this early stage of his writing to locate characters in a living environment. The reader receives indications of Steinbeck working toward this in *To a God Unknown*—in the curious village customs, the mysticism revealed in the peasants' daily lives and habits, their ornery and attractive personalities, and their deep, rhythmic relationship to the land. In *The Pastures of Heaven*, Steinbeck focused on such events solely, content to let the mystery grow out of the land and its people, thereby, in this subdued and realistic accounting, achieving his first clear artistic success.

While *Cup of Gold* and *To a God Unknown* evidence artistic failures, Steinbeck achieved a mature and sophisticated artistry in both of his early collections of short stories, *The Pastures of Heaven* and *The Long Valley*. He moved from surreal adventure and unreal mysticism to simple, dramatic portraits of characters and places he knew firsthand. Several of these short works achieve greatness; all are concerned to some degree with the theme of human freedom and the constraints of social conventions. Several of the most successful sketches also bear on artistic freedom in society.

BACKGROUND TO THE WRITING

The Pastures of Heaven is in the form of a collection of
sketches,[1] unified in a quasi-novelistic structure by the narrative frame of the wayward Spanish soldier who first saw
the verdant valley and the equally wayward bus driver
(both of whom herd a line of "slaves"). The title is ironic
since these pastures of heaven are inhabited by human beings who manifest every joy but also every perversity and
tragedy imaginable. In May, 1931, Steinbeck wrote to Ted
Miller of his thematic plan for the work, discussing how
happy the valley was until a certain family moved into it:

> They were just common people, they had no particular pro-
> fundities or characters except that a kind of cloud of uninten-
> tional evil surrounded them. Everything they touched went rot-
> ten, every institution they joined broke up in hatred. Remember,
> these people were not malicious nor cruel nor extraordinary in
> any way, but their influence caused everybody in the valley to
> hate everybody else. . . . This is a true account of it. I am simply
> taking a number of families and showing the influence of the un-
> conscious evil of the M———s. You see each family will be a
> separate entity with its own climax and end, and they will be
> joined by locality, by the same characters entering into each and
> by this nameless sense and power of evil. Do you think that is a
> good plan or not. At any rate, that is what I am working on, and I
> think the ironic name The Pastures of Heaven and the nebulous
> parallel of the M———s with the Miltonian Lucifer is fairly
> good.[2]

Further unifying the sketches is the theme of exercising
dominion and control over the land, a symbol of the order
of the characters themselves. Opening the sketches with
the Munroe family exorcising the ghosts of the old Battle
farm is no accident; order may be imposed, but still the
ghosts in this xenophobic valley linger. T. B. Allen points
out to Bert Munroe that "'maybe your curse and the farm's
curse has mated and gone into a gopher hole like a pair of

rattlesnakes. Maybe there'll be a lot of baby curses crawling around the Pastures the first thing we know'" (*PH*,
p. 20). And to a certain extent this is true as other inhabitants come to subdue their ghosts. Edward ("Shark")
Wicks, with his actual poverty and imaginary wealth, discovers that his actual wealth lies in what he had imagined
to be his poverty—the land itself and the "healing genius"
of his wife. Some, like the Lopez sisters, whose sketch was
excerpted from an early draft of *To a God Unknown*, bring
to the valley robust good health and a curious morality,
while others like Helen and Hilda Van Deventer bring torment that they hope to lay to rest. In each instance, however, the Pastures comprises its own little civilization, exercising restraint, granting direction, often providing solace.
Whether one is in conflict with oneself or the world, the
Pastures is a world of its own where one can work out the
conflict and perhaps find freedom.

Except perhaps for the artist. It is not surprising that artistic freedom becomes a strong theme in Steinbeck's early
work, given the constraints Steinbeck himself felt as he
considered his work in terms of public and critical reception. While a number of scholars have observed this theme
in *Cup of Gold*, particularly in the tension between the
poet Merlin who sings in Avalon and the congenital over-
reacher Morgan who battles his sins in an overwhelming darkness, the theme becomes more specific in several
sketches from *The Pastures of Heaven* and in several short
stories from *The Long Valley*. The analysis here focuses on
that theme in several key stories.

"TULARECITO"

The theme is evident first of all and perhaps most clearly in
the captivating story of Tularecito, the little frog, the squat,
outcast toad of society who nonetheless has a gift for making art. Like the hero in the western tradition of literature,
Tularecito's origins are uncertain: "The origin of Tularecito

is cast in obscurity, while his discovery is a myth which the folks of the Pastures of Heaven refuse to believe, just as they refuse to believe in ghosts" (*PH*, p. 47). In this heroic tradition, as it stretches back at least to the Oedipus Cycle, ambiguity of parentage always suggests a divine visitation—that the uncertain lineage may originate ultimately in the gods and therefore the person has divine gifts. Tularecito is an odd hero, however, wholly at odds with this tradition. His ugly, distorted features suggest a diabolic rather than Olympian origin.

Yet his divine gift is quickly recognized. He has, Franklin Gomez recognizes, "planting hands"—"tender fingers that never injured a young plant nor bruised the surfaces of a grafting limb." Planting hands, a gift also possessed by Elisa Allen of "The Chrysanthemums," is a divine gift for Steinbeck, one closely allied with artistic endeavor.[3] These hands of Tularecito are capable of ornate carving:

Also Tularecito had an amusing gift. With his thumbnail he could carve remarkably correct animals from sandstone. Franklin Gomez kept many little effigies of coyotes and mountain lions, of chickens and squirrels, about the house. . . . Pancho, who had never quite considered the boy human, put his gift for carving in a growing category of diabolical traits definitely traceable to his supernatural origin. [P. 49]

The gift is also recognized by the schoolteacher, Miss Martin, who effusively encourages him:

Miss Martin was overcome with the genius of Tularecito. She praised him before the class and gave a short lecture about each one of the creatures he had drawn. In her own mind she considered the glory that would come to her for discovering and fostering this genius.

"I can make lots more," Tularecito informed her.

Miss Martin patted his broad shoulder. "So you shall," she said. "You shall draw every day. It is a great gift that God has given you." Then she realized the importance of what she had just said. She leaned over and looked searchingly into his hard eyes while she repeated slowly, "It is a *great gift* that God has given you." Miss Martin glanced up at the clock and announced crisply, "Fourth grade arithmetic—at the board." [P. 51]

But Miss Martin is a philistine, one who bestows praise like pennies from heaven, and then sweeps up the change. Hardly done with her encomium, she swoops to the board and wipes out God's gift. Arithmetic will take precedence over art as she sturdily erases the board. The classroom erupts into pandemonium as Tularecito battles to save his art; and why shouldn't he? Isn't it God's gift?

Fortunately Miss Martin has a minor nervous breakdown after the brawl and is replaced by Molly Morgan, who not only recognizes the gift of her ugly charge but also knows how to control it. Molly blocks off a section of the blackboard where Tularecito may draw to his heart's content. By providing limits, definition, and appropriate space, she confirms the artist. This is an ongoing tension in Steinbeck's work, the need for recognition of art but also a need for clear limits and definition, a kind of compromise between individual freedom and society, a recognition of importance and significance through recognition of place.

Finally, however, and despite the best efforts of Molly, the tension is doomed in this story. As the artist pushes ever outward in the exercise of his gift, so too Tularecito strays beyond the confines of his blackboard. Enchanted with gnomes and the surreal, imaginative world of faery, he identifies himself with those gnomes, and in an effort to find his true people, he trespasses on the Munroe property. When Bert tries to drive him off, Tularecito battles back and is summarily incarcerated in the insane asylum.

How far can the artist compromise? How far does he pursue his instincts and gifts before others call him insane and lock him away? While Steinbeck was on the verge of finding this out personally in his two great social novels, *In Dubious Battle* and *The Grapes of Wrath*, he also pursued it artistically in "The Chrysanthemums" from *The Long Valley*.

"THE CHRYSANTHEMUMS"

This is probably Steinbeck's most popularly successful short story—the one, along with "Flight" and "How Mr. Hogan Robbed the Bank," most likely to be included in anthologies. It is a well-paced and lively story, full of the multiple levels of meaning that Steinbeck cherished and intentionally scaled into his fiction. Steinbeck wrote in a February 25, 1934, letter to George Albee that "I shall be interested to know what you think of the story, The Chrysanthemums. It is entirely different and is designed to strike without the reader's knowledge. I mean he reads it casually and after it is finished feels that something profound has happened to him although he does not know what nor how" (*LL*, p. 91). Steinbeck wanted to capture the reader in a net of words so that the reader could not escape seeing multiple levels. Jackson Benson describes his effort:

Phrased one way or another, the idea of striking "without the reader's knowledge" was an aim commonly expressed by [Steinbeck] during these years [the early nineteen thirties], as if he plotted a channel of communication in each work that somehow bypassed or circumvented the brain, giving the reader an experience which then generated an emotion. His discussion along these lines indicates that he felt that the best fiction was that which brought its theme to the reader subliminally, and that the problem with criticism was that too many critics were insensitive to experience, operating too much by intelligence directed by expectation.[4]

The particular significance of the technique in "The Chrysanthemums" is that the story, while critically construed as one about a woman's place, as one dealing with rejection, or as a simple portrait of the Salinas Valley, is also clearly a story about artistic sensibility. Steinbeck supplies certain clues. Like Tularecito, Elisa Allen possesses "planter's hands," but ironically she wards them with "heavy leather gloves" except to work with her chrysanthemums or for her ritual cleansing.[5] The tinker who rejects her gift, on the contrary, has "calloused hands [that] . . . were cracked, and every crack was a black line" (*LV*, p. 14).

The tinker and Elisa form the essential tension of the story, and it is a tension richly woven and carefully arranged. In the initial description the valley is described as a closed-off, cloudy world sealed by the mountains: "The high grey-flannel fog of winter closed off the Salinas Valley from the sky and from all the rest of the world. On every side it sat like a lid on the mountains and made of the great valley a closed pot" (p. 9). The image foreshadows the tinker, who mends old pots but also throws out Elisa's carefully potted chrysanthemums, which he persists in pronouncing "chrysantheums." The contrast between these two characters is further developed. While Elisa is described as bursting with energy—"Her face was eager and mature and handsome; even her work with the scissors was over-eager, over-powerful" (p. 10)—the tinker is haunted by a sad, ponderous slowness. While Elisa works in wet sand to bring her chrysanthemums to life, she also says of the road that the tinker must take leading out of the valley, "I don't think your team could pull through the sand" (p. 14). Her valley is also closed in by wet sand; she is confined by it. Moreover, while her chrysanthemums rise sturdily from wet sand, the tinker's "horse and donkey drooped like unwatered flowers" (p. 13).

Elisa's world is one of careful neatness, one in which she "smoothed . . . and patted firm" the soil for her plants, which she had set in immaculate parallel rows. The tinker's slovenly wagon drips black paint "in sharp little points beneath each letter" of the word *Fixed*, suggesting that his fixing of things is also slovenly. This carefully structured tension between Elisa and the tinker is described by James Gray as a tension between the energy of the artist and the studied ignorance of society:

"The Chrysanthemums" . . . presents the problem of the artist in conflict with philistinism. It does so in a way that makes a familiar, but often drearily detailed, complaint seem immediate and moving because the storyteller has offered a small, unexpected, fully dramatized instance. . . . Imbedded in the narrative, which is tense despite its seeming casualness and powerful despite the modesty of its material, is the further implication that to be touched by meanness, even accidentally, is to be a little tainted by it.[6]

But the tension also occurs in Elisa herself. Her gift is constrained partly by her husband Henry Allen's wish that she would use her "planter's hands" more practically, to grow more fruit that can be sold as a profitable commodity rather than for the pragmatically useless artistry of her chrysanthemums. While for Elisa, as for John Keats, "'Beauty is truth, truth beauty,'—that is all / Ye know on earth, and all ye need to know," beauty is insufficient reason for its own being in the world of her Salinas Valley, and she compromises this artistic beauty partly in her garb in order to nurture it. She dresses her huge energy, which society might construe as "unsuitable" for a woman, in a man's wardrobe:

Her figure looked blocked and heavy in her gardening costume, a man's black hat pulled low down over her eyes, clod-hopper shoes, a figured print dress almost completely covered by a big corduroy apron with four big pockets to hold the snips, the trowel and scratcher, the seeds and the knife she worked with. She wore heavy leather gloves to protect her hands while she worked. [P. 10]

While she is at work, however, Elisa's energy nearly bursts from her. There may be autobiographical reasons for the garb Elisa wears. Jackson Benson points out the Elisa-Carol resemblance: "They are both strong, large-boned, and competent; both wear masculine clothes (Carol wore jeans and sweatshirts that nearly matched her husband's). Both are seen—Carol by those who knew her at the time—as handsome, rather than pretty."[7] Regardless of that, however, the implication in the story is clear, for the tinker recognizes her as a woman. He affirms her dreams, and suddenly it seems to Elisa that it may be right for a woman to exercise these creative gifts and to have dreams. Under his flattering, albeit deceiving, words, "she tore off the battered hat and shook out her dark pretty hair," revealing more of herself as a woman, an act that quickly becomes associated with her gift of the chrysanthemums to him. As she explains the mystery of planting hands, Elisa opens herself more and more as a woman:

"I can only tell you what it feels like. It's when you're picking off the buds you don't want. Everything goes right down into your fingertips. You watch your fingers work. They do it themselves. You can feel how it is. They pick and pick the buds. They never make a mistake. They're with the plant. Do you see? Your fingers and plant. You can feel that, right up your arm. They know. They never make a mistake. You can feel it. When you're like that you can't do anything wrong. Do you see that? Can you understand that?" [Pp. 18–19]

This is a significant passage for understanding Steinbeck's artistry, for the planting hands are metaphorical for the artist at work. In the passage above one could insert "the artist" for "hands" and "the story" for "the plant" and have a fairly accurate assessment of Steinbeck's view of the creative process.

In this passage of the story the hands become inseparably allied with Elisa's womanhood, as if she offers both to the tinker for verification and benediction. The passage becomes increasingly sexual as it reveals the heart of Elisa and her gift, culminating in the scene that Steinbeck left out of the original version and later reinserted. Elisa crouches before the greasy tinker "like a fawning dog." The scene is important, because as she has sublimated her artistic gift so too she has sublimated her womanhood. She now almost dares believe that she can be free to be a woman *and* an artist. But quickly the tinker retreats, "It ain't the right kind of a life for a woman," and we find the inevitable rejection of her artistic gift foreshadowed as he withdraws from her offer. Elisa knows at this point that she has been used.

The tinker departs into what she calls "a bright direction. There's a glowing there." For a moment he inadvertently opened a door an inch or so on possibility, but also on her realization of the fragility of her dream, which is dashed like the snapped-off chrysanthemums wilting in the road.

As if divesting herself of the dream and regaining her accustomed role, she undergoes a ritual cleansing:

In the bathroom she tore off her soiled clothes and flung them into the corner. And then she scrubbed herself with a little block of pumice, legs and thighs, loins and chest and arms, until her skin was scratched and red. When she had dried herself she stood in front of a mirror in her bedroom and looked at her body. She tightened her stomach and threw out her chest. [P. 20]

The words are decidedly masculine once again—"legs and thighs, loins and chest and arms." And so Henry finds her when he comes banging in the door: "'Why—why Elisa. You look so nice!'" When she queries him, "'Nice? You think I look nice? What do you mean by "nice"?'" his "nice" changes to "strong." This is what she wants to hear; yes, there is strength in being an artist, and also in being a woman, "'I never knew before how strong.'" But her strength is as fragile as the snapped chrysanthemums lying in the road; she has been used, and she reverts to the sure, safe path she has led—her art and her strength hidden. There will be no prize fight; there will be only a "good dinner" and Elisa "crying weakly—like an old woman." [8]

While several of Steinbeck's sketches and stories of this early period deal symbolically with the dream of the artist, the artist's freedom of expression, and the constraints of society upon that freedom, nearly all the work does have the theme of freedom and constraint woven into it somehow. This may be dramatically cast in such well-known stories as "Flight," where Pepe's dream of manhood becomes woefully synonymous with murder, and he is hunted down like animal prey. We see it in Junius Maltby, who seems a prototype of Samuel Hamilton. The tension is particularly well focused in the Pat Humbert sketch from *The Pastures of Heaven* and in "The Harness" from *The Long Valley*.

PAT HUMBERT

With the possible exception of Helen Van Deventer living under the curse of a tyrannical dream of ordering her household and her psychotic daughter (a dream exploded in her murder of the daughter), no one in *The Pastures of Heaven* seems to feel the tyranny of the past more terribly than Pat Humbert. He was reared in a tight little cell of rectitude nailed shut by resentment: "Pat Humbert's parents were middle-aged when he was born; they had grown old and stiff and spiteful before he was twenty. All of Pat's life had been spent in an atmosphere of age, of the aches and illness, of the complaints and self-sufficiency of age. While he was growing up, his parents held his opinions in contempt because he was young" (*PH*, p. 177). And so Pat grew up without opinions, because if he were to have them, they would be worthless. In a sense Pat Humbert is the male counterpart of Elisa Allen.

Pat first tastes the heady wine of freedom when his parents die. Although his parents loathed the life they had been given, they fought desperately to retain it. Pat is thirty when they die, but a child in terms of responsibility to himself. The ghosts of his parents linger in the old house, sitting in judgment on every move he makes, every dream he dares entertain. But for the first time he realizes that he does not have to do it, that he is in fact free to do what he wants: "He felt like a boy who breaks school to walk in a deep and satisfying forest" (p. 184). In his revolt lies his freedom, but there is no joy in it. He has locked a door on the ghosts but has opened no new ones; the ghosts continue to rattle the chains of duty in his brain.

A ten-year period of searching desperately for companionship follows; the farm is flourishing healthy and straight under the spur of his lonely labor when one day Mae and Mrs. Munroe walk by, and Pat receives his vision of freedom. He will transform the house, and Mae will be his bride. A flame heats his mind as he broaches the parlor housing his parents' ghosts:

Pat knew where lay the centre of his fears. He walked rapidly through the room brushing the cobwebs from his eyes as he went. The parlour was still dark for its shutters were closed. Pat didn't have to grope for the table; he knew exactly where it was. Hadn't it haunted him for ten years? He picked up table and Bible together, ran out through the kitchen and hurled them into the yard. [P. 193]

In a frenzy of motion he hurls all reminders in a pile and burns them: "'You *would* sit in there all these years, wouldn't you?' he cried. 'You thought I'd never get up the guts to burn you. Well, I just wish you could be around to see what I'm going to do, you rotten stinking trash'" (p. 194). He has purged himself with fire; perhaps the dream can grow like a phoenix out of the ashes.

At first it seems to. With unstinting labor Pat remakes the house into his idealized Vermont cottage, always framing it for the bride whom he would bring there: "Now she was entering the kitchen. The kitchen wouldn't be changed, for that would make the other room a bigger surprise. She would stand in front of the door, and he would reach around her and throw it open" (p. 196). As the time for fulfillment of the dream arrives, he rides to propose to Mae, tragically on the very evening when she is celebrating her engagement to another. The dream has overridden Pat; he stands devastated by the reality he never accounted for, and he returns wearily to a house full of ghosts.

"THE HARNESS"

Pat Humbert cannot be freed; he is chained to his ghosts by a past that he cannot change and a present that he cannot control. It seems that all his dreams are doomed. Peter Randall of "The Harness," originally entitled "The Fool," etches the message even more deeply: we all wear a harness either of social constraint or of the constraints imposed by our own minds. Real or imaginary, it amounts to the same thing, a horrible kind of imprisonment from which one can never wholly break free. But beneath Peter's authoritative, harnessed demeanor lies "a force held caged."

Like Shark Wicks in *The Pastures of Heaven*, Peter Randall is a leader in the valley, a grave, stalwart man to whom others look for advice and pattern. Unlike the farmers, whose bodies are bent from long leaning to the earth, Peter stands with the straight rigidity of one who has conquered; but, we discover, his straightness of posture is artificial, imposed on him by his wife, who insists that he be trussed in a cumbersome harness. After twenty-one years of marriage Peter and Emma have a house as perfect as a museum piece, a magnificent farm, no children, and very little if any love. When Emma dies, Peter sets out to divest himself of her ghost. He explains to an embarrassed Ed Chappell:

"I don't know how she got me to do things, but she did. She didn't seem to boss me, but she always made me do things. You know, I don't think I believe in an after-life. When she was alive, even when she was sick, I had to do things she wanted, but just the minute she died, it was—why like that harness coming off! I couldn't stand it. It was all over. I'm going to have to get used to going without that harness." He shook his finger in Ed's direction. "My stomach's going to stick out," he said positively. "I'm going to let it stick out. Why, I'm fifty years old." [*LV*, p. 118]

During all these years, however, Peter has exercised his one small bit of freedom in annual, week-long drunken sprees in San Francisco. To these too he has become a kind of slave; this too is a pretense that chains him: "'I'm a natural fool! For twenty years I've been pretending I was a wise, good man—except for that one week a year.' He said loudly, 'Things have been dribbled out to me. My life's been dribbled out to me'" (p. 120).

For a time after Emma's death Peter discovers a new freedom in his land, planting the rich earth in sweet peas for no other reason than that he wants to and that he likes their scent. Free of the harness, he slouches over the land and is rewarded with a sea of flowers, a heaven-sent aroma, and an unexpected bonanza of wealth from the crop:

If the year and the weather had been manufactured for sweet peas, they couldn't have been better. The fog lay close to the ground in the mornings when the vines were pulled. When the great piles of vines lay safely on spread canvasses, the hot sun shone down and crisped the pods for the threshers. The neighbors watched the long cotton sacks filling with round black seeds, and they went home and tried to figure out how much money Peter would make on his tremendous crop. [P. 126]

The only problem Peter has is what to do with his wealth. His life has been a lurching series of steps toward dead ends. This one opens no new road: he winds up in San Francisco once more, unable to shake the constraints of the past:

Peter's swaying head rose up slowly. He stared owlishly at Ed Chappell. "She didn't die dead," he said thickly. "She won't let me do things. She's worried me all year about those peas." His eyes were wondering. "I don't know how she does it." Then he frowned. His palm came out, and he tapped it again. "But you mark, Ed Chappell, I won't wear that harness, and I damn well won't ever wear it. You remember that." [P. 126]

"I won't wear the harness," he vows. He doesn't have to. He has it imprinted on his spirit.

In his brief discussion of Steinbeck in *Writers in Crisis,* Maxwell Geismar asks this question: "Dwelling in those green pastures of the world, humanity, which as the young Steinbeck views it is potentially good, finds itself constantly thwarted, its little visions of peace endlessly crushed. What is, then, the curse which defeats us?"[9] Geismar cannot find a satisfactory answer to the question, as in fact Steinbeck himself could not at this point. Steinbeck does attest to the fact that hope rises ever renewed, that the hopeful vision recurs with each generation. Yet individual freedom seems constantly dashed by the constraints society places on one. Perhaps the answer lies in part in *Cup of Gold*, with Morgan's compromise with civilization. Perhaps it lies in another book of the thirties, *Tortilla Flat*, which finds an undiluted joy in simple acceptance of life as it is given and says that by drawing in the horizons of one's world a bit one may live fully and joyfully while the rest of the world, with its mad, ulcer-eaten tigers, destroys itself.

The theme of freedom and constraint can be traced in other works of Steinbeck during the first decade, but it reaches an apex in *Of Mice and Men*, where the individual dream is tragically destroyed by society and in *In Dubious Battle*, where, in the valley of destruction, the plea for freedom becomes the ringing shout of the mob.

Vintage of the Earth: *In Dubious Battle* and *Of Mice and Men*

INTERLUDE: *The Red Pony*

WHILE "THE CHRYSANTHEMUMS" merits attention because of the accomplished suggestiveness of its artistry, and while stories such as "The Harness" bear witness to Steinbeck's theme of individual freedom and social constraint, *The Red Pony* almost seems set apart from the works of this period as an enduring classic. The story cuts through all levels, enjoyed by children in appreciation for the adolescent protagonist Jody Tiflin, and enjoyed by many for its expert rendition of the so-called animal genre that has been popular for years in books ranging from *Lad* and *Lassie* to *Old Yeller* and *Sounder*. Further, it has been enjoyed for years by college students and other academics for its moving portrayal of a people's dreams, their struggle with a land and society, and their finding of a place to call home.

The "pony story," as Steinbeck first called it, was probably begun in late 1932 (soon after the publisher of *The Pastures of Heaven* went bankrupt) and continued into 1933 under most trying conditions. Steinbeck's mother was dying, and much of the work was under constant interruption: "I am typing the second draft of the pony story. A few pages a day. This morning is a good example. One paragraph—help lift the patient on bed pan. Back, a little ill, three paragraphs, help turn patient so sheets can be changed. Back—three lines, nausea, hold pans, help change bedding, back."[1] Still, the work progressed, and during that summer McIntosh and Otis had placed the first two of the projected four "stories" of the novella with the *North American Review,* one of the most prestigious monthlies of the time. The stories were published in November and December, 1933. During the winter and spring of 1934 Steinbeck wrote the remaining two stories of the novella but, although the *North American Review* had accepted three other Steinbeck stories by this time, it turned down further "pony" stories. In a May, 1934, entry in his journal Steinbeck noted that it was time to start blending the "five stories . . . about Jody" into one book (one story was either discarded or, more likely, not actually written). At Covici's urging, the work was brought out in a limited, signed edition in 1937 (699 numbered copies).

The story having been written under the trying circumstances of his mother's illness, it is not surprising that death has a major role in the events of the novella. The deaths range from the hard and brutal death of the red pony to the rather mystical passing of old Gitano. Combined with the deaths, of course, is the major theme of renewal of life, symbolized particularly in the new colt that is lifted from old Nellie's dead body.

Working through the major themes of death and renewal, of dreams such as Grandfather's and the confines of civilization upon it, is also the theme of freedom and constraint that especially marks the tension between Carl and Jody Tiflin. Probably like any other boy his age, Jody feels that the restriction dominates the freedom:

When the wood-box was full, Jody took his twenty-two rifle up to the cold spring at the brush line. He drank again and then aimed the gun at all manner of things, at rocks, at birds on the wing, at the big black pig kettle under the cypress tree, but he didn't shoot for he had no cartridges and wouldn't have until he was twelve. If his father had seen him aim the rifle in the direction of the house he would have put the cartridges off another year. . . . Nearly all of his father's presents were given with reservations which hampered their value somewhat. It was good discipline. [P. 13]

Gabilan, then, represents a new horizon in Jody's freedom, freedom to ride and explore, but also the freedom for Jody himself to be the one to discipline and train. But in any such fine tension life holds an unaccountable trick: death itself. Death seems to appear in different fashions in the novella: the death of Gabilan, the surrealistic death of Gitano riding Easter upward into the misty mountains, the death of Old Nellie, which brings forth the new colt, and the lingering death of Grandfather, who is not yet dead but who stopped living when the great dream of westering collided with the sea and civilization began pressing on its heels. Each story begins in hope and promise; each hope and promise collide with inevitable demise.

Are all dreams doomed? Jody says to Grandfather: "'Maybe I could lead the people some day.'" And Grandfather tells him: "'No place to go, Jody. Every place is taken. But that's not the worst—no, not the worst. Westering has died out of the people. Westering isn't a hunger any more. It's all done. Your father is right. It is finished'" (p. 119). But still the hunger arises in man; somehow the hunger is renewed.

The hunger is renewed especially in *In Dubious Battle* and *Of Mice and Men*. The popular success of *Tortilla Flat* in 1935 seemed to give wings to Steinbeck's writing, an assurance of worth and confidence in technique that exploded into a frenetic labor culminating in *The Grapes of Wrath*. Each of these novels provides variations on the dream for a better life and the tension between individual freedom to pursue that dream and social constraints upon it, but each does so in radically different ways, as if the three were to fold in on each other for some final answer. Clearly, in the writing of *In Dubious Battle*, Steinbeck was finding a new artistic and thematic path for finding that answer.

In Dubious Battle

The writing of *In Dubious Battle* began in mid-August, 1934, but the roots of the story go considerably further back. Discovering those roots is important, for in part such knowledge counters the frequent charge against Steinbeck that in the works of the mid- to late 1930s he was concerned with ideology rather than people, that his characters were pawns rather than living beings, and that he idealized a situation and a people of whom he had little firsthand knowledge. In terms of aesthetic consideration the issue is one of sincerity, and because of the contention that arose over Steinbeck's work in this decade, the issue warrants close attention.

While it is not an aesthetic defect for an author to have no firsthand, personal knowledge of the subject matter he deals with, one appreciates a sense of sincerity in the author when he deals with social issues.[2] Such sincerity, as Lionel Trilling pointed out, should be understood as authenticity—providing a realistic account of the events as they happen—and presupposes some involvement by the author in those events as well as his belief that those events hold significance. Unlike Émile Zola's exhortation to artistic impersonality at the turn of the century (particularly in his essay "The Experimental Novel," where he argued that the writer must be only a scientist, whose work must have the certainty, the solidity, and the practical application of a work of science),[3] Steinbeck believed that the artist could be, in fact, should be, personally very much involved in his subject matter. In this belief Steinbeck may have found himself allied in aesthetic attitude with Trilling, who argued many years later against the point of view Zola represented:

The doctrine of the impersonality of the artist was loyally seconded by the criticism that grew up with the classic modern literature. In its dealing with personality this criticism played an elaborate, ambiguous and arbitrary game. While seeking to make us ever more sensitive to the implications of the poet's voice in its unique quality, including inevitably those implications that are personal before they are moral and social, it was at the same time very strict in its insistence that the poet is not a person at all, only a *persona*, and that to impute to him a personal existence is a breech of literary decorum.[4]

Sincerity, in Trilling's estimation, had degenerated in the modern age to a kind of artistic solipsism. "To thine own self be true" represents sincerity that denies the real life that the artist must sooner or later find himself in. Confronted on the one hand with the cult of impersonality as set forth by Zola and on the other hand with the cult of Rousseauistic sentimentality passing itself off as sincerity, Trilling encourages the artist to authenticity. If one accepts Trilling's terms, Steinbeck is sincere in that he is authentic, grappling straightforwardly with a life of which he is a part. This is not to say that the author takes an interested view of that life, that is, that he has a personal, vested motive at stake, for he can be disinterested, objective, and still profoundly a part of it.

Many early critics questioned the worth of works such as *In Dubious Battle, Of Mice and Men,* and *The Grapes of Wrath* by charging that Steinbeck had created an artificial world of which he had little or no direct knowledge. That they were wrong did not stop them from their contention. Yet it is true that a certain respectability and validity are warranted to an author who has in fact had some firsthand experience of the events he records, the materials he artistically arranges. This clearly applies to Steinbeck in this instance for several reasons.

One might consider the pattern of his early working career, particularly at the Spreckels Plant, where he dealt directly and daily with migrants and paisanos off and on for several summers in and before the early 1920s. This in itself is not noteworthy, since many people order workers around without knowing them in the least. But the biographical evidence suggests that from the start Steinbeck's interests were with the people who worked there and that he formed a strong and immediate understanding with them. His work at the Spreckels Plant had two immediate effects on his writing. First, as Thomas Kiernan tells it, Steinbeck became dissatisfied with the ethereal and abstracted nature of the writing he had attempted to this point and began to see the need to root his writing in real people and places:

Steinbeck did begin to sense during his stay at the Spreckels ranch that his conception of writing was all wrong. He sensed it undoubtedly through his aborted attempts to write complete stories. Facilely able to begin a work, as he proceeded he found it more and more difficult to credibly sustain it, to develop the action and characters believably within the grandiose thematic scope that had inspired his story. Most of the time he would get halfway through a piece of writing and then throw down his pencil and tear up the pages in despair, knowing that it didn't work but not knowing why.[5]

Second, he obtained the opportunity for work alongside the people in the fields when he resigned his position of "civil engineer" and worked on the Spreckels ranches around King City and Santa Clara with the migrants, bindlestiffs, and bums who peopled his novels of the later thirties.

Another factor in Steinbeck's experience of the migrants and lower-class people of his novels, however, comes directly from his own youth. Jackson Benson fills in this overlooked and important side of Steinbeck's childhood:

Some have the impression that Steinbeck got much of his information about the Mexican-Americans and *paisanos* second- and third-hand, but he knew them well from childhood on. His friend Max Wagner had lived in Mexico until he was twelve, and together they were friendly with a number of Mexican families in Salinas, expecially the Sanchez brothers, with whom Steinbeck ran around in his late teens. From his association with the Mexican nationals who worked at Spreckels, he picked up several of the characters and stories that he used later in Tortilla Flat.[6]

A third factor accounting for Steinbeck's interest in, attraction to, and knowledge of these Salinas Valley migrants and working men would derive from his voracious appetite for valley news and a retentive memory that fastened like hooks on human details. Steinbeck was never a neat and thorough notetaker, but odd tidbits of information stuck with him, and years later he could reconstruct that information, not only in its facts but in its living environment, whole and clean. A large part of his early work was based on events in the Salinas Valley, from *The Pastures of Heaven*, which, he often pointed out in correspondence, derived from real-life events, to stories like "The Vigilante" from *The Long Valley*, derived directly from newspaper accounts of a hanging in Carol's home town.[7] However valuable newspaper accounts were as a stimulus and a framework, they never took precedence with Steinbeck over arrangement, the artistic creation of character and scene. Nonetheless, a dramatic reversal of technique occurs in the mid-thirties. While *Cup of Gold* and *To a God Unknown* were written in closed-off places as cerebral exercises, during the writing of *In Dubious Battle*, Steinbeck often ventured to the fields to test the speech, habits, and mannerisms of his characters against living people. The scrupulous attention to detail and accuracy that gave his journalism of the period its power also gave power and authenticity to his fiction. The portrait of Steinbeck during the thirties, then, is that of a knowledgeable and deeply sensitive artist. He was a particularly appropriate candidate to handle the historical drama behind *In Dubious Battle* in artistic fashion.

And it was a historical drama, as Jackson Benson and Anne Loftis have convincingly demonstrated in their "John Steinbeck and Farm Labor Unionization: The Background of *In Dubious Battle*." Convinced that the novel "is dramatically effective and convincingly realistic," Benson and Loftis pursue the question: "But how historically accurate is the novel, actually?"[8] Beyond the puzzle of who the purported Communist sympathizers were who gave Steinbeck information and in which valley the strike took place (whether the Pajaro Valley near Watsonville or some other),[9] Benson and Loftis attempt, and succeed in the effort, to reconstruct the entire artistic and historical background of the novel.

Their scrupulous historical research can be summarized as follows. Recovering from an economic slump in the late

twenties, agricultural production in California increased
during the early thirties. Wages, however, continued the
downward spiral of the prior decade. Protest strikes began
to break out but were easily quelled by the greater power
of the growers, the ineffectiveness of the strike leaders, and
the vast supply of cheap labor from the newer, Depression-
era migrants. Clearly the workers needed leadership, which
was supplied in late 1932 when the Communist party organized the Cannery and Agricultural Workers' Industrial
Union. According to Benson and Loftis:

> The skill of the C. & A. W. I. U. took the growers by surprise. For a
> year there were more victories (usually modest gains in hourly
> wages) than defeats. While the organization had weaknesses—it
> was badly split between the doctrinaire party leaders in the cities
> and the pragmatic organizers in the field—it did have the great
> strength of being able to mobilize support, moral and material,
> among those sympathetic to the farm workers' plight.[10]

The significant parts of this movement for Steinbeck were
that, first, he knew the workers, and second, he gained the
acquaintance, through a Carmel area sympathizer, Francis
Whitaker, of several of the strike leaders, including the
valley prototypes of Mac and Jim Nolan. Thus began an intimate and informed knowledge of the whole labor movement. In his biography of Steinbeck, Benson details one of
several means by which Steinbeck garnered information.
After the 1934 San Joaquin Valley strike a key movement
organizer named Cicil McKiddy had fled to the home of a
local farm-labor leader in Seaside (a residential-commercial
community a few miles north of Monterey). There he continued his organizational activities under cover and in hiding. According to Benson:

> Steinbeck has talked to McKiddy for hours at a time over the
> course of several weeks, questioning him in great detail. I should
> add, however, that although McKiddy was Steinbeck's major
> source for *In Dubious Battle*, he talked to other men involved in

farm-labor organizing as well. Also, he had, of course, his own background in farm labor (there had been talk of organizing even in those days, as the influence of the I.W.W. swept down from the Northwest), and he went out himself, during the summer of 1934, to the migrant camps in the Salinas area to listen to the workers talk.[11]

That Steinbeck had access to important firsthand information is clear, but equally clear is that his aim by no means was to provide a history. Nonetheless, parallels emerge between the historical strike site and Steinbeck's fictional one, as Benson and Loftis point out:

Although not a small apple-growing valley dominated by a few large growers, the Tagus Ranch did present some similarities to Steinbeck's Torgus [*sic*] Valley. Off highway 99 below Fresno and about six or seven miles above Tulare, the ranch spread over four thousand acres, all planted in peaches. The ranch was divided into a half-dozen sections, each with a camp for migrant workers. The workers were Mexicans plus Dust Bowl migrants. The ranch had a company store and issued company tokens to be used at the store. Pat Chambers claims that they had people working there for three or four seasons that had never seen any cash paid out by the ranch. To insure careful handling, most fruit picking, whether apples or peaches, was paid for by the hour, and the price offered by the management of the Tagus Ranch in the summer of 1933 was identical to that offered by the Growers Association in Steinbeck's novel—fifteen cents an hour.[12]

But here also arise several key differences between history and fiction. There is a marked difference between party leader Pat Chambers' and Mac's attitudes toward their men. While Mac "uses" them like ciphers in development of his movement, Chambers seemed to be motivated by a genuine admiration for the men and commitment to them. Benson and Loftis quote from an interview with Chambers in which the party leader says:

As human beings go, I don't think you'll find many better than
farm workers. . . . The overriding purpose was [to improve] conditions; wages were a part. . . . To achieve that, you had to create
unity. After that, if any organization came, that was a bonus. Your
first consideration was the needs of working people. You ask
nothing from them. You don't try to build an organization at their
expense.[13]

Other differences are noted by Benson and Loftis. Chambers and another leader, Caroline Decker, had to be very
cautious about the mixed ethnic backgrounds of the workers: blacks, Hispanics, migrants. The issue does not enter
In Dubious Battle. Chambers and Decker avoided ideology
but openly called the workers "comrades." Mac and Jim
avoid that term but are unswerving in their party loyalty.

Other details of a fascinating historical background are
provided by Benson and Loftis, some parallels to the novel
and some differences. Finally they poise us on the thin line
between fact and fiction. In early reviews *In Dubious Battle*
was proclaimed as "a straight story" of real human events[14]
and as "one of the most courageous and desperately honest
books that has appeared in a long time."[15] And in early criticism *In Dubious Battle* was proclaimed to be a story about
"perversion of justice in the interest of owners, destruction of property and life, danger of violent revolution."[16]
The focus of attention lay decidedly in the historical accounting of the novel. In fact, the historical background did
profoundly affect Steinbeck, and he steeped himself in it;
but then he put it in the subconscious background as he
crafted a wholly new—if parallel—world in his novel.

But if he was not content merely to give a historical rendition, if he was in fact "rearranging" an artistic perception
of reality into a new artistic work, what was it that Steinbeck was creating in *In Dubious Battle?* What motivated
and guided his rearrangement in the production of an artistic work? There are two responses to the question. The first
lies in Steinbeck's exploration of what he called the Phalanx, the mob psychology of humanity. And this raises addi-

tional questions: Are human beings merely animals working collectively in one large organism? The answer is that
humans can be but that they are not necessarily so. And
that answer leads to the second fundamental response: the
small struggles to achieve human dreams and establish human freedom in the quasi-Miltonic hell that is modern life.
Benson and Loftis consider the final point:

We cannot fault Steinbeck for being convincing, nor can we
blame him for having chosen from his sources what he wished for
his own purposes. The trouble lies in our persistent tendency to
view the novel on our own, usually political and journalistic,
terms. There is a darkness in this book that is pervasive. It runs
from dark nights of confusion and muttering nightmares, to sullen, cloudy days of rain-soaked mobs, to dimly lit tents and their
whispered conspiracies, into the souls of the bitter, suspicious
men. This may not be Milton's hell, but it is certainly hell, nevertheless. That this depiction of hell, this parable of man's self-
hatred, should still be thought of as one of our most journalistically
truthful novels is an ironic comment on our times, our taste, and
the relationship of our literature to our historical perceptions.[17]

A curious thing happened in the transformation of actual
event to novelistic event in that Steinbeck's own ideas also
underwent change. In his earliest references to the novel,
Steinbeck often described it as the Phalanx novel; enrap-
tured as he was at the time with his conception of the group
organism, it seems he wanted to make his conception concrete in fiction. In a letter of June 21, 1933, to Carlton
Sheffield, in which Steinbeck described his Group Man
theory at length, he announced his intentions:

And, when the parts of this thesis have found their places, I'll
start trying to put them into the symbolism of fiction.
The fascinating thing to me is the way the group has as a soul, a
drive, an intent, an end, a method, a reaction and a set of tro-
pisms which in no way resembles the same things possessed by
the men who make up the group. These groups have always been
considered as individuals multiplied. And they are not so. They

are beings in themselves, entities. Just as a bar of iron has none of the properties of the revolving, circling, active atoms which make it up, so these huge creatures, the groups, do not resemble the human atoms which compose them. [*LL*, p. 76]

Again, in a letter of approximately the same period to George Albee, Steinbeck discusses his Phalanx theory at length and announces: "I can't give you this thing completely in a letter, George. I am going to write a whole novel with it as a theme, so how can I get it in a letter?" (*LL*, p. 81). Steinbeck goes on to mention that Ed Ricketts had provided the "scientific" basis for the theory that virtually obsessed him during these months.

By the time he was well into the writing of *In Dubious Battle*, however, Steinbeck realized that he had something that was much larger than a novelistic portrayal of a highly speculative philosophy. To be sure, the Group Man theory still is imbedded in the story, but a deeper sense of the novel seemed to arise out of the many little dramas of the characters' lives. Thomas Kiernan believes that this change was the direct result of Steinbeck's firsthand involvement in the migrant experience itself:

In one sense the novel had gone badly. By the time he was well into it, Steinbeck had discovered that his characters would not behave according to his thematic plan. His phalanx theory remained intact, but it seemed not to work as an envelope for his story of migratory apple harvesters and Communist efforts to organize them. When he tried to impose upon the characters behavior and motivation that accorded with his theory, the action became leaden. Finally he abandoned his larger thematic purpose and concentrated on letting the characters follow their own inclinations. As a result, he produced a different book than he had set out to.[18]

Steinbeck himself realized the change, as he noted in a letter to George Albee dated January 15, 1935:

I had planned to write a journalistic account of a strike. But as I thought of it as fiction the thing got bigger and bigger. It couldn't be that. I've been living with this thing for some time now. I don't know how much I have got over, but I have used a small strike in an orchard valley as the symbol of man's eternal, bitter warfare with himself. [*LL*, p. 98]

Here he recognizes that the book is as much about characters as about a movement:

I'm not interested in strike as means of raising men's wages, and I'm not interested in ranting about justice and oppression, mere outcroppings which indicate the condition. But man hates something in himself. He has been able to defeat every natural obstacle but himself he cannot win over unless he kills every individual. And this self-hate which goes so closely in hand with self-love is what I wrote about. [*LL*, p. 98]

In its final form—although a much contested form in the editorial offices of Covici-Friede—the focus of the novel, taken from the epigraph from Milton's *Paradise Lost*, is on the dubious battle waged in the hearts of people, and is now centered in a character study of how one "uses" humanity. The central irony of the novel is that Mac and Jim Nolan use people every bit as much as the landowners do. Therefore, the battle is dubious, but the warfare may be won in the spirit of innumerable minor persons like Doc and Joy and London.

In Dubious Battle: USE VERSUS FREEDOM

The novel opens with Jim Nolan pictured as the man who has hit bottom, his life a dark litany of loss. His joining the Communist party is a reaction against loss rather than any direct commitment to principles. "'Why do you want to join the Party?'" asks Harry Nilson, to which Jim replies: "'Well—I could give you a lot of little reasons. Mainly, it's this: My whole family has been ruined by this system!'" (p. 5). He is a character motivated by desperation. The active commitment is not there initially, for, as Jim says, "'I feel dead.'" His rebirth is engineered by the party. When

Jim says, "'Hell, I've got nothing to lose,'" Harry responds:
"'Nothing except hatred. You're going to be surprised when
you see that you stop hating people. I don't know why it is,
but that's what usually happens'" (p. 9). It is questionable
whether Jim loses his hatred in the novel or merely re-
directs it to the landowners.

The descriptive framework for the opening of the novel
matches the deathlike despair of Jim Nolan. He comes in to
Harry from dark streets cast in a red glow:

> At last it was evening. The lights in the street outside came on,
> and the Neon restaurant sign on the corner jerked on and off, ex-
> ploding its hard red light in the air. Into Jim Nolan's room the sign
> threw a soft red light. For two hours Jim had been sitting in a
> small, hard rocking-chair, his feet up on the white bedspread.
> Now that it was quite dark, he brought his feet down to the floor
> and slapped the sleeping legs. [*IDB*, p. 1]

Joseph Fontenrose links this opening passage to the opening of *Paradise Lost:*

> This will be a novel about Reds, but the red light means much
> more than that. For *Paradise Lost* opens with Satan lying in de-
> feat, "rowling in the fiery Gulfe" (PL 1:52); there in a "dis-
> mal Situation waste and Wilde" he was surrounded by flames:
> "yet from those flames / No light, but rather darkness visible,"
> in regions where "hope never comes / That comes to all" (PL
> 1:60–67). Images of fire and of contrasting darkness pervade
> both *Paradise Lost* and *In Dubious Battle.*[19]

There are clear parallels with *Paradise Lost* in the novel,
although perhaps not quite so many as Fontenrose sees.[20]
The key items in this initial setting, however, are that Jim is
lifted from a dark abyss of despair by the party and is given
light (at first the "hard white light" by which he types party
letters) and direction. As Jim and Mac set off in that direction, hopping a freight at the railyards for the Torgas Valley,
the physical light is fresh and powerful: "The sun was just
clearing the buildings of the city. . . ." In terms of the
light-dark imagery with which Steinbeck so often frames

his fiction, it is significant that a great deal of the action, the dubious battle in the Torgas Valley, takes place by night or in murky, rainy, gray weather. The uncertain light and shifting weather are symbolic counterparts to the hazy battle of the strikers.

As Jim and Mac enter the Torgas Valley, the central theme of "using" is developed. It is established subtly at first, evident in the small techniques that Mac passes along to Jim, such as learning to smoke so he can establish his comradery with others, but it escalates rapidly into a forceful pattern. Mac sets it down as a creed:

"How are you going to go about getting started?" Jim asked.

"I don't know. We've got to use everything. Look, we start out with a general plan, but the details have to be worked out with any materials we can find. We use everything we can get hold of. That's the only thing we can do." [P. 43]

The first practice of the creed occurs when Jim and Mac enter the migrant jungle: "'Somebody's sick,' Mac said softly. 'We didn't hear it yet. It pays to appear to mind your own business'" (p. 45). Like a trap, Mac's mind snaps down on opportunity, no matter how he has to lie or cheat to turn it to his advantage. In this instance the opportunity is London's pregnant daughter, an opportunity Mac uses masterfully and ingeniously to unite the men. The only person who might suffer is Lisa, since Mac has no more idea how to deliver a baby than does any other man there. But it fits the creed: "'Well, there's just one rule—use whatever material you've got.'" The creed becomes overwhelming, and when the materials increasingly become human lives, one wonders what difference there is between Mac and the growers themselves. Both have their own, separate ends, but the means differ hardly at all.

The examples of such use of human life multiply. Old Dan, the former Wobblie and tree topper, is preyed upon not so much because he is a leader as because when his leg breaks he can be used. Mac's response to Old Dan's tragedy is simple:

Mac said, "Well, it's happened. I kind of expected it. It doesn't take much when the guys feel this way. They'll grab on anything. The old buzzard was worth something after all."

"Worth something?" Jim asked.

"Sure." He tipped the thing off. We can use him now." [P. 90]

Similarly, they will use Mr. Anderson. Here Mac is almost as wily as Milton's Satan, first using the dogs to win Anderson's favor and then using Anderson himself. When Jim objects, Mac responds: "'Don't you go liking people, Jim. We can't waste time liking people'" (p. 103). A third person tragically reduced to "use" is the brutalized party brawler, ironically named Joy. When Joy is cut down by a strikebreaker's bullet, Mac can afford no emotion for the life of a man who had given that life for the party. Here is the standard for Mac: "'He's done the first real useful thing in his life'" (p. 148). Declaring that "'we've got to use him to step our guys up, to keep 'em together,'" Mac bears up Joy's body like a bloody banner and parades through the camp. When the migrant leaders Dakin and London object, Mac exclaims: "'What we got to fight with? . . . We *got* to use him'" (p. 154). It is a sad and oppressive litany.

So thorough is Mac in the creed that he indoctrinates Jim only too well. The "use" theory does not permit men to be men; it sucks them up in the vortex of the Mob. Staggered by fever from his gunshot wound, Jim becomes the terrible phoenix, like Yeats's rough beast slouching toward Bethlehem, reborn from the ashes of Anderson's farm and the fiery energy of Mac's all-consuming plan. Mac recognizes it first, as well he should—this is his product: "'You're getting beyond me, Jim. I'm getting scared of you. I've seen men like you before. I'm scared of 'em. . . . Jim, it's not human. I'm scared of you'" (p. 249). Jim points out that "'I wanted you to use me. You wouldn't because you got to like me too well. . . . Now I'll use you, Mac. I'll use myself and you'" (p. 249). Finally, the movement, any movement, becomes an uncontrolled beast that devours humanity. The language of the creed is now thoroughly Jim's. After Sam

sets a neighboring ranch ablaze in retaliation for Anderson's
ruined ranch, Jim says calmly, "'We can use him, if he
comes back.'" In typical imagery of this period, Steinbeck
images Jim as an animal. Here he is described lying in fevered sleep:

The face was never still. The lips crept back until the teeth
were exposed, until the teeth were dry; and then the lips drew
down and covered them. The cheeks around the eyes twitched
nervously. Once, as though striving against weight, Jim's lips
opened to speak and worked on a word, but only a growling
mumble was said. [P. 254]

Jim has become bestial, has lost human individuality, and is
now the Group Man incarnate, like some strange and terrible force unleashed on the world.

The migrants, too, are now described as "a mechanism"
or in animal imagery. As the mob psychology escalates to
the same fevered pitch that possesses Jim, Mac comments
on how the strikers will handle the landowners' barricade:

"That's not what I mean. The *animal* don't want the barricade. I
don't know what it wants. Trouble is, guys that study people always think it's men, and it isn't men. It's a different kind of animal.
It's as different from men as dogs are. Jim, it's swell when we can
use it, but we don't know enough. When it gets started it might
do anything." [Pp. 288–89]

And like an animal pack, when one leader is killed off, another steps into its place. When Jim is killed, Mac steps
to the rude camp platform, the slain body propped gro-
tesquely behind him, and once again intones the words
from the "funeral" of Joy: "He moved his jaws to speak,
and seemed to break the frozen jaws loose. His voice was
high and monotonous. 'This guy didn't want nothing for
himself—' he began. His knuckles were white, where he
grasped the rail. 'Comrades! He didn't want nothing for
himself—'" (p. 313).

The narrative ends in a hopeless cycle. What ending

can there be? Steinbeck himself recognized this open-
endedness. He wrote to Mavis McIntosh:

> I hardly expect you to like the book. I don't like it. It is terrible.
> But I hope when you finish it, in the disorder you will feel a
> terrible kind of order. Stories begin and wander out of the pic-
> ture; faces look in and disappear and the book ends with no
> finish. A story of the life of a man ends with his death, but where
> can you end a story of a man-movement that has no end? No
> matter where you stop there is always more to come. I have tried
> to indicate this by stopping on a high point but it is by no means
> an ending. [*LL*, pp. 105–106]

The novel reveals the brutal inability of the Group Man
psychology to arrive at any significant answer, but if there
had been a transition in Steinbeck's thinking, from the
projected Phalanx novel to a novel about people, where
and how did this occur? Primarily in the character of Doc
Burton, a literary type of Ed Ricketts, as most critics agree,
but more precisely a spokesman here for Steinbeck himself.
The presence of Doc Burton is adroitly set up by Steinbeck. With the move to Anderson's farm, Mac needs the
sanction of the Health Department and immediately thinks
of Doc Burton. His description of Doc is telling and prophetic of the thematic role he will play in the novel: "He's a
queer kind of a duck, not a Party man, but he works all the
time for the guys" (p. 85). From the outset Doc is the man
set apart—neither migrant nor landowner, neither party
man nor townsman, but merely his own man. Doc tests all
parties, and he does so neither with judgment nor with
vested interest, but in a kind of probing Socratic argument
that studies all options to discover the one kernel of truth.
Interestingly enough, in their first of several dialogues together it is Mac who tests Doc about where he stands:

> Mac spoke softly, for the night seemed to be listening. "You're a
> mystery to me, too, Doc."
> "Me? A Mystery?"

"Yes, you. You're not a Party man, but you work with us all the time; you never get anything for it. I don't know whether you believe in what we're doing or not, you never say, you just work. I've been out with you before, and I'm not sure you believe in the cause at all." [P. 129]

In response, Doc points out the impossibility of finality in human affairs, an argument very much like Ricketts' in *The Sea of Cortez* as well as in his personal life. Because things constantly change, Doc personally holds the option of seeing things for what they are, not as they are colored by some cause: "'I don't want to put on the blinders of 'good' and 'bad,' and limit my vision. If I used the term 'good' on a thing I'd lose my license to inspect it, because there might be bad in it. Don't you see? I want to be able to look at the whole thing'" (p. 130). His argument proves true in the instance of this particular strike; the thing is a ceaseless movement, but only by pausing to study it carefully can one wrest any significance out of it. Therefore, Doc focuses on particular individuals rather than the group. Such a view as his does not risk "using" people by subsuming them under a cause. Rather it retains the freedom to see individual significance in each person, as Doc does, in fact, in his careful treatment of each of his patients—Old Dan, Lisa, and others. Opposed to the blind allegiance the party demands, an allegiance which also blinds it to individual needs, Doc advocates a view of humanity rooted in common sense that allows for sympathy for the individual.

In subsequent appearances in the novel Doc remains firm in his belief. At one point Mac presses him: "'It's a funny thing, Doc. You don't believe in the cause, and you'll probably be the last man to stick. I don't get you at all.'" To which Doc replies: "'I don't get myself. . . . I don't believe in the cause, but I believe in men'" (p. 176).

The particular genius of *In Dubious Battle* lies in this subtle conflict of points of view that undergirds a powerful story. It is the more effective because Doc's role is anything but heroic. He resides in the background of the volcanic emotions and events that rip the valley. But that is precisely his role; it is consonant with his philosophy. Where there is a need, he will do his best to assuage it, but he is a far remove from, for example, the mantic heroism of a Joseph Wayne.[21] Doc has found his place: helping individuals who are wounded by the malignancy of the Phalanx.

A further contrast between Mac and Jim, on the one hand, and Doc Burton, on the other, focuses on teleological versus non-teleological thinking as set forth in *The Log from the Sea of Cortez*. In this instance Mac and Jim typify the teleological thinkers who, in striving for a goal, are subsumed by that goal and ultimately lose touch with life around them. F. W. Watt points out that "the man who devotes himself utterly to an ideology, who goes to the ultimate stage in 'wanting nothing for himself,' becomes *nothing*, literally, a faceless inhuman being."[22] Doc represents the alternative, although he is actually the man who wants "nothing for himself" except to see clearly the life environment around him. Richard Astro observes of Doc Burton that for all his understanding of the cause he is "incapable of directing its movements and so enriching the lives of its unit-men."[23] Which is to say that Doc chooses to act in small ways, and not at the spearhead of the Phalanx, for surely he has, perhaps without due recognition of those about him, enriched the lives of the strikers by his quiet and earnest labor.

The motif of freedom and constraint coupled with the dreams of little men that one observes so often in Steinbeck's fiction is present here too, but more by way of implication than by overt theme. It lies, for example, behind the entire strike movement, which may be seen as a battle for freedom from the constraint of the owners. In this sense Steinbeck's theme of freedom and constraint focused in group conflict does echo Marx's theory of the never-ending struggle by the proletariat for freedom from political and economic dominance of the bourgeoisie. Where Mac talks about using every man, Marx says: "Now and then the workers are victorious, but only for a time. The real fruit of their battle lies, not in the immediate results, but in the ever expanding union of the workers."[24] In a calm moment Mac might have said the same words. Moreover, the narrative plot itself follows a Marxist pattern, for as Marx borrowed the Hegelian dialectical framework for an ever-expanding thesis-antithesis-synthesis cycle of worker versus owner, so too in *In Dubious Battle* each small cycle generates a larger one, culminating—but surely not ending—in the novel's close, which suggests an endless repetition.

All of this is to say that Steinbeck knew Marxism, which is not surprising, since he also knew the party leaders in the Tagus Ranch strike. Curiously enough, the very arguments that a philosopher might raise in an objective analysis of Marxism are precisely the arguments that Doc Burton raises in the novel. For example, Marx tended to see man as little more than an animal. Marx does grant man volitions, feelings, and conscience, which are unpredictable and therefore can be used to change the movement of history, but he fails to account for humanity's capacity for self-transcendence, for consciousness of personhood and for dreaming or aspirations—consciousness of the person in a different and perhaps better condition. For Marx, at best the proletarian *Unmensch* will receive through his liberation a spiritual nature. But this nature is tied to the movement, and given Marx's theory of the movement in his materialistic view of history, one wonders whether it is ever an individual spiritual nature. This can occur only when one sees humans as possessing individual worth and freedom. This is precisely Doc Burton's alternative in the novel.

It is an error to view *In Dubious Battle* as a Marxist manifesto. Such charges, and they were numerous, inflamed Steinbeck. Probably thoroughly worn out and disgusted with such contention, Steinbeck wrote with uncharacteristic vitriol to Mavis McIntosh:

That is the trouble with the damned people of both sides. They postulate either an ideal communist or a thoroughly damnable communist and neither side is willing to suspect that the communist is a human, subject to the weaknesses of humans and to the greatnesses of humans. I am not angry in the least. But the blank wall of stupid refusal even to look at the thing without colored glasses of some kind gives me a feeling of overwhelming weariness and a desire to run away and let them tear their stupid selves to pieces. If the fools would only change the name from Communist to, say, American Liberty Party, their principles would probably be embraced overnight. [*LL*, p. 108]

The last words belong to Doc, and they are his last words in the novel:

Mac studied him. "What's the matter, Doc? Don't you feel well?"

"What do you mean?"

"I mean your temper's going. You're tired. What is it, Doc?"

Burton put his hands in his pockets. "I don't know; I'm lonely, I guess. I'm awfully lonely. I'm working all alone, towards nothing. There's some compensation for you people. I only hear heartbeats through a stethoscope. You hear them in the air." [P. 232]

Of Mice and Men

Fortunately, few people have been deterred from serious consideration of *Of Mice and Men* by Maxwell Geismar's surprising judgment: "How thin 'Of Mice and Men' is after all, how full of easy sensations it appears upon a little reflection."[25] Lamenting the thinness of the characters— "Lennie . . . seems rather more like a digestional disturbance than a social problem"—Geismar declares that

"Of Mice and Men" is a tribute to Steinbeck's narrative power, to the brilliance with which he clothes such mechanical literary types, to the intensity which somehow gives breath to these poor scarecrows. We see here the dominance of the creative fire over common sense, so that we are held by such apparitions as these characters who, when removed from the framework of the play, crumble under the weight of their own improbability.[26]

Those are a few of his kinder judgments, but regardless of such early reactions, readers have found themselves very much intrigued by Steinbeck's scarecrows. The popular reception of Steinbeck's work had, in fact, grown to the point where he would mutter that fame was "a pain in the ass," partly, of course, because of the demands on time that he would rather give to writing. By the same token, one cannot measure aesthetic excellence by popular reception,[27] but there are excellences in the work itself that account for its enduring appeal.

Shortly after *In Dubious Battle* was published, Steinbeck considered revising that novel into dramatic structure for the stage. After several thwarted attempts at blocking the novel, he gave up the effort. It was probably an impossible task. Although while he was writing *In Dubious Battle*, Steinbeck concentrated on conveying action through dialogue and providing clear character portraits that in novelistic form contain a forceful sense of concentrated action, the novel itself was too unwieldy for successful adaptation to the stage. It is curious that while more films have been made of Steinbeck's work than of the work of any other modern novelist, no film has been made of *In Dubious Battle*—curious because the *movements between* the concentrated actions and the tight sequence of the novel, while difficult for the narrower confines of the stage, lend themselves very nicely to cinematic art.[28] *Of Mice and Men*, however, was written with deliberate staging design; in fact, over 80 percent of the lines went directly into the play. Joseph Fontenrose comments on the artistic technique of the work:

Each of the six chapters is confined to one scene and opens with a description of the scene; there follows dialogue with entrance and exit of characters. Every descriptive or narrative remark can be considered a stage direction (of the Shavian kind at any rate). The chapters can easily be converted, as they stand, into acts or scenes; and this is nearly what was done when *Of Mice and Men* was published and produced as a play in November, 1937. The dialogue was altered very little, and the conversion of description and narrative required more changes in form than in content. As drama or novel *Of Mice and Men* is economical, tightly knit, carefully constructed.[29]

The effect is clear in the novel. *Of Mice and Men* is one of Steinbeck's most compressed and unified works. Nonetheless, it achieves an artistic richness of structure and theme that ranks it among the best of his works. Three items in particular distinguish the novel: the framing and foreshadowing through structure, the development of Lennie's character and the theme of friendship, and the nature of human dreams.

The novel opens with the objective specificity of locale that would mark stage directions, or perhaps cinema. Like a long pan of the camera, the opening scene traces the Salinas River where it "drops in close to the hillside bank and runs deep and green" near Soledad. Following the flow of the river, the scene narrows and becomes more specific in detail, moving from the broad expanse of the "golden foothill slopes" of the Gabilan Mountains to the very small setting of "the sandy bank under the trees," where we find details as minute as "a lizard makes a great skittering" and "the split-wedge tracks of deer." The narrowing vision provides a smooth and gentle transition to the two bindlestiffs hunkered by a fire in the evening of the day. The light, too, narrows and focuses, from the broad, golden flanks of the Gabilans to the evening duskiness and the shade "that climbed up the hills toward the top."

The expertly framed opening is precisely echoed and inverted at the close of the novel, where the same two bindlestiffs stand by "the deep green pool of the Salinas River" in the evening of the day. Once again shade pushes the sunlight "up the slopes of the Gabilan Mountains, and the hilltops were rosy in the sun." We find the same, familiarly routine skitterings of birds and animals by the sandy bank, only now a small something has happened. The original title of the novel, "Something That Happened," is precisely the point here; a small thing occurs, however momentous and tragic in the lives of Lennie and George, that goes virtually unnoticed in the ways of the world. Antonia Seixas comments in her article "John Steinbeck and the Non-Teleological Bus" that "the hardest task a writer can set himself is to tell the story of 'something that happened' without explaining 'why'—and make it convincing and moving."[30] Again, as if viewing the scene through a movie camera, we observe the "what" without the explanatory "why." While Lennie stares into the sun-washed mountains, George recreates the dream as he levels the Luger at the base of Lennie's skull.

The mountains that frame the story, as they frame the little thing that happened in the lives of George and Lennie, always carry large significance for Steinbeck. In *The Grapes of Wrath* crossing the mountains represents the entrance into the promised land for the Okies. In *East of Eden*, Steinbeck provides two mountain ranges, one dark and one light, which symbolically frame the struggle between good and evil in the valley between those ranges. In *The Red Pony*, as in *To a God Unknown*, the mountains represent mystery; in the former work old Gitano goes to the mountains on Easter to die; in the latter Joseph Wayne witnesses strange, ancient rituals. In *Of Mice and Men* also, the darkening mountains represent the mystery of death, carefully sustained in the minor imagery of the heron seizing and eating the little water snakes.

In between the two scenes of the mountains on those two evenings, and in the serene willow grove that, as Peter Lisca points out, symbolizes "a retreat from the world to a primeval innocence,"[31] we have the quiet drama of George and Lennie's dream unfolding and unraveling. But this dream is doomed, and Steinbeck provides ample foreshadowing in the novel, most notably in Candy's dog. According to Carlson, Candy's dog has to die because he is a cripple, out of sorts with the normal routine of society, something in the way. With careful detail Carlson describes how he would shoot the dog so that it would not feel any pain: "'The way I'd shoot him, he wouldn't feel nothing. I'd put the gun right there.' He pointed with his toe. 'Right back of the head. He wouldn't even quiver'" (p. 82). Candy's huge regret is that he didn't do so himself. It would have been kinder to have the dog die by a familiar and loved hand than to have a stranger drag him to his death. The same feeling motivates George as he leads the social cripple Lennie to his dream world. For Steinbeck this act constitutes a rare heroism. Years later he wrote in a letter to Annie Laurie Williams:

M & M may seem to be unrelieved tragedy, but it is not. A careful reading will show that while the audience knows, against its hopes, that the dream will not come true, the protagonists must, during the play, become convinced that it will come true. Everyone in the world has a dream he knows can't come off but he spends his life hoping it may. This is at once the sadness, the greatness and the triumph of our species. And this belief on stage must go from skepticism to possibility to probability before it is nipped off by whatever the modern word for fate is. And in hopelessness—George is able to rise to greatness—to kill his friend to save him. George is a hero and only heroes are worth writing about. [*LL*, pp. 562–63]

Lennie is not the only dreamer in the novel, however, and each of the other dreamers also seems afflicted with the loneliness of nonattainment. Most notable is the woman known only as "Curley's wife," a mere thing possessed by her flamboyant husband. From the start George recognizes the incipient danger posed by Curley's wife, a recognition that proves prophetically true: "'She's gonna make a mess. They's gonna be a bad mess about her. She's a jail bait all set on the trigger'" (p. 92). But Curley's wife is also caught in a hopeless little valley of small dreams. She dreamed of being an actress, of sweeping Hollywood, but when Curley came along he simply represented escape, and that was better than nothing. When Lennie shares his dream in response to her candor, she exclaims: "'You're nuts. . . . But you're a kinda nice fella. Jus' like a big baby. But a person can see kinda what you mean'" (p. 156). Similarly, Crooks, the stable hand and another small outcast, has his dream, one of companionship to assuage the terrible, haunting loneliness: "'Books ain't no good. A guy needs somebody—to be near him. . . . A guy goes nuts if he ain't got nobody'" (p. 127). And Candy too, another social outcast, is captivated by the dream: "'Sure they all want it. Everybody wants a little bit of land, not much. Jus' som'thin' that was his. Som'thin' he could live on and there couldn't nobody throw him off of it. I never had none'" (p. 133).

But through his careful foreshadowing Steinbeck suggests that each dream is doomed. Curley, the flamboyant fighter, stands ever ready to goad someone into a fight, particularly those larger than he, and who is larger on the ranch than Lennie? The dead mouse that Lennie strokes prefigures the dead girl's hair and the impossible dream of rabbits. And George knows these things; he senses the inevitable end. Early in the novel he tells Lennie to remember good hiding places, even as he tells him once more of the dream farm and the "fatta the lan'."

What keeps these little social outcasts going? What motivates them when all dreams seem doomed? In a sense the large-scale battle of *In Dubious Battle* is played out here in a small, quiet, but equally tragic scene, as if George and Lennie are the Everymen in a microcosmic universe. They are drawn together by the human need born of loneliness. George's words to Lennie, which form a dark refrain in the book, might have occurred equally well in *In Dubious Battle* or *The Grapes of Wrath:* "'Guys like us, that work on ranches, are the loneliest guys in the world. They got no family. They don't belong no place. They come to a ranch an' work up a stake and then they go into town and blow their stake, and the first thing you know they're poundin' their tail on some other ranch. They ain't got nothing to look ahead to'" (p. 28).

Even though the dream seems inevitably doomed, that is also at once man's glory—that he can dream and that others participate in the dream. Finally, this sets Lennie

apart from the animal that he is imaged as being. At first
the novel seems to set forth one more reductionistic pattern
of imagery so familiar to Steinbeck's work. Lennie seems
little more than an animal in human form: "Behind him
walked his opposite, a huge man, shapeless of face, with
large, pale eyes, and wide, sloping shoulders; and he walked
heavily, dragging his feet a little, the way a bear drags his
paws" (p. 9). Lennie bends to the water and drinks "with
long gulps, snorting into the water like a horse" (p. 10).
After drinking, he "dabbled his big paw in the water and
wiggled his fingers so the water arose in little splashes"
(p. 11). But as Tularecito rises above the animal by virtue of
his creative gift, Lennie also rises above the animal in several ways. He is, for example, marked by kindness, a trait
that at once sets him above Curley. Lennie is sensitive to
the small and the forlorn, and it is no accident that Crooks
and Curley's wife confide freely in him. But he does lack
the rational acuity to survive in this society; killing Curley's
wife is not qualitatively different for Lennie from killing the
mouse. As Howard Levant points out, "The relative meaninglessness of his victims substitutes pathos for tragedy."[32]
Clearly, Lennie is not a tragic figure, for he has nothing of
the required nobility about him. But in a sense the deeper
tragedy lies in his pathos; there is no place for a Lennie in
society. Yet in the novel there is a kind of subtle reversal of
animal imagery that makes animals of those who establish
society's norms that disallow the survival of a Lennie. In
the story of Tularecito, Miss Martin is closer to the animal
in her fanatical insistence that Tularecito be whipped. In
Of Mice and Men, Curley is closer to the animal in his
predatory desire to fight. Oppression of any life is the animalistic trait, the struggle for survival that kills off or hides
away the weaker members. For Steinbeck, on the other
hand, that human life, which might be observable upon
first glance as animalistic, often carries a warm dignity.
While Lennie is a social misfit, it may be because society
itself is ill.

Although *Of Mice and Men* quickly became one of Steinbeck's most popular works, it met with a great deal of puzzlement. Readers may have expected another angry *In Dubious Battle* from him and got instead this sad little drama of something that happened, something so small it escapes common attention. George walks away at the end just one more bindlestiff. Yet part of Steinbeck's success here lies in investing those small, barely noticeable lives with both pathos and dignity. If, as Carlson points out, there is a right way to kill a cripple, one still wonders why the cripple has to be killed.

But Steinbeck himself was dissatisfied with the novel, largely on aesthetic grounds. With the failed effort to block *In Dubious Battle* for the stage, he wanted very much to succeed with this effort. Steinbeck referred to the book as an experiment "designed to teach me to write for the theatre" (*LL*, p. 132), and he often spoke of it in perjorative terms such as a "simple little thing," or "the Mice book."[33] Whatever his attitude, the dramatic adaptation, like the novel, was a commercial success, opening at the Music Box Theatre in New York on November 23, 1937, and running for 207 performances.

Steinbeck at this time, however, was back home in California, well into the background work for his greatest achievement, *The Grapes of Wrath*.

The Wine of God's Wrath: *The Grapes of Wrath*

The Grapes of Wrath may well be the most thoroughly discussed novel—in criticism, reviews, and college classrooms—of twentieth-century American literature. It is a treasure trove, ceaselessly yielding up new jewels under the probing hands of historians, theologians, and critics of every caste, method, and meaning. A thorough bibliography of articles and book chapters on the novel would cover pages, and anyone reading all these discussions comes away amazed at the ingenuity of those who wrote them. Doing so also deepens one's admiration for the original, which rewards readers time after time with new insights. That it marks Steinbeck's permanence in American literature no one questions; that it was the basis for the Nobel Award given twenty-three years later few people doubt.

In his concluding Chronicle of Narnia, *The Last Battle*, C. S. Lewis described heaven as an onion with the inside bigger than the outside, so that with each ring you peel off you seem to go further in but also further out into new visions and new understanding. The analogy may apply as well to all great works of literature. The challenge becomes, finally, to excise one ring whole and clean rather than attempting to lift a great many tangled chunks of the onion that is the work. In this chapter I focus on just two of those "inner rings" of the novel, and they form an essential part of the whole. Further, they are allied with the themes Steinbeck was exploring during the entire decade of the 1930s. First, in the portrait of Ma Joad and her dream of "the fambly of man," Steinbeck provides a clear response to the ongoing tension between the individual and the Group Man, freedom and restraint. Like Cathy Ames in *East of Eden*, Ma Joad is the pivot of *The Grapes of Wrath*. Second, in his realistic characterization and particularly in the use of profanity, Steinbeck developed an important aesthetic approach to the issue of censorship, an issue that has attended the novel from its publication until the present.

BACKGROUND TO THE NOVEL: STRUCTURAL TECHNIQUE

In early 1936, Steinbeck began writing what he called his "flock of experimentation," which was to develop into *Of Mice and Men*. Although interrupted by the growing critical interest in *Tortilla Flat* and by the move from the Pacific Grove cottage (which was being too frequently visited by the critics and the merely curious) to the cabin at Los Gatos, the work began in earnest in March. Steinbeck completed the second writing in August. About that time, George West, of the *San Francisco News*, approached him with the idea of writing a series of articles on disturbing conditions in the agricultural belt of the San Joaquin Valley. The focus was to be on the plight of the migrants and the government's efforts to supply sanitary camps for them.

The idea appealed to Steinbeck immediately. Outfitting an old bakery truck in a manner foreshadowing the 1960 trip in *Rocinante*, he set out for the squatters' camps in the company of the director in charge of management of migrant-camp programs, Eric H. Thomsen. Such camps were hardly a new experience for Steinbeck. Hobos and migrants were familiar people to him. Even Salinas had a so-called Little Oklahoma on its outskirts. But somehow this trip imprinted the human misery and need on him as never before. His response can be sensed from the articles he wrote for the *News*. The sentences are terse, clipped, unornamented. Portrait after heartrending portrait emerged on those pages. And it was clear from the outset that the journalist was also the novelist with a larger story to tell, the story behind that misery and need.

The Dust Bowl migration, which had begun around 1930, had reached an apex at the time Steinbeck undertook his trip down the San Joaquin Valley. Over 80,000 new migrants had wandered into California that year alone. Throughout the decade between three and four hundred thousand migrants—fiercely independent people who were also terribly dependent on new jobs that did not exist—entered the agricultural fields. The portraits submitted to the *News* brought individual stories to light, but Steinbeck's literary instinct was for the large story, the whole life environment of the people. As he traveled farther with Thomsen, Steinbeck arrived at the Arvin Sanitary Camp, or "Weedpatch," run by Tom Collins. Collins supplied Steinbeck with innumerable firsthand experiences, with his own journals and camp reports, and also with his unique idealism centered in the common man. The reports in particular provided a valuable resource for *The Grapes of Wrath*. Beyond the mandatory statistics they were filled with anecdotes and details that brought to reality the large story sought by Steinbeck.

It was nearly two years before Steinbeck could fully assimilate and objectify his material and experiences. In a sense he had grown too close to the reality. In time he found the necessary artistic distance to write a story rather than a diatribe. During those two years, however, he was never far from the story, writing occasionally, mulling it over, revising. By March, 1938, the work had reached a crisis. He confessed to Elizabeth Otis that "I want to put a tag of shame on the greedy bastards who are responsible for this" (*LL,* p. 162). By April he had finished a draft of the satirical work that he called "L'Affaire Lettuceberg," a draft that profoundly disappointed him. Within weeks he had decided to burn the manuscript and begin anew.

The new work started in early June and proceeded rapidly through its completion in December, 1938. The fact that Steinbeck wrote a 200,000-word novel in this half-year period is daunting enough, but the hard work was exacerbated by all kinds of demands on his time and energy, including Carol's serious illness with a strep infection in August and the bankruptcy of Pascal Covici's publishing company. That he wrote so many words is a feat in itself; that he told a powerful story is incredible. But surely the most fascinating aspect lies in the stylistic skill with which the novel is written. The artistic complexity that provides the novel its hard, focused energy may, indeed, be a partial result of the feverish conditions under which it was written.

Several items of that stylistic technique may seem the result of fortunate coincidence. For example, as was observed in chapter 1, titles were often a matter of large significance—and no small difficulty—for Steinbeck. He wanted titles that somehow suggested at once the narrative accounting, the tone of the accounting, and its symbolic significance.

Steinbeck credited Carol with the selection of "The Grapes of Wrath," and he was ecstatic over the choice, even insisting to Elizabeth Otis that the entire "Battle Hymn of the Republic," "one of the great songs of the world," be published—music and words—on a page at the beginning. He further suggested to Otis that "as you read the book you will realize that the words have a special meaning in this book" (*LL*, p. 173). Indeed they do, at several symbolic levels. The first level, of course, derives from the song itself. "He is trampling out the vintage where the grapes of wrath are stored" encapsulates the rage of the oppressed, prophesies the overthrow of suppression, and envisions a strong freedom.

The most familiar biblical analogue, at a second level of symbolism, occurs in Revelation 14:19–20: "And the angel thrust in his sickle into the earth, and cast it into the great winepress of the wrath of God. And the winepress was trodden without the city, and blood came out of the winepress, even unto the horse bridles, by the space of a thousand and six hundred furlongs."[1] Someone who has read the Bible as carefully as Steinbeck would observe that the actions of the avenging angel, sent here by the Lamb, follow the oppression of the Beast detailed in previous chapters. The familiar New Testament passage, however, is rooted solidly in the Old Testament. In passages such as Deuteronomy 32:32, "For their vine is of the vine of Sodom, and of the fields of Gomorrah: their grapes are grapes of gall, their clusters are bitter," and Jeremiah 31:29, "In those days they shall say no more, The fathers have eaten a sour grape, and the children's teeth are set on edge," grapes are used symbolically as prefiguration of divine retribution upon the oppressor.

Ironically, however, in the Bible the grapes of wrath are juxtaposed and contrasted to the equally strong theme of the grapes of plenty. Such instances are found, for example, in Numbers 13:23–27, where the spies come to the Brook of Eshcol in Canaan and return with a huge branch of grapes as a sign of "the land of milk and honey." This parallels the prophecy of Deuteronomy 23:24 that the Israelites would eat their fill of grapes. Steinbeck perceived the contrast, of course, for the dream of grapes of plenty recurs in *The Grapes of Wrath*. Grampa dreams of it: "'Jus' let me get out to California where I can pick me an orange when I want it. Or grapes. There's a thing I ain't never had enough of. Gonna get me a whole big bunch of grapes off a bush, or whatever, an' I'm gonna squash 'em on my face an' let 'em run offen my chin'" (p. 112). Again, Grampa proclaims: "'They's grapes out there, just a-hangin' over inta the road. Know what I'm a-gonna do? I'm gonna pick me a wash tub full a grapes, an' I'm gonna set in 'em, an' scrooge aroun', an' let the juice run down my pants'" (p. 126). And yet a third time: "'I'm gettin' hungry. Come time we get to California I'll have a big bunch a grapes in my han' all the time, a-nibblin' off it all the time, by God!'" (p. 141). For Grampa, grapes represent the possible dream of the promised land, imaged in an almost sexual and animal indulgence. But the promised land is a fallen land, riddled by greed, and as the prophecy of the sweet grapes is replaced by the reality of thin stew, the grapes of wrath take root in their place.

Other techniques of structural unity and symbolic suggestiveness focus the novel. Perhaps the most conspicuous (and intriguing) such technique is the artistic use of the intercalary chapters, which can be observed to function in several ways.

The intercalary chapters, first of all, provide aesthetic

richness by symbolic analogies that frame or support the narrative plot. Perhaps the most notable example occurs in chapter 3, where the turtle functions as a symbol of the migrants. The turtle carries its house on its back as the migrants carry their households on the backs of ancient vehicles. The turtle's "horny beak" and his "fierce, humorous eyes" resemble both the grim determination and the quick capacity for joy in the migrants but especially resemble the description of Grampa Joad with "his shrewd, mean, merry eyes," and also Jim Casy with his "nose, beaked and hard." The turtle's instinctive sense of direction toward the southwest, even after being upset by Tom's boot, resembles the Okies' dogged determination to arrive in California despite the obstacles in their way. The turtle's awkward gait, as it "jerked itself along," resembles the lurching, overloaded migrant trucks. And, finally, the turtle is one of the oldest of reptiles, resembling this oldest of urges in man to move on to a new place, what Grandfather in *The Red Pony* calls the "Westering" urge. Further use of animal imagery in the novel, and particularly in the intercalary chapters, could be explored at some length. In chapter 16, as the Wilson's car breaks down, the shadow of a buzzard flits over the earth. In intercalary chapter 17, Steinbeck uses insect imagery, a recurring pattern discussed by Robert J. Griffin and William E. Freeman in their essay on the topic, "Machines and Animals: Pervasive Motifs in *The Grapes of Wrath*."[2]

The intercalary chapters also provide historical background that throws the narrative event into relief. Chapter 5, for example, evokes the historical environment through the Bank-as-Monster image that frames the immediate plight of the Okies. Such passages also serve to universalize the story for the reader; by being placed in historical context, the Joads become part of our own story. Chapter 9 functions the same way, as a vast farmering consciousness allows the author to compress history and retain focus on the narrative. Chapter 21 serves as another example of how the intercalary chapters fill in historical detail to frame the

narrative. In such chapters the narrator speaks in the same
omniscient "overvoice" that we find in such works as *Cup
of Gold*, *East of Eden*, and *Sweet Thursday*.

Furthermore, the intercalary chapters provide aesthetic
pace or rhythm to frame the events of the narrative plot.
Chapter 7, the intercalary chapter on car sales, follows immediately on the sense of loss and movement in the preceding chapter. It is an important chapter because the car will
become a character in its own right in the novel, and here
we get to know the "character" well. More important, however, the caroming pace of chapter 7 plays off against the
hollowness that ends chapter 6. The forty-two-word final
sentence of that chapter spirals downward with a particular
emphasis on heavy *o* and *u* sounds: "They were silent, and
gradually the skittering life of the ground, of holes and bur-
rows, of the brush, began again; the gophers moved, and
the rabbits crept to green things, the mice scampered over
clods, and the winged hunters moved soundlessly over-
head" (p. 82). The syntactical pace of chapter 7 opens like
the crack of a whip as short prepositional phrases careen
across the page. Steinbeck uses elliptical syntactical structures with the main verbs eliminated for the impressionistic
quickness and crispness of roaring engines. The pace quick-
ens until it roars through staccato sentences that average
about five words each. Similarly, chapter 23, which recounts the dance at Weedpatch, breaks into the ring-shout
pattern of the square dance:

> Look at that Texas boy, long legs loose, taps four times for ever'
> damn step. Never seen a boy swing aroun' like that. Look at him
> swing that Cherokee girl, red in her cheeks an' her toe points out.
> Look at her pant, look at her heave. Think she's tired? Think she's
> winded? Well, she ain't. Texas boy got his hair in his eyes, mouth's
> wide open, can't get air, but he pats four times for ever' darn step,
> and he'll keep a-goin' with the Cherokee girl. [P. 449]

These are the caller's lines, used here to provide the festive
beat of Weedpatch.

Mary Ellen Caldwell has pointed out, in one of the more consistent studies of the intercalary chapters, that these chapters as a whole fold in on the central chapter 15 of the book by chapter count and by theme. Caldwell says of chapter 15 that "neither [is it] a purely intercalary chapter as the others are nor is it a part of the Joad narrative. It is an epitome of the whole book, having its own narrative paragraphs and intercalary paragraphs."[3] In this chapter Steinbeck juxtaposes the rush of the highway with the one small act of kindness to a migrant family. Significantly, this chapter is preceded by one detailing the first coalescence of the people from "I" to "we":

Here is the anlage of the thing you fear. This is the zygote. For here "I lost my land" is changed; a cell is split and from its splitting grows the thing you hate—"We lost our land." The danger is here, for two men are not as lonely and perplexed as one. And from this first "we" there grows a still more dangerous thing: "I have a little food" plus "I have none." If from this problem the sum is "We have a little food," the thing is on its way, the movement has direction. . . . This is the beginning—from "I" to "we." [P. 206]

Chapter 15 provides the "how" of the equation. The chapter begins with the same pounding rhythm of the highway notable in other intercalary chapters. Billboards march by in a blur; legends slap at weary eyes. But here we find a change from the car and junk dealers of chapter 9 who deal in "junked lives" to little kindnesses that grow and balance the cruelty. In Caldwell's estimation, "Chapter 15 is not only a microcism of *The Grapes of Wrath* but also a microcosm of the United States."[4]

Taking Steinbeck at his word that "its structure is very carefully worked out,"[5] that structure is evident in the careful interweaving of the intercalary chapters and the way in which they fold in, both stylistically and thematically, on chapter 15. In precisely the same way that chapter 15 becomes a structural pivot in the novel, Ma Joad becomes a thematic pivot between the "I" and the "we" forces with her concept of the "fambly of man." She is the spiritual pivot with her enduring faith and loving-kindness.

Ma Joad's thematically pivotal role can best be considered in the general context of Steinbeck's female characters.[6] Female characters play a significant role in Steinbeck's fiction, and their roles, as well as the author's comments on them, merit close attention. If one of his ongoing concerns is freedom and constraint and individual dreams of fulfillment, female characters play an important part as examples of that theme.

Not surprisingly, the vast majority of female characters in Steinbeck's work are there without particular sanction or censure; they are there simply as human characters in the ceaseless drama of life that he witnessed. One such grouping is the whorehouse women, who are generally characterized in the fiction as spirited and wholesome. Several of these rise to major roles in the fiction; for example, Fauna, the indomitable matron of the Bear Flag, who "could easily have been chairman of the board of a large corporation," who tutors her girls in fine etiquette, and who keeps her "star board" of those girls who marry well. Another might be Suzy of *Sweet Thursday*, who possesses such native grace that she can make a cottage of a cast-off boiler. Suzy also struggles mightily to clean up her language to fit the ladylike portrait Fauna provides for her. In another grouping we find the rambunctious paisano women of *Tortilla Flat*, whose volcanic emotions sometimes threaten to blow up Monterey Bay. And in yet another grouping we find the stirring human portraits from the short fiction: Helen Van Deventer of "The White Quail," who struggles with her psychotic daughter; Mary Teller, a fascinating literary counterpart to Elisa Allen; and the ladies of the Long Valley, who contend with themselves, their husbands, and their families, and who sometimes find peace. Women are the focal point of many of these stories, and perhaps one of the most notable is Molly Morgan of *The Pastures of Heaven*, whose interview with

John Whiteside forms a kind of intricate psychoanalytic journey into her past.

Several women gain preeminent roles. Curley's wife in *Of Mice and Men* is a significant character despite her namelessness. She is selfish, but not evil in the way that Cathy Ames is. She is lonely, comparable perhaps to Crooks and Candy in the novel, and thereby a part of George's general lament, "We're the loneliest guys in the world." She is a victim of accident, it seems, the worst accident being her marriage to Curley. To Claire Booth Luce, who played Curley's wife in the stage play, Steinbeck elaborated on her character with surprising specificity:

> Now, she was trained by threat not only at home but by other kids. And any show of fear or weakness brought an instant persecution. And she learned she had to be hard to cover her fright. And automatically she became hardest when she was most frightened. She is a nice, kind girl and not a floozy. No man has ever considered her as anything except a girl to try to make. She has never talked to a man except in the sexual fencing conversation. She is not highly sexed particularly but knows instinctively that if she is to be noticed at all, it will be because some one finds her sexually desirable. [*LL*, p. 154–55]

Steinbeck goes on to describe her loneliness, and how it is allied with her sexuality:

> If anyone—a man or a woman—ever gave her a break—treated her like a person—she would be a slave to that person. Her craving for contact is immense but she, with her background, is incapable of conceiving any contact without some sexual context. With all this—if you knew her, if you could ever break down the thousand little defenses she has built up, you would find a nice person, an honest person, and you would end up by loving her. [*LL*, p. 155]

But, more important, Steinbeck points out that "I've known this girl and I'm just trying to tell you what she is like" (*LL*,

p. 155). That is the key; she also emerges from Steinbeck's perception of and experience in the living drama.

One of the strongest female characters is Juana, who is discussed in chapter 7 of this book, as is Cathy Ames in chapter 8. Cathy, like Ma Joad, is the pivotal character of a novel but is Ma Joad's diametrical opposite—a thoroughly evil center in contrast to Ma Joad's thoroughly good center.

While he frequently uses female protagonists, Steinbeck's personal comments on women should be separated from his characters since the comments usually reflect his psychological state in relation to his marriages. Thus after his divorce from Gwyn, when he announces to Bo Beskow that "I do not think now I will remarry," Steinbeck engages in a long reflection comparing American women to their European counterparts (*LL*, pp. 342–43). The comments—such as "American married life is the doormat to the whore house"—should be understood in their personal context and no other. At times these personal reflections lap over into the fiction in generalized statements. Describing Elizabeth in *Cup of Gold*, Morgan reflects: "She was a thing of mystery. All girls and women hoarded something they never spoke of. His mother had terrific secrets about biscuits, and cried, sometimes, for no known reason. Another life went on inside women—some women—ran parallel to their outward lives and yet never crossed them" (*COG*, p. 21). In *East of Eden*, Lee reflects on his mother in general terms: "My father said she was a strong woman, and I believe a strong woman may be stronger than a man, particularly if she happens to have love in her heart. I guess a loving woman is almost indestructible" (*EOE*, p. 357).

In short, with the exception of Cathy Ames, Steinbeck observes with appreciation the following character traits in his major female characters: endurance through adversity, a patient ability to ride with changing circumstances and yet retain an individual point of view, and a loving-kindness that, while not immune to adversity, nonetheless finds a straight and sure path through that adversity. Each of these traits is exemplified particularly well in Ma Joad as, despite the pull of a solipsistic individualism on the one hand and a subsuming into a great, amorphous Group Man force on the other, she strikes a path she calls the "fambly of man." Consider first her thematic counterparts in the novel, and then the way in which these counterparts, as the intercalary chapters fold in on the pivotal 15th chapter, gather around Ma Joad for thematic resolution.

THEMATIC CONFLICT

The background conflict of the novel, rich versus poor, is established at the outset when Tom Joad, newly released from McAlester Penitentiary, tries to hitch a ride with the truck driver. When the driver points to the "No Riders" sticker, Tom responds: "Sure—I seen it. But sometimes a guy'll be a good guy even if some rich bastard makes him carry a sticker" (p. 11). The brief exchange foreshadows the tragedy of the devastated farms, amalgamated by the "Machine" of the nameless rich into one vast possession. The first person Tom meets on that blasted farmland is the former "Burning Busher," the Reverend Jim Casy, who has forsaken his call from the Holy Spirit in search of the spirit of man.

Casy is one of the most significant characters in the novel, and through him Steinbeck establishes the broad view typified in earlier works by a character like Doc Burton. Richard Astro has argued that Doc Burton and Jim Casy are figures of Ed Ricketts, and to a certain extent both Burton and Casy represent the non-teleological view of Ricketts. Astro sees Casy as a more successful spokesman than Burton for that view in that "unlike Burton, whose vision of the whole is never converted into meaningful action, Casy knows that 'we got a job to do' and applies the principles of his perceptions to help 'the folks that don' know which way to turn.'"[7] Casy becomes a spokesman for the movement from "I" to "we" and assumes a degree of leadership in it before he is cut down by the landowners' goons. But it is precisely that futility of leadership of a mob that stands apart from Ma

Joad's enduring loving-kindness toward the family. In a sense Ma Joad is closer to Doc Burton's character than Jim Casy's; not a "party" person, she merely battles in her quiet way for human dignity. It is these quiet, almost forgotten people, like George and Lennie, that Steinbeck brings to public recognition and in whom he finds a resilient nobility.

Casy plays a significant role in the dramatic action of *The Grapes of Wrath*, however, and one can better understand Ma Joad's character by a closer examination of Casy. He has, as he says, forsaken the Holy Spirit (which he sees as being apart from man) for the human spirit. In his initial conversation with Tom, Casy provides rather unclear reasons for his conversion. He says, first, that "'the Sperit ain't in the people no more'"; they seem forsaken, lost, and lonely. Second, "'The Sperit ain't in me no more,'" a statement that he qualifies immediately by saying that the spirit is still strong in him but has changed from an abstract divinity to concrete action. He does not fully understand this new spirit that calls him to be a part of the people rather than apart from the people, but he recognizes that "'I got the call to lead the people, an' no place to lead 'em.'" His effort now is to come to grips with what he calls the "human sperit." While Casy has been popularly interpreted as a Christ figure and dozens of convincing analogies are provided in the text (analogies that I would suggest Steinbeck uses to provide backdrop or "coloring" for Casy's actions), it is necessary that Casy be seen first in aesthetic terms, as a profound and moving psychological study of a man grappling with sin and human nature.

From the early portraits of Tom Joad and Jim Casy one can trace two primary themes developing in the novel. The first, which we may call theme A, observable immediately in the scene of Tom and the truck driver, suggests that, when threatened by the huge force of the "machine" or "monster," each person must care for himself. Every man for himself will be answered in the novel by Ma Joad's idea of the family of man—although Tom also finds his own response in the family of strikers. Theme B is represented by

Jim Casy and may be considered as parallel to A, the movement from some ideal outside and imposed on humanity to
the spirit in humanity. Ma Joad finally ties these two together, perhaps as theme C. We consider first Steinbeck's
careful development of the two themes, A and B, to appreciate fully Ma's response.

As Tom and Jim trek over the land, gouged by the iron
claws of the tractor, theme A, each man for himself, is exemplified by Joe Davis's boy and his migrant counterpart,
the sad and irascible Muley Graves. Joe Davis's boy puts his
own needs ahead of others. When reminded by a tenant
farmer that "'nearly a hundred people have to go out and
wander on the roads for your three dollars a day,'" Joe
Davis's boy responds: "'Can't think of that. Got to think of
my own kids. Three dollars a day, and it comes every day.
Times are changing, mister, don't you know?'" (p. 50). Muley
Graves, whose character is exemplified by both his names,
stubbornly refuses to leave the land of ruined lives and
dreams. His life is a portrait of desolation, his whiskered
face a study in bereavement, as he tries to understand how
others can think only of themselves. Casy is right when he
says to Muley, "'You're lonely—but you ain't touched.'" But
touched by the malignant hand of the monster, Muley too
is reduced to the man living only for himself, unable to
leave, as he says, wandering "'aroun' like a ol' graveyard
ghos.'"

In the novel the movement of the migrants is from the
"I" of each man for himself to the "we" where people,
partly out of desperation, are driven to a unit. The first
mention of this occurs when Grampa dies. When the family sets out, they are anything but a unit. In fact, although
cast together by the necessity of the journey, each harbors
his or her own individual motivations and dreams, from
Grampa, who wants to frolic in a tub of grapes, to Connie,
who builds a little dream world that leaves no room for
either his wife or their unborn child. In this novel the familiar dream motif can actually threaten the family. But
around the rude grave of Grampa's burial, in a sodden little

ditch shared with the Wilsons, "the family became a unit" (p. 189). And that unity is echoed in the following intercalary chapter with its refrainlike measures:

One man, one family driven from the land; this rusty car creaking along the highway to the west. I lost my land, a single tractor took my land. I am alone and I am bewildered. And in the night one family camps in a ditch and another family pulls in and the tents come out. The two men squat on their hams and the women and children listen. Here is the node, you who hate change and fear revolution. Keep these two squatting men apart. [P. 206]

That unity is not easily maintained, however, and will be strained throughout the novel. The threat is made clear by the returning migrant who, in chapter 16, explains the handbill ruse and the landowners' theory of bring together, divide, and conquer. Significantly, this occurs in a camp where the owner exemplifies the theme of each man for himself by overcharging the Okies for their night's lodging. That theme prevails to the end of the novel. After Tom decides to take up Casy's banner, he says to Ma Joad, "'I know now a fella ain't no good alone,'" and he quotes Ecclesiastes 4:9-12 to verify it. While Tom does not quote the first verse of that chapter, it provides the significant context for the later verses as well as for Tom's decision:

So I returned, and considered all the oppressions that are done under the sun: and behold the tears of such as were oppressed, and they had no comforter; and on the side of their oppressors there was power; but they had no comforter. [Eccles. 4:1]

At the close of the novel the two sides of theme A, the "I" and the "we," clash dramatically—not just landowners versus migrants, but the migrants among themselves, so that the unity is threatened from within. This time the causes emanate from nature itself in the relentless rain and the rising flood. As children sicken, the migrants pound desperately on doors for help and are turned away, collecting in a hard, hopeless unit at the railroad yards. Quietly at first the whispers of desperation run through the unit:

"Wainwright said, 'We was jes' talkin'. Seems like we oughta be gettin' outa here'" (p. 595). The strain deepens. As Rose of Sharon's birth pangs start, the floods continue their inexorable tide, and Pa Joad tries to unify the men to build a dam:

Pa sloshed through the mud to the stream. His marking stick was four inches down. Twenty men stood in the rain. Pa cried, "We got to build her. My girl got her pains." The men gathered around him.
"Baby?"
"Yeah. We can't go now."
A tall man said, "It ain't our baby. We kin go."
"Sure," Pa said. "You can go. Go on. Nobody's stoppin' you. They's only eight shovels." He hurried to the lowest part of the bank and drove his shovel into the mud. The shovelful lifted with a sucking sound. He drove it again, and threw the mud into the low place on the stream bank. And beside him the other men ranged themselves. [P. 599]

For a time the men coalesce in a frenetic battle against the flood, but finally the families are forced to separate, and the Joads wander to the old barn, where once again the unit, the family of man, is reestablished by Rose of Sharon offering her breast to the starved man.

Theme B, the movement from a transcendent spirit to a spirit immanent in man, parallels the "I" to "we" theme, and is focused in the developing character of Jim Casy. Casy has to find this spirit in himself before he can find it in others, and the development of his character parallels this discovery. Before his "conversion" Jim Casy struggled desperately against his human drives and could find no sanctification for them. After preaching, he would roll with a girl in the bushes. He seemed set apart by the word he preached, but actually he had set himself apart by his failure to account for human fallibility. That recognition dawns on him slowly. After Tom tells the slightly risqué story of Willy Feeley's heifer, Jim Casy laughs softly and reflects: "'You know . . . it's a nice thing not bein' a preacher no more.

Nobody use' ta tell stories when I was there, or if they did I couldn' laugh. An' I couldn' cuss. Now I cuss all I want, any time I want, an' it does a fella good to cuss if he wants to'" (p. 94). His self-recognition deepens when he is driven into reciting a breakfast "prayer." What can he say that will articulate his belief? With whom will he commune in the human spirit? The prayer edges him another step forward in his thinking:

"An' I got to thinkin', on'y it wasn't thinkin', it was deeper down than thinkin'. I got thinkin' how we was holy when we was one thing, an' mankin' was holy when it was one thing. An' it on'y got unholy when one mis'able little fella got the bit in his teeth an' run off his own way, kickin' an' draggin' an' fightin'. Fella like that bust the holiness. But when they're all workin' together, not one fella for another fella, but one fella kind of harnessed to the whole shebang—that's right, that's holy." [P. 10]

Again, Casy is driven to prayer at Grampa's rude committal service, and here he finds inspiration in Emerson: "All that lives is holy." The third time Casy is driven to prayer, when Sairy Wilson is dying, he can find no words at all but merely bows his head in silence, to which Sairy responds: "'That's good. . . . That's what I needed. Somebody close enough— to pray'" (p. 298). What she needed was simply someone *close enough*, and Casy's silent presence seals his transformation.

It is not surprising, then, that at the California migrant camp Casy gives himself up in place of another. If, as so many critics have argued, Jim Casy is a Christ figure, he is a thoroughly humanized one, acting as man for man: "Far down the line Floyd came in sight, sprinting for the willows. The deputy, sitting on the ground, raised his gun again and then, suddenly, from the group of men, the Reverend Casy stepped. He kicked the deputy in the neck and then stood back as the heavy man crumpled into unconsciousness" (p. 361). Casy gives himself up, but is not to be held long, not with the jail cells jammed with migrants, and upon his release he takes up the cause of man that leads to his death. He dies with the echo of Christ on his lips: "'You fellas don' know what you're doin'. You're helpin' to starve kids'" (p. 527). His transformation is complete and extends beyond his death. He has changed his loyalty to the spirit of man and that spirit will endure, as is exemplified by Tom's picking up the bloody banner of the cause.

MA JOAD AS THEMATIC PIVOT

Between the poles of Tom Joad and Jim Casy, Ma Joad is the lodestar that evinces calm and grants direction. Her concept of the family of man, which she holds intuitively from the start, is the final point at which the others arrive like grim pilgrims, knowing the place for the first time. The enigmatic ending of the novel in this instance is indeed a thematic fulfillment, and it is no wonder that Steinbeck fought his editors to retain it. Strip away that ending and one destroys the thematic structure of the novel. The ending represents the direction Ma Joad has been traveling since the start of the novel, and it is no accident that Rose of Sharon's action occurs at Ma Joad's behest. But to arrive properly at that ending, we consider first the character development of Ma Joad in relation to the thematic development—this woman who says, "'I ain't got faith,'" but whose faith finally proves sufficient to undergird the whole family.

Ma Joad is typified from the outset by a generosity that, along with patient loving-kindness, will guide her actions in relations to the family of man throughout. She is, in a sense, the female counterpart to Doc Burton in her steadfast performance of altruistic deeds. When Pa Joad plays his little trick of introducing Tom and Casy as strangers, "'Ma, there's a couple fellas jus' come along the road, an' they wonder if we could spare a bite,'" Ma's reaction is immediate: "'Let 'em come. . . . We got a'plenty'" (p. 99). That they do not have a'plenty is undeniable, but not as undeniable as the need of others that Ma will always try to meet. This idea of the woman as matriarchal "Feeder" is important in twentieth-century southern fiction and char-

acteristic of real migrant families on their long pilgrimage to California. The father is the worker-provider, the
mother the nourisher-feeder—source of spiritual as well as
physical nourishment.

Among the migrants Steinbeck would, no doubt, have
witnessed the "feeder" ritual dozens of times. One such
scene may have had direct impact on *The Grapes of Wrath*.
Migrant-camp director Tom Collins had asked Steinbeck
to write a foreword to his manuscript "Bringing in the
Sheaves," written under the pseudonym Windsor Drake.
In the foreword Steinbeck recollects an experience in the
migrant camps with Collins:

> I dropped to sleep in my chair. A baby's crying near at hand
> awakened me. Windsor was gone. He came back in a few mo-
> ments and stood turning the burnt bacon.
> "What happened?" I asked.
> "Baby lost the breast. Mother was too tired to wake up."
> "What did you do?"
> "Found the breast and gave it back to the baby."
> "Didn't the mother wake up then?"
> "No,—too tired. Been working all day in the rain."
> Later in the year Windsor and I traveled together, sat in the
> ditches with the migrant workers, lived and ate with them. We
> heard a thousand miseries and a thousand jokes. We ate fried
> dough and sow belly, worked with the sick and the hungry, lis-
> tened to complaints and little triumphs.
> But when I think of Windsor Drake, I remembered first, the
> tired eyes, and I think of the baby that lost the breast in the
> night, and the mother too tired to wake up. [8]

With the starvation rampaging among the migrants, the
"Feeder" attained a role of huge significance. Her very
food became symbolic of hope and unity and spiritual nourishment. In Collins's manuscript another stirring scene is
related:

> We frightened the little children we found in the tent, the two
> little children. . . . And the bulging eyes of those two children,
> the sunken cheeks,—the huge lump on the old bed,—they

frightened John [Steinbeck] and me. Inside the tent was dry because it was on high land, but it was an island in a sea of mud and water all around it. Everything under that bit of canvas was dry—Everything—the make-shift stove was without heat; all shapes of cans were empty; pans, pots and kettles—all were dry. Everything, for there was not a morsel of food—not a crumb of bread.

"Mommy has been like that a long time. She won't get up. Mommy won't listen to us. She won't get up." Such was the greeting cried to us by the two little children.

Mommy couldn't get up. She was the lump on the old bed. Mommy was ill and she hadn't eaten for some time. She had skimped and skimped so that the children would have a bite. A bite is a banquet when there is nothing but a bite. [9]

Steinbeck himself records one such scene in *The Grapes of Wrath* at the first California migrant camp. The scene is preceded by intercalary chapter 19, which raises the cry of hunger as a backdrop: "How can you frighten a man whose hunger is not only in his own cramped stomach but in the wretched bellies of his children? You can't scare him—he has known a fear beyond every other" (p. 323). In chapter 20 the Joads find the reality of the intercalary chapter at the Hooverville camp. Over and over the refrain rises: "'S'pose they's a hundred men wants that job. S'pose them men got kids, an' them kids is hungry. S'pose a lousy dime'll buy a box a mush for them kids. S'pose a nickel'll buy at leas' somepin for them kids'" (p. 334). And in the center of that raging hunger Ma Joad fixes the family meal, while the camp children watch with wolfish eyes: "The children, fifteen of them, stood silently and watched. And when the smell of the cooking stew came to their noses, their noses crinkled slightly" (p. 344). Finally Ma, the Feeder and Nourisher, ladles out her stew for the others, saying as she does so, "'I can't send 'em away . . . I don't know what to do'" (p. 351). This same Feeder motif operates at the end of the novel, where Ma asks Rose of Sharon to give her breast to the starved man, an ending structurally and thematically anticipated from the first meeting with Ma Joad.

Gradually, in the development of the novel, as the men are torn between the "I" and the "we", Ma Joad also takes over the dominant male role of the family so that her generosity and loving-kindness will prevail. She is no one's apathetic servant. As Feeder, she must be indomitably strong, for if the Feeder weakens, the family falls apart. Her fight is for the family—and indeed for the family of man—rather than for herself.

Ma Joad is not immune to the sense of catastrophe and of hope mixed with fear, that accompanies the migrant exodus. In fact, she finds some solace in the sheer numbers of people leaving, and at one point she anticipates the war cry of the California migrant camps:

She came near to him then, and stood close; and she said passionately, "Tommy, don't you go fightin' 'em alone. They'll hunt you down like a coyote. Tommy, I got to thinkin' an' dreamin' an' wonderin'. They say there's a hundred thousand of us shoved out. If we was all made the same way, Tommy—they wouldn't hunt nobody down—." [p. 104]

There is steel in this woman's hope. And when hopelessness first begins to descend upon the others, in chapter 16, Ma Joad begins to exert control, threatening Pa with a jackhandle until she gets her way. While Pa gives in with some obligatory curses, Tom questions her: "'What's the matter'th you anyways? You gone johnrabbit on us?'" To which Ma responds: "'You done this 'thout thinkin' much. . . . What we got lef' in the worl'? Nothin' but us. Nothin' but the folks'" (p. 230). To protect the family she will stand up to anyone, even her own.

Ma's steel-like courage and control are strengthened on the desert crossing. While Connie and Rose of Sharon try in their desperate little privacy to make love, Ma Joad cradles the dying Granma's head in her lap, and even after Granma dies, Ma retains the courage to bluff her way past the border inspection. Spiritually and psychologically she assumes control over the family.

The Weedpatch camp poses a crisis for both the psycho-

logical well-being of the family and the spiritual control of
Ma Joad. Having sojourned in tribulation, having been de-
meaned by the common epithet "Okies" on the lips of calloused and angry men, the family has its dignity reaffirmed
at Weedpatch. Ma sighs, "'Why, I feel like people again.'"
The camp is marked by small items that seem to validate
human worth: from flush toilets to dances to the dignity of
labor as a commodity for barter. And while the dubious
battle rages outside the walls of Weedpatch, one feels that
one could harbor in its port forever. But ironically Weedpatch has its own psychological nettles. For example, it
robs the people of their will. At ease with their heaven-sent
manna, the migrants do not want to risk the struggle into
Canaan. In the camp the migrants find themselves becoming more and more dependent, depleted in will and direction. The Joad resources prove insufficient to sustain the
family. Ma rises to goad them on, and the argument that
rises to meet her is precisely the desirability of being at
ease. "'This here hot water an' toilets—'" Pa argues, to
which Ma responds, "'Well, we can't eat no toilets.'" Again
Ma exerts her authority and issues the command:

Ma plunged the dish into the bucket. "We'll go in the mornin',"
she said.

Pa sniffled. "Seems like times is changed," he said sarcastically.
"Time was when a man said what we'd do. Seems like women is
tellin' now. Seems like it's purty near time to get out a stick."

Ma put the clean dripping tin dish out on a box. She smiled
down at her work. "You get your stick, Pa," she said. "Times when
they's food an' a place to set, then maybe you can use your stick an'
keep your skin whole." [Pp. 480–81]

And again, it is Tom who presses her for her reasons, to
which Ma responds:

"Take a man, he can get worried an' worried, an' it eats out his
liver, an' purty soon he'll jus' lay down and die with his heart et
out. But if you can take an' make 'im mad, why, he'll be awright.
Pa, he didn't say nothin', but he's mad now. He'll show me now.
He's awright." [P. 481]

Yet a third time the issue of control rises, notable here because Ma uses the occasion to reflect on the nature of women. Suffused with a vast loneliness for his old homestead and feeling lost in the new land, Pa Joad exclaims: "'Funny! Woman takin' over the fambly. Woman sayin' we'll do this here, an' we'll go there. An' I don' even care.'" Ma soothes him by responding: "'Woman can change better'n a man. . . . Woman got all her life in her arms. Man got it all in his head. Don' you mind.'" After a short pause Ma adds: "'Man, he lives in jerks—baby born an' a man dies, an' that's a jerk—gets a farm, an' loses his farm, an' that's a jerk. Woman, it's all one flow, like a stream, little eddies, little waterfalls, but the river, it goes right on. Woman looks at it like that. We ain't gonna die out. People is goin' on— changin' a little, maybe, but goin' right on'" (p. 577).

Like Faulkner's Dilsey in *The Sound and the Fury*, Ma Joad endures; somehow she sees past the fiery emotions of the moment to one sure light that guides her path. In so doing she keeps the dream alive, nurtures and feeds it, of a "fambly" of man united in the same love and generosity she exhibits. The spirit is infectious, in a sense replacing—or perhaps the alternative to—the Group Man infection of the Mob that Doc Burton analyzes in *In Dubious Battle*. In Ma's hour of need, Mrs. Wainwright reciprocates:

> Ma fanned the air slowly with her cardboard. "You been frien'ly," she said. "We thank you."
>
> The stout woman smiled. "No need to thank. Ever'body's in the same wagon. S'pose we was down. You'd give us a han'."
>
> "Yes," Ma said, "we would."
>
> "Or anybody."
>
> "Or anybody. Use' to be the fambly was fust. It ain't so now. It's anybody. Worse off we get, the more we got to do." [P. 606]

A new movement has started, and its beginning—not its ending—is exemplified at the close of the novel as Ma's eyes and Rose of Sharon's meet in acknowledgment:

> "Hush," said Ma. She looked at Pa and Uncle John standing helplessly gazing at the sick man. She looked at Rose of Sharon

huddled in the comfort. Ma's eyes passed Rose of Sharon's eyes,
and then came back to them. And the two women looked deep
into each other. The girl's breath came short and gasping.
She said "Yes."
Ma smiled. "I knowed you would. I knowed!" [P. 618]

From the dust-filled skies of Oklahoma to the rain-laden
skies and scudding clouds of California, Ma Joad points a
straight path for her family. Similarly she is the thematic
center of the novel.

Ma Joad represents a quality of the novel too often overlooked, that is, the warm, sympathetic, and often humorous portrayal of character. Too often readers focus on the
fiery scenes in California and miss the quiet little nights
that provide enduring illumination. If the turtle symbolizes
the Okies, it is easy to focus only on its hard shell and hard,
horny beak and to miss its fierce, humorous eyes. That humor attends the migrants also. We see it in the comedy of
Grampa Joad fumbling with his pants buttons, casting lech-
erous glances at Granma, or dreaming of a tub bath in
grape juice. It is there too when Granma Joad falls asleep in
the privy:

"Where is Granma?" Rose of Sharon asked.
"I dunno. She's aroun' here somewheres. Maybe in the out-
house."
The girl went toward the toilet, and in a moment she came out,
helping Granma along. "She went to sleep in there," said Rose of
Sharon.
Granma grinned. "It's nice in there," she said. "They got a patent toilet in there an' the water comes down. I like it in there,"
she said contentedly. "Would of took a good nap if I wasn't woke
up." [P. 178]

Humor is there also in the frolicking dance at Weedpatch.
These thoroughly human touches continually mitigate the
anger of the book and make it finally a book about people
rather than a political tract.

As a book about people, captured in all their ornery and
humorous and noble and despicable reality, *The Grapes of*

Wrath also raises the issue of profanity and censorship. The issue warrants attention for two reasons: first, it has fueled many censorship campaigns against *The Grapes of Wrath,* and, second, it is revealing of Steinbeck as a literary artist. The literary history of *The Grapes of Wrath* is, in part, a history of literary censorship in America.

PROFANITY, THE ARTIST, AND CENSORSHIP

Although Steinbeck advised his agent, Elizabeth Otis, against a large print run of *The Grapes of Wrath* under the opinion that "this will not be a popular book," the novel quickly seized the attention of the nation. Despite Steinbeck's prediction, "It will be a loss to do anything except to print a small edition and watch and print more if there are more orders" (*LL,* p. 173), Covici could hardly keep ahead of sales. By April, 1939, advance sales were past 90,000 copies. By November the book was selling 11,000 copies a week, and Steinbeck had just sold the movie rights for $75,000. The novel remained on the best-seller lists for much of 1940.

From the start the novel was accompanied by censorship, and for two major reasons. The first was clearly political, as Martin Shockley has able demonstrated in "The Reception of *The Grapes of Wrath* in Oklahoma."[10] But political censorship diminished with the passage of time. With the onset of World War II, the migrants found new jobs. Regional suspicions waned. Political and ideological charges eventually died down. But also from the start there was a second torrent of censorship that remains very much alive today, that is, censorship owing to the book's profane language. As Jackson Benson points out, in the early period the charges of profanity may have been in fact politically motivated:

Charges of filth against the novel were widespread and led to bannings and burnings in several localities, including Buffalo, New York; East Saint Louis, Illinois; and Kern County, California. (Since these early responses, the book has remained among the most frequently banned, as reported by school and library associations.) But this aspect of the controversy didn't bother Steinbeck nearly as much as the one that was essentially political (although, as [Joseph Henry] Jackson noted, some of the charges of obscenity were no doubt politically inspired.[11]

But the issue had predated that; it had, in fact, occurred in the editorial offices of Viking Press before publication:

The manuscript had gone on to Viking, where there was much concern over the novel's language. It was felt that if some passages were not changed and some words altered, bookstores would simply refuse to handle the book and it would be banned throughout much of the country. The problem was a delicate one. Viking would not censor the offensive language, yet the editors were quite aware that Steinbeck would not willingly alter anything, especially for reasons of placating an audience or insuring sales.[12]

It is clear, however, that Steinbeck both recognized the issue and dealt with it from the start and that he had an artistic theory of language that included profanity and guided him throughout his career.

For Steinbeck the heart of the issue lay in his effort to capture the whole life environment of a character and in his recognition that in certain groups of people and certain environments profanity is a customary form in which characters express emotions or convictions. The words chosen for this expression do not necessarily carry the same meaning or weight of meaning that they do for other people in other environments. The novelist's task, however, is to capture accurately the people and environment of his story and not to appease readers from a wholly other environment. An early indication of this belief occurs in *Cup of Gold*. When Henry Morgan ventures forth on ship for the first time, "To his lips came the peculiar, clean swearing of sailors; phrases of filth and blasphemy and horror, washed white by their utter lack of meaning in his mouth" (pp. 46–47). In this environment, from the lips of these people, profanity is a natural thing, "washed white" by the lack of profane intention.

Steinbeck wrote at some length about this relativity of language to people and environment in *The Log from the Sea of Cortez*. The passage is important in relation to the novelist's task, which is, like the marine biologist's, fidelity to the truth of the people and environment he perceives:

We have wondered about the bawdiness this book must have if it is to be true. Bawdiness, vulgarity—call it what you will—is such a relative matter, so much a matter of attitude. A man we knew once long ago worked for a wealthy family in a country place. One morning one of the cows had a calf. The children of the house went down with him to watch her. It was a good normal birth, a perfect presentation, and the cow needed no help. The children asked questions and he answered them. And when the emerged head cleared through the sac, the little black muzzle appeared, and the first breath was drawn, the children were fascinated and awed. And this was the time for their mother to come screaming down on the vulgarity of letting the children see the birth. This "vulgarity" had given them a sense of wonder at the structure of life, while the mother's propriety and gentility supplanted that feeling with dirtiness. If the reader of this book is "genteel," then this is a very vulgar book. [P. 70]

While he was at work on *Tortilla Flat*, Steinbeck observed the problem, emphasizing the novelist's prerogative to see things his own way: "Dad doesn't like characters to swear. But if I had taken all the writing instructions I've been given, I would be insane. I try to write what seems to me true. If it isn't true for other people, then it isn't good art. But I've only my own eyes to see with. I won't use the eyes of other people" (*LL*, p. 90). This attitude crystallized while Steinbeck was at work on *In Dubious Battle*. His acute consciousness that he must keep his fictional characters faithful to real-life prototypes affected his language: "The talk, and the book is about eighty percent dialogue, is what is usually called vulgar. I have worked along with working stiffs, and I have rarely heard a sentence that had not some bit of profanity in it. And in books I am sick of the noble working man talking very like a junior college professor" (*LL*, p. 99).

Throughout this period, with a growing sense of sureness and purpose in his own artistry, Steinbeck was adamant in what he called "the sound of authenticity." Any tampering with that would lessen and cheapen a work. A revealing episode occurred in November, 1937, when Jack Kirkland was given the task of providing the dramatic adaptation of *Tortilla Flat*. Seeing the script for the first time, Steinbeck alternated between outrage and "howls of laughter" at the linguistic mangling. A week and a half after firing off an angry salvo at Kirkland, Steinbeck reflected a bit more temperately:

These are little things but I have a feeling that unless they are taken care of, the play is not going to have any sound of authenticity. You can argue that it doesn't matter because no one in the east ever heard of these people, anyway. Just remember some of the phony dialect in pictures and you will see that it does matter. No one believes that, in fact scorns it. [*LL*, p. 150]

This "sound of authenticity" became a creed for Steinbeck as novelist.

It is clear that Steinbeck had sharply formed attitudes toward language and authentic characterization by the time of *The Grapes of Wrath*. He anticipated problems with the profanity and did not avoid them. When the editors questioned the language, he remained firm in his conviction.

Elizabeth and I went over the mss and made some changes. I made what I could. There are some I cannot make. When the tone or overtone of normal speech requires a word, it is going in no matter what the audience thinks. The book wasn't written for delicate ladies. If they read it at all they're messing in something not their business. I've never changed a word to fit the prejudices of a group and I never will. The words I changed were those which Carol and Elizabeth said stopped the reader's mind. I've never wanted to be a popular writer—you know that. And those readers who are insulted by normal events or language mean nothing to me. [*LL*, p. 175]

Steinbeck never varied in this attitude. Seldom did he use profanity gratuitously—perhaps only in *The Winter of Our Discontent,* in which the profanity seems somewhat at odds with character and environment. With the publication of *Travels with Charley* and its notorious "cheerleaders" scene, he faced a conflict similar to that of *The Grapes of Wrath.* Steinbeck's letter to Elizabeth Otis of February 1, 1962, bears an interesting statement. Because of the danger of sensationalism there was a concomitant danger of losing the truth. Therefore Steinbeck worked out the cheerleader passage by suggestion and implication rather than quotation:

What started out as a simple piece of truth now wears all the clothing of sensationalism and has lost every vestige of its purity. It doesn't feel clean to me any more. The only value of the passage lay in its shock value. Now it has become that book with the dirty words and by a magical turnabout the dirty words are no longer the cheer leaders' but mine. When I get the galleys I shall see what I want to do. I know that by simple suggestion I can make them much uglier without saying them. [*LL*, pp. 733–34]

In its final form the simple suggestiveness goes like this:

No newspaper had printed the words these women shouted. It was indicated that they were indelicate, some even said obscene. On television the sound track was made to blur or had crowd noises cut in to cover. But now I heard the words, bestial and filthy and degenerate. In a long and unprotected life I have seen and heard the vomitings of demoniac humans before. Why then did these screams fill me with a shocked and sickened sorrow?

The words written down are dirty, carefully and selectedly filthy. But there was something far worse here than dirt, a kind of frightening witches' Sabbath. Here was no spontaneous cry of anger, of insane rage.

Perhaps that is what made me sick with weary nausea. Here was no principle good or bad, no direction. [*TWC*, pp. 227–28]

Clearly, this is more than "suggestiveness." It is also con-
demnation for the feral gratuitousness of the language of
the cheerleaders whose sole purpose was to express hatred,
to vilify and to demean, being therefore absolutely opposed
to Steinbeck's whole point of view. The language was sordid, ugly, and obscene by virtue of willfulness. In *The
Grapes of Wrath* Jim Casy quotes Emerson, "All that lives
is holy"; Casy says this with awe and reverence for the mystery that is life. Although John Steinbeck expressed no particular fondness for D. H. Lawrence, he might have agreed
with Lawrence that obscenity constitutes anything that de-
grades the holiness of life. As a matter of fact, Lawrence's
derision for pornography roughly parallels Steinbeck's derision for obscenity such as the cheerleaders'. In his essay
"Pornography and Obscenity," Lawrence wrote:

> Pornography is the attempt to insult sex, to do dirt on it. This
> is unpardonable. Take the very lowest instance, the picture post-
> card sold underhand, by the underworld, in most cities. What I
> have seen of them have been of an ugliness to make you cry. The
> insult to the human body, the insult to a vital human relationship!
> Ugly and cheap they make the human nudity, ugly and degraded
> they make the sexual act, trivial and cheap and nasty.[13]

The same can be said about Steinbeck's view of language as
used by the cheerleaders. When language threatens the
family of man, it is, like the brute power of the landowners
in *In Dubious Battle* and in *The Grapes of Wrath*, an obscene and malevolent thing.

Critics have sometimes spoken of a series of apexes in
Steinbeck's work, with *The Grapes of Wrath* representing
the highest and a series of lesser heights represented in
East of Eden and finally *The Winter of Our Discontent*.
While one might find fault with such a scheme because of
the great variety of Steinbeck's work—that is, *The Pearl*
may be an apex as parable, *Tortilla Flat* as comedy, *Of Mice
and Men* as novella—it is true that Steinbeck achieved a
work of rare complexity and merit in *The Grapes of Wrath*.

When he spoke of five layers of meaning he put into the novel, he probably did not guess that readers would easily double the number of layers. In terms of thematic complexity and artistic skill, however, the work stands also as one of the masterpieces of American literature.

6

Angels in Midheaven: The Cannery Row Novels

THE MONTEREY PENINSULA is a squat little cusp of a peninsula thrusting out into the Pacific. From the spine that ridges it, hills angle down to the sprawl of streets that form the tight little city of Monterey. Founded in 1770 by Fray Junipero Serra, Monterey was the first capital of a California that was still a land of Indians and Mexicans and Spaniards, a land of great forests, mountainous ridges hiding mines of gold and silver, and fertile valleys that eventually yielded the richest lode of all—vegetables.

In Monterey, the official edifices of rule still stare at the sea, well-preserved mementos of a Spanish colonial past.

In the city proper, curious little streets fit the contours of the land, snaking between buildings, twisting among shops as varied as the winds that play in the bay. Up against the hills that roll on to Pacific Grove and Pebble Beach lie the flats of upper Jefferson Street. They are wedged between streets bearing presidential names—Jackson, Van Buren, Madison, Roosevelt—streets recalling Spanish origins—Calle Principal, Alvarado, Bonifacio—and streets that are simply American—Larkin, Artillery. On these flats sprawl the small clapboard houses and shanties that housed generations of cannery workers and the residents of Tortilla Flat. All the streets empty into the mouth of the bay and Cannery Row, "a stink, a grating noise, a quality of light, a tone, a habit, a nostalgia, a dream." Here is the home of the Pacific Biological Laboratories at 800 Cannery Row, the home of the Wing Chong Market at 835 Cannery Row— now the Old General Store, the home of La Ida's Cafe—

now Kalissa's International Restaurant, the home of the
Bear Flag, and the home of the "Steinbeck Tree," an
old cypress reputed to be one of several shady reposing
grounds for Mack and the boys. The house that Steinbeck
purchased in 1944 at 460 Pierce is now a doctor's office.

Cannery Row is a lazy bustle, punctuated by the frantic
clanging of cannery bells, the shrill of their steam valves,
and the lazy movements of fishermen casting lines along
the shore in the evening. At the Old General Store one can
buy *Cannery Row: A Pictorial History*[1] and surplus can-
ning labels bearing such brands as "Captain Silver Monterey Sardines," "Portola California Squid," "Don Palma
Horse Mackerel," and "El Carmel Sardines." Milton Little's
ranch that overlooked the bay in 1851 was transformed by
the ingenuity of F. E. Booth, who in 1895 decided to harvest fish from the ranch of the Pacific. In came the Italians,
Mexicans, Portuguese, Japanese, and Chinese, each in separate living areas. On the north, migrants started Seaside.
A forest of smokestacks sprouted along the bay, and the
ethnically diverse population of Monterey converged at the
great sprawling factories.

The canneries are for the most part empty now—the
bustle and stink and grating noise replaced by the quiet
click of change on store counters.

BACKGROUND TO THE NOVELS

Curiously, Monterey thought it would not survive *Tortilla
Flat*. It was, after all, a cannery town. When the first loads
of tourists descended on the town looking for the remains
of Danny's house, reactions ranged from directions to "Tortilla Flat" tolerantly given to outrage at the imposition.
Tortilla Flat was the first of Steinbeck's books to earn national recognition, and as it changed the structure of Monterey Bay it also changed the author. Steinbeck records the
change in Monterey Bay in a letter to Elizabeth Otis: "One
very funny thing. Hotel clerks here are being instructed to
tell guests that there is no Tortilla Flat. The Chamber of
Commerce does not like my poor efforts, I guess. But there

is one all right, they know it" (*LL,* p. 111). Later in that
same letter Steinbeck hints at the growing encroachment
on his own time: "The publicity on TF is rather terrible out
here and we may have to run ahead of it. Please ask CF
[Covici-Friede] not to give my address to anyone. Curious
that this second-rate book, written for relaxation, should
cause this fuss. People are actually taking it seriously"
(p. 111). Thomas Kiernan elaborates on the publicity attracted to Steinbeck:

Before the publication of *Tortilla Flat,* Steinbeck had at once
enjoyed and suffered anonymity in the tiny house in Pacific Grove.
In his desire for recognition, he had endured his anonymity as a
symbol of the public's unjustified rejection of his work. By September his notoriety made him wish for a return of his former
obscurity. Tourists, literary pilgrims, newspaper interviewers
and a varied assortment of cranks and beggars made their way to
the cottage in droves.[2]

The reaction was perplexing to Steinbeck, since it came
from a book which he considered a light diversion, written
partly to offset the oppressive burden of illness in his own
family (the book was released on May 28, 1935, just five
days after his father's death). Steinbeck made note of this
when he first started the book in the late summer of 1933:

My father collapsed a week ago under the six months' strain
and very nearly landed in the same position as my mother. It was
very close. Paradoxically, I have started another volume [*Tortilla
Flat*] and it is going like wildfire. It is light and I think amusing
but true, although no one who doesn't know paisanos would ever
believe it. I don't care much whether it amounts to anything. I am
enjoying it and I need something to help me over this last ditch.
[*LL,* p. 88]

In much the same vein, he wrote to Edith Wagner in November, 1933:

When we came over a month ago, I got to work finally and did
three fourths of a book. I thought I was going to slip it through,
but dad's decline beat me. This is indeed writing under difficulty.

The house in Salinas is pretty haunted now. I see things walking
at night that it is not good to see. This last book is a very jolly one
about Monterey paisanos. Its tone, I guess, is direct rebellion
against all the sorrow of our house. [*LL*, pp. 89–90]

The significance of such comments should not be missed.
To a large degree Steinbeck's work of the early and mid-
thirties was in transition from writing fiction whose purpose was chiefly to elaborate an abstract theme, shaping
the plot to express that theme, to writing fiction that was
rooted in reality and allowed the reality in its own way to
sustain its theme. In effect, his artistic vision was transforming from an inward, cerebral vision to an outward, objective, and experiential vision. Looking outward from the
trying circumstances of his home life, he found the paisanos
of Monterey. While at work on *To a God Unknown*, Steinbeck wrote: "It will probably be a hard book to sell. Its
characters are not 'home folks.' They make no more attempt at being human than the characters in the *Iliad*.
Boileau insisted that only gods, kings and heroes are worth
writing about. I firmly believe that."³ And in *To a God Unknown*, Steinbeck wrote of a god-king-hero only to find that
the creature he had dreamed up was as unlike real life as
the sirens of Homer were to the clanging cannery bells of
Steinbeck's own Monterey. The change was from Polyphe-
mus ("Much-Fame"), associated with Odysseus, to Anti-
phates ("Against-Renown"), the Laestrygonian king who
neither knows the famed Odysseus nor much cares about
him. A new heroism arises, in the decidedly ungodlike
shapes of Danny, Pilon, Mack, and Hazel. *Tortilla Flat* is
the fulcrum that tipped Steinbeck from the mystical to the
real.

One wonders, then, how seriously to take Steinbeck's
comments about the theme of *Tortilla Flat* announced in a
letter to Mavis McIntosh during the negotiations over the
novel. Putting aside the issue of the intentional fallacy, one
would judge that it is best to take Steinbeck's announce-
ments to his agents quite seriously. Few authors have had

as astute a conceptual grasp of their own work.[4] In the McIntosh letter Steinbeck actually announced two intentions for his work. Curiously, only the first, the Arthurian theme, has received critical attention.

The Arthurian story had lingered in Steinbeck's mind since his childhood reading of *Morte D'Arthur*, and Steinbeck claimed to have used its rough elements as a kind of superstructure for *Tortilla Flat*. To McIntosh, however, he acknowledged that the attempt was not successful:

The book has a very definite theme. I thought it was clear enough. I have expected that the plan of the Arthurian cycle would be recognized, that my Gawaine and my Launcelot, my Arthur and Galahad would be recognized. Even the incident of the Sangreal in the search of the forest is not clear enough I guess. The form is that of the Malory version, the coming of Arthur and the mystic quality of owning a house, the forming of the round table, the adventure of the knights and finally, the mystic translation of Danny. [*LL*, pp. 96–97]

Perhaps critical analysis of comparisons between *Tortilla Flat* and *Morte D'Arthur* is attractive because Steinbeck himself suggested the relationship and therefore any such study seems to carry the author's sanction. Careful examination, however, demonstrates that, while *Morte D'Arthur* may have had a suggestiveness that inspired certain sections of *Tortilla Flat*, firm analogies fail to hold; there are in fact more dissimilarities than similarities.

In the McIntosh letter Steinbeck acknowledges the similarities. Danny is a bit like Arthur in that he assembles his friends about him in a new Round Table graced with fruit jars of grappa and dollar-a-gallon wine. The quest on Saint Andrews' Eve for the great treasure may be like the quest for the Sangreal insofar as any quest is like the archetypally fulfilling Grail quest. But the contrasts are so many that one hesitates to start listing them.

Is *Tortilla Flat* "colored" by *Morte D'Arthur*? Certainly. Steinbeck notes the ways in which this occurs in the McIntosh letter and refers the reader to them in the preface. Is

Tortilla Flat analogous to *Morte D'Arthur?* Certainly not.
Peter Lisca details a few in the interminable list of dissimilarities:

It is not possible to identify with certainty and consistency his
"Gawaine and Launcelot," his "Arthur and Galahad." If Danny is
the Arthur of the saga, since he owns the property which corresponds to the Round Table, his identity is confused when, like
Launcelot, he goes mad. Pilon, Jesus Maria, Danny, Big Joe
Portagee: all are seduced by fleshly pleasures. While there are
numerous examples in Malory of knights being seduced or
tempted, none of the episodes seems to bear any resemblance to
incidents in *Tortilla Flat.* Percival is not mentioned in the letter,
but The Pirate bears him some resemblance in coming to the
group from a boorish existence in the country. This similarity is
strengthened by the fact that The Pirate's dogs see a vision of St.
Francis. However, it is in Chretien's *Percival* that Percival sees
the Grail; in Malory it is Galahad, the son of Launcelot.[5]

Finally, and quite accurately, Lisca concludes that "Steinbeck may have exaggerated the book's parallel to Malory
in order to impress some publisher."[6] This would not be
surprising in view of Steinbeck's own desperate quest for
significant publication in the mid-thirties and the artistic
transformation from the grandiose (Malory) to the concrete
(paisanos).

A second item in that same McIntosh letter, however,
warrants closer attention. Repeatedly Steinbeck spoke of
the work as "light diversion," a comedy to offset his personal tragedies. The McIntosh letter continues: "But the
little dialogue, if it came between the incidents would at
least make clear the form of the book, its tragi-comic theme.
It would also make clear and sharp the strong but different
philosophic-moral system of these people" (*LL*, p. 97). The
key here lies in Steinbeck's description of *Tortilla Flat* as
tragicomic in theme. Lisca has been one of the very few
Steinbeck scholars to make anything of this, and he discusses it rather perfunctorily but accurately in his descrip-

tion of the novel's "mock-epic tone," which he locates particularly in the often inflated, pompous chapter headings.[7]

I believe that the tragicomic theme extends far beyond the chapter headings; in fact, it undergirds theme and structure in *Tortilla Flat* as well as its anglicized successors *Cannery Row* and *Sweet Thursday*.

Both artists and critics have been uncomfortable with efforts at exclusive distinction between tragedy and comedy. Aristotle provided the Western world with a language for distinguishing these genres, asserting that poetry "broke up into two kinds according to the differences of character in the individual poets; for the graver among them would represent noble actions, and those of noble personages; and the meaner sort of actions of the ignoble."[8] From this simple distinction he extrapolated the discussion in the *Poetics*, emphasizing that tragedy deals with noble events, actions, emotions and comedy with the ignoble, including "men worse than the average; worse, however, not as regards any and every sort of fault, but only as regards one particular kind, the Ridiculous, which is a species of the Ugly."[9] By the Ridiculous or Ugly, Aristotle means here someone from the common order of humanity who makes "mistakes" that cause no pain to others but merely produce bewilderment or confusion. These comic characters are very much like the denizens of Cannery Row.

In Renaissance and Elizabethan drama, with its explosion of creative dramatic energy, the issue again became an effort to make distinctions. While scholars of the time argued distinctions with cultivated asperity, the dramatists simply arranged as they saw fit, finding no infrangible rules for life itself. Shakespeare freely mingled genres, luring audiences to the brink of tragedy and saving them with a quick, sure tug of comedy.[10] Generally, the distinctions cherished by the scholars—Aristotle, Sidney, Jonson, Milton, Dryden—and ignored blithely by the dramatists follow a more or less prescribed pattern for generic purity.

Tragedy takes its name from the Greek *tragos oidia*,

"song of the he-goat," a song that begins admirably and
ends foul. *Comedy* derives from the *komos oidia*, "village
festival song." *Characters* of tragedy are generally distinguished figures of royal families or history such as kings,
princes, and political leaders; those of comedy are humble
persons usually with an obligatory clown or two. The *plot*
of tragedy begins happily and ends terribly; that of comedy
begins in confusion and turbulence and ends joyfully—the
resolution in a happy ending is required, and the confusion
is thereby ordered. The *style* of tragedy is elevated and poetic; that of comedy is colloquial and realistic. The *setting*
of tragedy is usually a terrible and imposing place—a battle-
field, a palace, or sometimes, as in *Hamlet*, the mind; the
setting of comedy is often a tavern, a bedroom, a forest, or
a field. The *atmosphere* of tragedy is grim, dark, and fore-
boding; that of comedy is light and frivolous. The *themes* of
tragedy include revenge, discovery of evil, terrible deeds
and the guilt thereof; those of comedy include sex, love and
marriage, and confused identities. Such categories are not,
of course, absolute but represent a kind of historical-critical
consensus.

On first appearance Steinbeck's Tortilla Flat and Cannery
Row characters would seem to reside firmly in the genre of
comedy. They are village characters; worse, they are what
many people would call bumpkins, apparent clowns if not
outright fools. The plots of these tales invariably begin in
some disorientation or even confusion—Danny's acquisi-
tion of two houses, Doc's seemingly incurable loneliness—
and each resolves itself in almost Bacchanalian festivity, a
Dionysian revel. The style of the novels is deliberately colloquial, although Peter Lisca is correct in noting the satire
of "a burlesque epic language and action" in *Tortilla Flat*.[11]
The setting of these works seems unmitigatedly comic, from
the pine flats of Monterey to the dingy lab of Doc to the
river bottoms of the frog hunt to the innumerable bedrooms
and drinking sprees. But finally the works cut across all genres. The large themes that unify the works are the tragic

threat of loneliness and the consolation of friendship, but a
suborder of comic themes of sex and love undergirds them.

The popular assumption of the trilogy is that Steinbeck
crafted breezy little comedies. Why, then, does Warren
French perceive the initial work thus: "As a heroic tale,
Tortilla Flat is ultimately a tragedy—another tragedy of
the man who tries to attain greatness but who does not succeed"?[12] The answer lies in Steinbeck's own designation for
the works; they are finally tragicomic, freely intermingling
traits of each genre. But "tragicomedy" carries a meaning
deeper than simply a facile juggling act. To appreciate fully
Steinbeck's achievement and his increasing dedication to
human realism, further implications of the term need to be
set forth.

Tragicomedy, although solidly rooted in Renaissance
drama, or earlier, in works like Chaucer's *The Miller's Tale*
or *The Pardoner's Tale*, has taken on a uniquely twentieth-
century form and meaning. It seems allied with man's sense
of frailty before great, earth-shaking powers that he can
hardly influence but whose influence on him is inescapable. Wylie Sypher discusses this mode in "The Meanings
of Comedy":

Our new appreciation of the comic grows from the confusion
in modern consciousness, which has been sadly wounded by the
politics of power, bringing with it the ravage of explosion, the
atrocious pain of inquisitions, the squalor of labor camps, and
the efficiency of big lies. Wherever man has been able to think
about his present plight he has felt "the suction of the absurd."
He has been forced to see himself in unheroic positions. In his
sanest moments the modern hero is aware that he is J. Alfred Pru-
frock, or Osric, an attendant lord—"Almost, at times, the Fool."
Or else Sweeney, the apeneck, seeking low pleasures while death
and the raven drift above.[13]

Tragicomedy begins in an awareness of the world as chaotic
and beyond human control, essentially a tragic place threat-

ening to humanity. The concept seems inherent in literary
Naturalism as discussed in the first chapter. If, in tragedy,
as George Steiner has argued in *The Death of Tragedy*,
there "can be no recourse to secular or material remedies,"
then the modern world appears irredeemably tragic."[14]

With the unrelenting realism of twentieth-century literature the neat, rational distinctions of Aristotle seem
obliterated. Every man seems potentially tragic, potentially ridiculous or ugly, for the world itself seems tragic.
Therefore, playwright Christopher Fry ponders the need
to account for the potentially tragic before comedy can be
attempted:

> The bridge by which we cross from tragedy to comedy and
> back again is precarious and narrow. We find ourselves in one or
> the other by the turn of a thought; a turn such as we make when
> we turn from speaking to listening. I know that when I set about
> writing a comedy the idea presents itself to me first of all as trag-
> edy. The characters press on to the theme with all their divisions
> and perplexities heavy about them; they are already entered for
> the race to doom, and good and evil are an infernal tangle skin-
> ning the fingers that try to unravel them. If the characters were
> not qualified for tragedy there would be no comedy.[15]

Typifying modern tragicomedy, then, is a straightforward
engagement with the potentially tragic realities of modern
life. Such an engagement clearly marked Steinbeck's artistry from the mid-thirties on. If tragicomedy is a probing
engagement with real life, and if there seem to be no temporal remedies to the difficulties in this life, then salvation
from the tragic must arise in man himself, and this is typified by his indomitable ability to laugh. Such laughter
should not be construed as an escape from life. Rather, the
fondness of modern authors for tragicomedy inheres in the
wholeness of this view of life as a symbiosis of tears of
laughter and tear of sorrow. The tragicomic novelist Peter
De Vries said in an interview with Roy Newquist that "it's
false to separate elements from counterparts with which
they are inseparably intermingled in reality. You can't talk

about the serious and comic separately and still be talking about life, any more than you can independently discuss hydrogen and oxygen and still be dealing with water."[16] DeVries carefully distinguishes his work from satire, an important point also for Steinbeck in relation to the Monterey characters. Some critics have, in fact, misunderstood Steinbeck as subjecting the paisanos to satire. DeVries observed: "I'd say roughly that the difference between a satirist and a humorist is that the satirist shoots to kill while the humorist brings his prey back alive. Swift destroyed the human race; Mark Twain and Thurber enabled it to go on."[17] If, on the one hand, Steinbeck's intention is not, as Peter Lisca argues, "to *apotheosize 'natural'* man," neither is it to denigrate that natural man.[18] Finally, Steinbeck's aim, in concert with the non-teleological thinking of *The Log from the Sea of Cortez,* is to bring to light a set of characters and their natural environment on a life stage where the tragic and the comic intermingle and offset one another.

If the novels should be read not as an apotheosis or as a satiric denigration of character, neither should they be regarded, as Howard Levant points out, simply as "local color":

The paisanos are undeniably a colorful people, and *Tortilla Flat* has been read often enough merely as a potpourri of exotic local color. If it were no more than that, it probably would not communicate the insights and the pleasure that it does. In reality, Steinbeck's linking a colorful people to a basically serious view of social and economic values tends to humanize the idea and to domesticate the people."[19]

In this lively environment with its dynamic characters, we see a bit of that human life we all share.

Matthew Winston has written, in "Black Humor: To Weep with Laughing," that "the comedy in black humor helps us overcome our fears," and that is an essential power of tragicomedy, including everyone in its drama.[20] What exactly is the fear in the Cannery Row novels? What is the threat that creates the potential for tragedy. In each of the

novels it is the fear of loneliness, which culminates, perhaps, in *Sweet Thursday* with Doc's relentless and consuming lament:

And there would be three voices singing in him, all singing together. The top voice of his thinking mind would sing, "What
lovely little particles, neither plant nor animal but somehow
both—the reservoir of all the life in the world, the base supply of
food for everyone. If all of these should die, every other living
thing might well die as a consequence." The lower voice of his
feeling mind would be singing, "What are you looking for, little
man? Is it yourself you're trying to identify? Are you looking at
little things to avoid the big things?" And the third voice, which
came from his marrow, would sing, "Lonesome! Lonesome! What
good is it? Who benefits? Thought is the evasion of feeling. You're
only walling up the leaking loneliness." [*ST*, p. 24–25]

The theme of loneliness marks all of Steinbeck's fiction of
this period, and it was probably heightened in *Sweet Thursday* by the recent death of his close friend Ed Ricketts:

I've just finished another book about the Row. It is a continuation
concerned not with what did happen but with what might have
happened. The one can be as true as the other. I think it is a
funny story, and sad too because it is what might have happened
to Ed and didn't. I don't seem to be able to get over his death. But
this will be the last piece about him. [*LL*, p. 474]

While the theme held special poignancy for Steinbeck's
personal life, it reinforces the themes of the individual versus social restraint and unfulfilled dreams in the other early
fiction. George's lament in *Of Mice and Men*—"Guys like
us, that work on ranches, are the loneliest guys in the
world. They got no family. They don't belong no place"—
applies equally to the paisanos of Cannery Row, except that
here the tragic theme of loneliness is offset by the comic
theme of friendship. "'In all the world,'" says Pablo,
"'there are few friends like thee, Danny. It is not given to
many to have such solace'" (*TF*, pp. 88–89). This tragi-

comic loneliness-friendship pattern can be seen in each of
the Cannery Row novels.

Tortilla Flat

If, as Northrop Frye observed in "The Argument of Comedy," "tragedy is really implicit or uncompleted comedy. . . . [and] that comedy contains a potential tragedy
within itself,"[21] consider first how Steinbeck structures the
potential for tragedy in *Tortilla Flat*. The casual glance will
immediately observe the comic characters in their squalid,
rustic satellite to Monterey and observe that, as in *Of Mice
and Men*,

> The best laid schemes o' mice an' men
> Gan aft a-gley
> An' lea'e us nought but grief an' pain
> For promis'd joy.

But the tragic potential is more precisely patterned here in
characteristic imagery of Steinbeck's that places man as
a curious animal in a naturalistic world. Although not as
overt as in a short story like "Flight," the animal imagery
functions to level the paisano existence, subtly enforcing
its rustic quality. At Danny's and Pilon's first meeting they
"huddled near the fire and sipped delicately at the bottle
like effete bees" (p. 23). In one of his early, glorious fights,
Danny butts a girl in the stomach, who then "went out the
door croaking like a frog" (p. 37). The notable Pirate has
eyes with "the secret look of an animal that would like to
run away if it dared turn its back long enough" (p. 93).
The irony of the Pirate's situation is that each of his five
dogs, with the exception of the commonplace Fluff, has
a specific name—Enrique, Pajarito, Rudolph, and Señor
Alec Thompson—while the Pirate has none; he is simply
"the Pirate," keeper of dogs and lover of Saint Francis. The
seductive ladies of Tortilla Flat are often imaged as bees,
such as Dolores "Sweets" Engracia Ramirez: "Dolores'

voice sounded as huskily sweet as the drone of a bumble-
bee" (p. 156). Teresina Cortez's nine children crawl after
boiled beans "with the intentness of little bugs" (p. 226).
Such examples are revealing. The animal imagery here is
not threatening or malevolent; it is quite different, for
example, from the snarling, vicious imagery that attends
Pepe of "Flight" or Cathy Ames of *East of Eden*. Rather, it
simply domesticates and locates the rusticity and com-
monality of these decidedly ignoble characters. It at once
places them in the camp of the comic by their rustic qualities but also opens them to the threat of the tragic by their
vulnerability.

The great threat to which they are vulnerable is the decidedly human one of loneliness. Coming home belatedly
from military careers entered on drunken impulse, endured with fractious élan, and returned from without glory,
honor, money, or wine, the paisanos wander back to the
battles of Tortilla Flat. Meeting with Pilon, Danny enters a
Beckett-like dialogue:

> Danny sighed and changed the subject, for he realized that he
> had prodigally used up the only acquaintance in any way fit for
> oratory. But the loneliness was still on him and demanded an out-
> let. "Here we sit," he began at last.
> "—broken hearted," Pilon added rhythmically.
> "No, this is not a poem," Danny said. "Here we sit, homeless.
> We gave our lives for our country, and now we have no roof over
> our head."
> "We never did have," Pilon added helpfully. [P. 24]

Danny's houses will become a haven for the lost and lonely,
but the world overflows with such, and the houses can
scarcely contain them all. Loneliness is the tragic threat to
the characters and lurks always in the wings of their stage
like a beast of prey. They fight against its dim, gray shape,
rescuing the perishing wherever possible.

The contrast between tragic loneliness and the comic is
emphasized in the storytelling match of chapter 14, "Of the
Good Life at Danny's House . . . ," where Steinbeck care-

fully distinguishes tragic story from comic story. Storytelling is essential and significant to the paisanos, providing
them with both a history and a direction. And they have a
sure sense of story. Pilon's creed echoes Steinbeck's: "The
story was gradually taking shape. Pilon liked it this way. It
ruined a story to have it all come out quickly. The good
story lay in half-told things which must be filled in out of
the hearer's own experience" (p. 74). In the storytelling
competition recorded in chapter 14, the paisanos distinguish between the tragic humor and comic humor. Sometimes people laugh at bad things; such laughter emerges
out of bitterness or loneliness, but it is not redemptive. It
provides no healthy perspective or renewal. An example of
tragic humor is the story of Tall Bob, who out of dreadful
loneliness and need for attention shoots off the end of his
nose. As Pablo tells the story: "'You have all seen Bob's nose,
with the end shot off. The people laughed; but it was a hard
kind of laughing, and they felt bad to laugh'" (p. 247). This
is the bad laughter—the laughter of tragedy which only de-
means and belittles and does not rejuvenate.

In the tale-topper sequence Jesus Maria broods on such
"bad" laughter:

Jesus Maria had been brooding, with his head back against the
wall. He observed, "It is worse than whipping to be laughed at.
Old Tomas, the rag sucker, was laughed right into his grave. And
afterwards the people were sorry they laughed.

"And," said Jesus Maria, "there is another kind of laughing,
too. That story of Tall Bob is funny; but when you open your
mouth to laugh, something like a hand squeezes your heart."
[P. 248]

Encouraged by Pilon, Jesus Maria tells the story of the
Rovanno family, wrenched apart by the loneliness at the
heart of all their tragedies. The cause of Rovanno's sorrow is
that he "was lonely when Petey was not there with him"
(p. 249). The story ends in taunting, jeering, and bitterness, and Pilon complains: "'It is not a good story. There
are too many meanings and too many lessons in it. Some of

those lessons are opposite. There is not a story to take into your head. It proves nothing'" (p. 257).

Juxtaposed to tragedy and "bad laughter" are comedy and healthy laughter. They are sustained in the novel stylistically; that is, in tone and language Steinbeck provides a backdrop for good-hearted laughter, and these techniques prevail throughout the Cannery Row novels. First, he uses the technique of ironic juxtaposition, so that the reader perceives a disparity between the thing stated and its reality. Into that gap humor enters. Such juxtaposition between what is stated and what is implied is always narrative. For example, when Danny's friends try to cheer him up, Steinbeck tells us that "they reported details of the love life of Tortilla Flat so penetrating that they would have been of interest to a dissection class" (p. 284). Tied together by the pun on "penetrating," the two opposing elements of the juxtaposition—emotional sexuality and objective dissection—bring together the hotly human with the coldly scientific and thus create an ironic jest: for the paisanos, love is a hot-blooded science. Another instance occurs in the description of Jesus Maria Corcoran, whose full name comes to include "that great-hearted man." Here he is described as the comforter of young women:

> It has been said that Jesus Maria Corcoran was a great-hearted man. He had also that gift some humanitarians possess of being inevitably drawn toward those spheres where his instinct was needed. How many times had he not come upon young ladies when they needed comforting. Toward any pain or sorrow he was irresistibly drawn. [P. 230]

The fact that his comforting of young women is ironically and thoroughly sexual is implied in the juxtaposition of his humanitarianism and the young ladies' need. What "great-hearted man" would not respond to their need?

A second stylistic technique for sustaining comic tone often occurs in understatement. When the paisanos get drunk, they are not revoltingly drunk; they sip delicately from "the bottle like effete bees." Understatement is used

often in descriptive passages, as of Danny's house: "At dinner they had used a piece of candle, but now only the light
from the stove cracks dispelled the darkness of the room.
To make it perfect, rain began to patter on the roof. Only
a little leaked through, and that in places where no one
wanted to sit anyway" (p. 32). In a later passage Danny's
house, which the realistic eye might see in such terms as
"dilapidated," "dingy," or "seedy," is lifted by understatement to a kind of squalid grandeur: "No curtains covered
the windows, but a generous Nature had obscured the glass
with cobwebs, with dust and with the neat marks of rain-
drops" (p. 239). To handle the magnificently reproductive
Teresina's desertion by her husband, Steinbeck uses understatement to mitigate the evil of the deed: "When she was
sixteen, Mr. Alfred Cortez married her and gave her his
name and the two foundations of her family, Alfredo and
Ernie. Mr. Cortez gave her that name gladly. He was only
using it temporarily anyway" (p. 223). Such understatement takes the edge off potential tragedy, domesticates it,
familiarizes it, making it humanly manageable.

A third artistic technique that offsets tragedy is the comedy of situation. The continual preying on Torelli, supplier
of wine and possessor of a lively wife, poses innumerable
comic situations, but also the threat of tragedy when Torelli
buys Danny's house for twenty-five dollars. Another such
example is the fifteen-dollar vacuum cleaner Danny buys
for two dollars and presents lavishly to Dolores. Dolores
rises thus to social eminence on the Flat, to be seen daily
pushing it back and forth while humming quiet little motor
sounds since her house was not wired for the machine.
Only when the vacuum is stolen and sold to Torelli do we
discover that it never had a motor.

A fourth stylistic technique marking the comic quality of
the work lies in characterization. Shakespeare's Timon of
Athens said, "Strange times that weep with laughing, not
with weeping." Translated to Tortilla Flat, he might have
said the same thing about Steinbeck's paisanos, for they are

the stuff of human laughter. That Steinbeck could make them first human characters, and not just buffoons or clowns, is a mark of his achievement. These characters lie at the heart of the comedy. In his theory of comedy elaborated in "The Bias of Comedy," Nathan Scott has concluded:

> This, then, is *the comic way:* it is a way that descends into the mundane, conditioned world of the human creature, moving confidently into all the diverse corners of man's habitation. And the difference between this way and the tragic way is not that the one leads into suffering and agony and that the other leads into rollicking mirth and jollity, for the men and women of comedy sometimes suffer too.[22]

Steinbeck's paisanos are not just clowns but inhabitants of that "mundane, conditioned world of the human creature." Their success depends on their diversity, as opposed to the stereotypicality of the clown. Danny is invested with a certain dignity and seriousness that serve as a ground for the others. In Pilon we find the man of "pitiless logic," a precursor of Hazel, one who strives mightily to find reasons for a conclusion he holds in advance. In Jesus Maria Corcoran we find the inimitable humanitarian: "Jesus Maria Corcoran was a pathway for the humanities. Suffering he tried to relieve; sorrow he tried to assuage; happiness he shared. No hard nor haunted Jesus Maria existed. His heart was free for the use of any one who had a use for it" (p. 173). Pablo, Big Joe Portagee, and the Pirate round out the inner circle, each with his own sharply defined and unforgettable personality, but equal care is devoted to the minor characters, often captured succinctly but thoroughly in one quick, impressionistic glance, as is Teresina Cortez's mother: "Her mother, that ancient, dried, toothless one, relict of a past generation, was nearly fifty. It was long since any one had remembered that her name was Angelica" (p. 221). The success of the work depends largely on the liveliness of such characters, who spring fully and humanly into the story.

Religion, too, plays an important part in the lives of these characters, but it is religion relativized to the Flat, an essential and inescapable part of their lives. The tone is established early in the book when the bifurcated spirit of Pilon soars to mystic reaches while retaining its firm base in reality. In that hour of purple dusk, overcome by the sheer, affirmative joy of living, the "good" Pilon praises Our Father in the evening while the feet of the "bad" Pilon momentarily pause in their ceaseless quest for a gallon of wine. The religious awareness of the paisanos inhabits their lives, emerging in quite traditional forms such as the Pirate's gold candlestick for Saint Francis and in quite untraditional forms in a religion they construct and interpret for their own ends. In the latter manifestation we see the personalities of the paisanos in full play: Pilon observes of Cornelia's father that he needs her masses for "he was a bad man and never went to jail for it" (p. 49). Jail is a more familiar form of absolution for the paisanos than is the confessional or Mass; and, after all, "'A mass is a mass,' said Pilon. 'Where you get two-bits is no interest to the man who sells you a glass of wine. And where a mass comes from is of no interest to God. He just likes them, the same as you like wine'" (p. 50). Frequently the paisanos demonstrate their intimate awareness of the mind of God. Similarly, traditional religious rituals stand in competition with a host of superstitious talismans and amulets. While the paisanos often ponder God with a theological certitude approaching Kantian proportions, in a time of need (such as seeking the lost treasure on Saint Andrew's Eve) they will embellish their knowledge with a plethora of superstitious tricks to seize a little power from the deity. Anything at all will do: signs of the cross or magic circles to keep evil spirits at bay. Such actions create a moral and philosophical base in the book, but the base, as Howard Levant argues, is foundation for the apex of human relations, friendship. Levant writes:

Tortilla Flat has a serious intention that fuses with its celebration of friendship. That is, the novel has a moral aim that rests on

a theological base. The *paisano* concept of friendship stems from
a source that is older and more profound than the Round Table.
The *paisanos* are children of Mother Church. They recognize the
basic Christian distinction between temporal and eternal things
and translate it into a specific distinction between the temporal
value of money and the eternal value of friendship. This specific
distinction governs the development of every episode. Again and
again some threat to friendship (and, thus, to the good life) is established in some detail. In the end, however narrow the margin,
the eternal value—friendship—is sustained in the minds and
hearts of the endangered *paisanos*.[23]

While Steinbeck carefully sustains a comic tone in the
novel, the thematic counterpart to the tragic theme of
loneliness inheres in the comitatus of friends. *Comitatus* is
a medieval term used often to describe Arthur's circle of
knights, those who swore allegiance to him and became one
body in their vows. A larger implication in the Cannery
Row novels is that civilization, the larger world outside the
Row, is predatory and divisive. Opposed to civilization's
power, as Arthur's Round Table stood in opposition to the
"beast" of the external world, is the camaraderie of the
paisano friends. A telling passage occurs when the painfully
lonely Joe Portagee comes off the train to seek friends:

> True friends he found none that night, but in Monterey he
> found no lack of those vile and false harpies and pimps who are
> ever ready to lead men into the pit. Joe, who was not very moral,
> had no revulsion for the pit; he liked it.
>
> Before many hours had passed, his wine was gone, and he had
> no money; and then the harpies tried to get Joe out of the pit, and
> he wouldn't go. He was comfortable there. [P. 123]

On the Flat, however, Joe can be assimilated and valued.
The first effect of the comitatus of friends is that it vests the
individual with an identity that the civilized world would
devour as it uses the individual. The comitatus lifts the individual out of the pit.

Moreover, the group of friends provides comfort, as the

Pirate, despite the bad motivations of Pilon, learns: "These were his friends, he told himself in the night, when the house was dark, when the dogs snuggled close to him so that all might be warm. These men loved him so much that it worried them to have him live alone. The Pirate had often to repeat this to himself, for it was an astounding thing, an unbelievable thing" (p. 112). Further, friends nurture each other, sometimes even when the friends do not want it, as in the desperate attempts of the comitatus to do something for their leader. Again, when Big Joe Portagee arrives, we see in the curious religious milieu of the Flat that friends take the place of beneficent angels: "Big Joe Portagee was happy to be with Pilon. 'Here is one who takes care of his friends,' he thought. 'Even when they sleep he is alert to see that no harm comes to them.' He resolved to do something nice for Pilon sometime" (p. 152).

The comitatus stands against the world, sharing with the slightly stooped shoulders of friends one another's burdens: "Danny sighed with relief that his problem was assumed by his good friends" (p. 167). But, finally, the group is united, despite the native chicanery of the individual paisanos, by trust, here represented by the Pirate's unbelievable horde of quarters: "The bag of money had become the symbolic center of the friendship, the point of trust about which the fraternity revolved. They were proud of the money, proud that they had never tampered with it" (p. 198).

That desire of the friends to share each other's burdens, to care for and nurture each other, sets up the cataclysmic ending of the book. If there is a Malorian influence upon the novel, as Steinbeck suggested, it is clearest in the conclusion. Several scholars have pointed out that the influence of Malory is clearest in the high language of the chapter heads, a device linking the episodic nature of the essentially short-story narrations, and probably inserted after the book's completion.[24] The heading of chapter 26 notes "How Danny Was Translated," a clear reference to the mystic passing of Arthur to Avalon. But the actual passing of Danny is more solidly rooted in tragicomedy.

Afflicted by an Arthurian-like ennui in the golden days of
his kingdom, unsettled by loneliness, Danny takes to the
field of battle once more, this time on the stony flats of his
own little Monterey kingdom. The scene is aggrandized in
the language of myth:

"No one?" Danny cried again? "Am I alone in the world? Will
no one fight with me?" The men shuddered before his terrible
eyes, and watched fascinated the slashing path of the table-leg
through the air. And no one answered the challenge.
Danny drew himself up. It is said that his head just missed
touching the ceiling. "Then I will go out to The One who can
fight. I will find The Enemy who is worthy of Danny!" [Pp. 300–
301]

As he stalks out after his personal Mordred, Danny—in a
farcical turn of events—tumbles down a drainage ditch to
his death. It takes four doctors, roused from their sleep by
harrying paisanos, to declare his demise, but the legend
endures:

"Danny was glad on mornings like this," said Pilon.
After their trip to the gulch, the friends sat for a while on the
front porch and celebrated the memory of their friend. Loyally
they remembered and proclaimed Danny's virtues. Loyally they
forgot his faults.
"And strong," said Pablo. "He was as strong as a mule! He
could lift a bale of hay."
The told little stories of Danny, of his goodness, his courage,
his piety. [P. 312]

And, like a sign of reciprocation by Pilon's beneficent angels, Danny's shack conflagrates: "Better that this symbol of
holy friendship, this good house of parties and fights, of
love and comfort, should die as Danny died, in one last
glorious hopeless assault on the gods" (p. 316).
But the tragic passing of Danny, inflated here into myth,
is also attended by all the trappings of comedy. Inherent in
the genre of comedy is the sine qua non that events, no
matter how close to the abyss of tragedy they stagger, must

resolve in joy and festivity. *Tortilla Flat*, like the Cannery
Row novels, ends in a party, a supercharged, rollicking festivity. In traditional comedy the closing festivity always
represents a restoration of order. No matter how askew
things may seem in this world, harmony will be restored.
In the marriage comedies of the Renaissance such parties
are frequently visited by Hymen, and marriages rattle off
right and left; the *Tortilla Flat* counterpart exists in Danny's
final, mythic, sexual undertaking: "No one kept actual
count, and afterwards, naturally, no lady would willingly
admit that she had been ignored; so that the reputed prow-
ess of Danny may be somewhat overstated. One tenth of
it would be an overstatement for any one in the world"
(p. 298). In traditional comedy the festivity is accompanied
by rolling out a barrel or two of ale; the *Tortilla Flat*
counterpart exists in a mythic flood of grappa: "It is passionately averred in Tortilla Flat that Danny alone drank
three gallons of wine. It must be remembered, however,
that Danny is now a god. In a few years it may be thirty
gallons" (pp. 298–299). In traditional comedy the festivity
is celebrated with dancing as symbol of the orderly harmony of the spheres and order among men; the *Tortilla
Flat* counterpart exists in a caterwaul of wounded instru-
ments: "The whole happy soul of Tortilla Flat tore itself
from restraint and arose into the air, one ecstatic unit. They
danced so hard that the floor gave way in one corner. The
accordions played so loudly that always afterwards they
were windbroken, like foundered horses" (pp. 296–97). In
traditional comedy the festivity is blessed by divine appearances; the *Tortilla Flat* counterpart exists in the appearance
of Pilon's Father in the Sky: "It is not always that Nature arranges her effects with good taste. Truly, it rained before
Waterloo; forty feet of snow fell in the path of the Donner
Party. But Friday turned out a nice day. The sun arose as
though this were a day for a picnic" (p. 311).

Steinbeck takes the traditional elements and explosively
inflates them; this is the comedy of Tortilla Flat. Although
each paisano wanders off, "and no two walked together," in

the spirit of comedy they walk back not into loneliness but unified: "Better that this symbol of holy friendship, this good house of parties and fights, of love and comfort, should die as Danny died, in one last glorious hopeless assault on the gods" (p. 316).

Cannery Row

Although all focusing on the same tangled little knot of human life that Steinbeck discovered in Monterey, the three novels, written almost exactly a decade apart, unravel that life in decidedly different ways. Having sworn to himself and the public that he would leave Danny's boys alone, Steinbeck nonetheless found himself irresistibly drawn to this throbbing little cluster that served him as a metaphor for all of life. *Tortilla Flat* appears as a tragicomedy in which the tears of sorrow are offset by the tears of laughter, but Steinbeck's vision darkens considerably in *Cannery Row*. While Steinbeck described the work to Webster Street as "a funny little book that is fun and it is pretty nice" (*LL*, p. 265), the fun is riddled with horror, as if one were laughing in a room filled with broken mirrors that slice through to the dark heart of man and show his own agony. It is a jarring, nervous book, in which the humor turns dark like "a poisoned cream puff." Warren French observes: "Those who carry away the impression that *Cannery Row* is a humorous book do so on the overpowering strength of the description of the parties toward the end of the book; one who stopped reading with the fourth chapter could hardly fail to find the novel profoundly depressing."[25]

Many of the same themes, so fundamental to the early work and to *Tortilla Flat*, persist here. For example (as also in *Sweet Thursday*), loneliness is a central issue. Instead of being redeemed by the comitatus, however, loneliness here is often inexorable and destructive, devouring those characters that it attacks. When the boy Andy looks into the eyes of the Chinaman in chapter 4, he looks into the infinite abyss of human loneliness: "And the loneliness—

the desolate cold aloneness of the landscape made Andy whimper because there wasn't anybody at all in the world and he was left. Andy shut his eyes so he wouldn't have to see it any more" (p. 24). Those outside the comitatus of Mack and the boys are generally typified by a torment of loneliness. William, the Bear Flag bouncer who longs desperately to be one of the group, finds his way out of the loneliness with an ice pick driven into his heart. The only qualifying comment is casually objective: "It was amazing how easily it went in" (p. 21). Henri, the ineffectual artist, has a vision of such demonic cruelty that it drives him "howling with terror." This is quite a different tone from the merry pranksterism of *Tortilla Flat*; this is the horror of the human spirit unleashed like a dragon on the narrow streets of the Row.

Compared to the generally fluid and episodic flow of *Tortilla Flat*, the structure of *Cannery Row* also differs, and this change in itself suggests the darker view. Steinbeck makes use of two principal techniques to create his theme: the intercalary chapter and multiple thematic, metaphorical levels that fold in on the central image of the tidal flat and the central character of Doc.

The most careful analysis of chapter structure in *Cannery Row* has been provided by Warren French, who sees the rise and ebb of narrative and intercalary chapters as analogous to "the pattern of a wave, growing slowly, hitting a reef or barrier, dividing and crashing prematurely, reforming, rising to a great height and crashing at last on the beach itself."[26] It is difficult to see this analogy as a consistent pattern imposed on the narrative events, because the interspersing of intercalary chapters is not perfect. If anything, they suggest the chaotic swirl of a tidal pool, a random series of swirling vortexes, quiet eddies, and still waters. If one considers that an intercalary chapter recounts an action other than that in the narrative plot development but one that adumbrates themes of the narrative or illuminates its action, then it is difficult to isolate a purely intercalary chapter sequence. Several chapters clearly fit the qualifications. Chapter 2's discourse on civilization points to a theme present in the work. Similarly, chapter 4, on Andy's overwhelming loneliness, functions in parallel to the narrative theme. Other such chapters roughly follow an even-numbered sequence, but while some of them are purely intercalary—apart from the narrative but applying thematically to it—others seem to mesh with the narrative itself. In the first category one would include Chapters 2, 4, 8, 12, 14, 16, 19 (here the even-numbered sequence breaks; Peter Lisca reports that the publishers dropped a chapter), 22, 24, 26, and 31. In the category of chapters meshing with the narrative, we find characters from the primary narrative involved in actions separate from the narrative plot. For example, in chapters 10 and 28 we find the significant relationship of Frankie to Doc operating as a thematic parallel to the plot: Frankie's pure, unquestioning love is set against the manipulative love of Mack and the boys. Similarly, chapter 6 involves Doc and Hazel on a collecting trip, which provides Steinbeck space for thematic suggestiveness that colors the primary narrative. In sum, while Steinbeck employs the technique of the intercalary chapters in *Cannery Row*, they are not as carefully structured and thematically consistent as, for example, those of *The Grapes of Wrath*. The intercalary chapters do provide him room for discourse, however, on the thematic structure of the novel.

The thematic content of the novel is man versus civilization, but it is worked into the novel on three separate levels. Whereas in *Tortilla Flat* the paisanos could withstand the beast of the civilized world in the unified comitatus, here the beast assumes monstrous dimensions, as may be seen on the first and most overt level. Here is the strictest boundary line between the Row and the rest of the world—the boundary of civilization with the external world pressing in on the Row. "Out there" lies a monster, "the world ruled by tigers with ulcers, rutted by strictured bulls, scavenged by blind jackals" (p. 15). This is the teleological world in which goals are eaten away by ulcers and aims prove as hollow as the vacancy in the Chinaman's eyes that finally discloses to Andy his own loneliness. "What can it profit a man to gain the whole world and to come to his property with a gastric ulcer, a blown prostate, and bifocals?" (p. 15). It seems at first, as Steinbeck suggests, that "Mack and the boys avoid the trap, walk around the poison, step over the noose while a generation of trapped, poisoned, and trussed-up men scream at them" (p. 15). They seem to avoid it; closer examination proves their world addled with its own kind of poison, inescapable and irremediable.

The boys seem to avoid civilization because their standards and customs differ: "In the pipes and under the cypress tree there had been no room for furniture and the little niceties which are not only the diagnoses but the boundaries of our civilization" (p. 13). But this is superficial. While in *Tortilla Flat* Danny's boys flop all over the shack save for Danny's sacred bed, set aside like a Siege Perilous, Mack carefully chalks out lines of demarcation on the Palace Flophouse floor: "Mack, with a piece of chalk, drew five oblongs on the floor, each seven feet long and four feet wide, and in each square he wrote a name. These were the simulated beds. Each man had property rights inviolable in his space. He could legally fight a man who encroached on his square" (p. 39). As Jackson J. Benson has demonstrated in his essay "John Steinbeck's *Cannery Row*: A Reconsideration," civilization has encroached upon the Row. Like Grampa's "Westering" in *The Red Pony*, civilization bumps into the bay. In a comparison of Steinbeck to Mark Twain, Benson argues:

Twain has been a major figure in the literary discussions of this thematic complex, and many critics have seen a direct line between James Fennimore Cooper's Natty Bumppo and Huck Finn (despite Twain's mockery of Cooper): Bumppo always moves out into the wilderness ahead of the encroachment by frontier settlements with their whiskey and restrictions, while Huck lights out "for the Territory ahead of the rest, because Aunt Sally she's going to adopt me and civilize me, and I can't stand it." Cannery Row, in a sense, is the end of the road; the Row is on the beach of the Pacific Ocean—the last frontier, now decayed. It is Natty Bumppo's last stand.[27]

But civilization has not just encroached *upon;* this is not Natty Bumppo's last stand. Civilization has encroached *within.* Like the poison to which Steinbeck so often compares it, civilization is in the system now, and the body is in torment. If the first level for understanding the effects of civilization lies in the world outside the Row, the second level lies in the Row itself.

Early in the novel the reader observes the fragile efforts of the Row's denizens to compromise with the beast without, and by such small compromises to keep the beast at bay. When Dora is dunned for local charities, she must put up more than her share:

If the police gave a dance for their pension fund and everyone else gives a dollar, Dora has to give fifty dollars. When the Chamber of Commerce improved its gardens, the merchants each gave five dollars but Dora was asked for and gave a hundred. With everything else it is the same, Red Cross, Community Chest, Boy Scouts, Dora's unsung, unpublicized, shameless dirty wages of sin lead the list of donations. [Pp. 17–18]

By such compromises Dora exists and functions in her rightful role on the Bay. but what happens when the beast raises its scaly head within the Row itself, as it surely does in this novel?

One observes this first in the brief intercalary chapter on the Malloys, a couple who find serenity and even a bit of comfort in the Hediondo Cannery boiler. But only for a time. When the canneries boom briefly, the Malloys begin renting out pipes and boilers as sleeping quarters; in effect, they become the civilized tigers in search of the clear goal of financial gain. The effect is quick and certain:

Mrs. Malloy had been contented until her husband became a landlord and then she began to change. First it was a rug, then a washtub, then a lamp with a colored silk shade. Finally she came into the boiler on her hands and knees one day and she stood up and said a little breathlessly, "Holman's are having a sale of curtains. Real lace curtains and edges of blue and pink—$1.98 a set with curtain rods thrown in." [P. 49]

The pattern is observable in a dozen little ways throughout the novel: William the outcast from an outcast group kills himself; Henri the hapless painter hopelessly adapts to each new fad; and why not include Lee Chong, whose sausage-like fingers tap the countertop as he and the boys try to outmaneuver each other? Despite Doc's flighty encomium on Mack and the boys, their story does not bear him out. Doc specifically contrasts the boys to civilization:

I think they survive in this particular world better than other people. In a time when people tear themselves to pieces with ambition and nervousness and covetousness, they are relaxed. All of our so-called successful men are sick men, with bad stomachs, and bad souls, but Mack and the boys are healthy and curiously clean. They can do what they want. They can satisfy their appetites without calling them something else. [P. 149]

Doc adds that "they could ruin their lives and get money," but Mack and the boys simply aren't the same sort as the tenderheartedly conniving paisanos. This is evident not only in their wheeling and dealing but in the very nature of the flophouse that reflects their characters. While Danny and his boys recline in a splendid ambience of untouchable cobwebs and the aroma of wine, the Palace Flophouse is touched everywhere by the qualities of civilization: "With the great stove came pride, and with pride, the Palace became home. Eddie planted morning glories to run over the door and Hazel acquired some rather rare fuchsia bushes planted in five-gallon cans which made the entrance formal and a little cluttered" (pp. 41–42). In short, while the beast reigns outside Cannery Row, the beast also insinuates its slow poison into the Row's very heart. *Cannery Row* is no easy book, with its good guys versus bad guys. It is a work in which the presumed heroes totter on feet of clay.

On the third level one observes civilization metaphorically in the tidal-flat imagery that is a kind of microcosm both of the Row and of the larger world. The beauty, grace, virtue, and viciousness are all there in the tidal flats. As Richard Astro correctly points out: "In many ways, *Cannery Row* is a fictional sequel to the *Log* section of *Sea of Cortez* in that Steinbeck applies directly to a work of fiction many of the philosophical premises he and Ricketts developed in the Gulf of California."[28] Clearly *Cannery Row* is Steinbeck's one thoroughly non-teleological book, presenting life as it is, unqualified by either romantic or scientific jargon. And that explains also the realism of the author in seeing the infestation of civilization at all levels. No matter what the organism—the civilization—whether it be the world at large, Cannery Row, or the tidal flat—the author is going to see it as it is. The initial question of the book guides the fictional method:

How can the poem and the stink and the grating noise—the quality of light, the tone, the habit and the dream—be set down alive? When you collect marine animals there are certain flat worms so delicate that they are almost impossible to capture whole, for they break and tatter under the touch. You must let them ooze and crawl of their own will onto a knife blade and then lift them gently into your bottle of sea water. And perhaps that might be the way to write this book—to open the page and to let the stories crawl in by themselves. [P. 3]

When Doc looks into tidal pools, they seem first to display peace and beauty and then to deepen into horror. Two examples make this clear. First, in chapter 6, Doc goes collecting with the truly remarkable Hazel—perhaps the anglicized counterpart to Pilon—in the Great Tidal Pool. Upon first glance the pool is a picture of serene grace: "It is a fabulous place: when the tide is in, a wave-churned basin, creamy with foam, whipped by the combers that roll in from the whistling buoy on the reef" (p. 30). From this romantic glimpse the author takes us down beneath the surface appearance into the reality. The life becomes ever more harried and savage, from crabs scuttling along their ocean highways to green fronds in frenzied motion to a thoroughly brutal warfare:

Here a crab tears a leg from his brother. The anemones expand like soft and brilliant flowers, inviting any tired and perplexed animal to lie for a moment in their arms, and when some small crab or little tide-pool Johnnie accepts the green and purple invitation, the petals whip in, the stinging cells shoot tiny narcotic needles into the prey and it grows weak and perhaps sleepy while the searing caustic digestive acids melt its body down. [P. 31]

This passage darkens commensurately to a hard, vicious pulse of words charged with murderous urgency:

Then the creeping murderer, the octopus, steals out, slowly, softly, moving life a gray mist, pretending now to be a bit of weed, now a rock, now a lump of decaying meat while its evil goat eyes watch coldly. It oozes and flows toward a feeding crab, and as it comes close its yellow eyes burn and its body turns rosy with the pulsing color of anticipation and rage. Then suddenly it runs lightly on the tips of its arms, as ferociously as a charging cat. It leaps savagely on the crab, there is a puff of black fluid, and the struggling mass is obscured in the sepia cloud while the octopus murders the crab. [P. 31]

From the creamy foam of waves we have moved to a world surcharged by feral, predatory language and actions that malignantly typify any civilization—particularly the war years during which the novel was written—not excluding the Row itself.[29]

Another instance of analogy between tide pool and civilization occurs in chapter 18, a terrible scene set up earlier by the exposure to the viciousness of the ocean floor and the clear suggestion early in the chapter that "on the bottoms lie the incredible refuse of the sea, shells broken and chipped and bits of skeleton, claws, the whole sea bottom a fantastic cemetery on which the living scamper and scramble" (p. 113). In this "cemetery" Doc will also encounter the detritus of civilization, now linked to the ocean bottom. The collecting starts normally, even serenely: "It was good hunting that day. He got twenty-two little octopi. And he picked off several hundred sea cradles and put them in his wooden bucket" (p. 113). But as Doc reaches the lip of the barrier reef, near the unknown gulf that might symbolize all we do not understand about either oceans or human civilization,

He grew rigid. A girl's face looked up at him, a pretty, pale girl with dark hair. The eyes were open and clear and the face was firm and the hair washed gently about her head. The body was out of sight, caught in the crevice. The lips were slightly parted and the teeth showed and on the face was only comfort and rest. Just under water it was and the clear water made it very beautiful. It seemed to Doc that he looked at it for many minutes, and the face burned into his picture memory. [P. 114]

The chapter closes with a dramatic irony—Doc tortured by the beauty of the girl and the hideousness of her death, and the man on the beach thinking of her in "civilized" terms—to collect a bounty for the discovery.

There is thus a careful thematic structure in *Cannery Row* as it focuses on the nature of civilization united in the central metaphor of the tide pool.[30] Just as important as a unifying factor is the character of Doc, who in a sense operates also as a non-teleological means by which we discover the characters in the tidal pool. Doc is a focal point both of narrative plot and of thematic unity. In the narrative plot, slim as it is, Mack and the boys decided to reciprocate Doc's innumerable kindnesses to the Row by giving him a party, and when the first party does more damage than good, they'll give him another until they get it right. More important, like Ma Joad in *The Grapes of Wrath* and Cathy Ames in *East of Eden*, Doc is a focal point for thematic unity and for character development. In relation to him we understand the characters of the Row and the significance of the Row. The temptation, however, is to see Doc as something larger than he is, both in *Cannery Row* and in *Sweet Thursday*. That temptation arises because the pervasive

religious aura of *Tortilla Flat,* which directly affects the
moral-philosophical actions of its inhabitants, is replaced
here by the Row inhabitants' apparent deification of Doc.
Readers might easily miss the ironic juxtaposition of an
early description of Doc: "He wears a beard and his face
is half Christ and half satyr and his face tells the truth"
(p. 28). One who reads Steinbeck carefully, however, cannot fail to appreciate the irony of the juxtaposition in its
conflation of myth. It is not right to stop with the Christlike
Doc; he is also the satyr, as much lascivious creature as
beneficent savior. The effect of the irony is not to deify Doc
but to humanize him. Like everyone on the Row, he is
good man—bad man. In a sense he is somewhat like the
man described by eighteenth-century sage Joshua Reynolds in his *Third Discourse on Art:* A man is not weak,
though he may not be able to wield the club of Hercules;
nor does a man always practice that which he esteems the
best; but does that which he can best do."[31] Doc does not
wield a superhuman club of Hercules. Despite his achievements (or, in *Sweet Thursday,* lack of achievements), he is
simply one man on the Row doing what he does best, and
the best that he does is being a kind of sounding board, as
Jackson Benson describes him, for the Row itself.

The aesthetic and the biological move in tandem throughout the
book, . . . and the two are brought together in the person of
Doc. Doc is the novel's central character largely because of this
juncture, not as a result of moving forward the plot—he doesn't—
or participating in most of the episodes—he doesn't. In a novel of
"being," he is the main character because of what he is, rather
than what he does. Although he is not present to see all that happens, he is also the observer, in the full sense of the word—a sen-
sory sounding board for the variety of life that surrounds him.[32]

Because he thereby incarnates the spirit of the Row, because he is, as Benson states, "the connector, the nucleus
for the orbiting Beauties, Graces, and Virtues which sur-
round him, and the lightning rod for those in trouble and
need,"[33] Doc serves as a kind of supernatural presence on

the Row, although surely not its sovereign deity. Doc may
be described as the One Who Is Available. In *Tortilla Flat*
the narrator reflects, "Ah, the prayers of the millions, how
they must fight and destroy each other on their way to the
throne of God" (p. 42). No such prayer chain exists in the
battling world of Cannery Row, but when there is need a
call goes through to Doc:

> Now a genuine panic came over the Palace Flophouse. Darling
> had come to be vastly important to them. Hughie and Jones in-
> stantly quit their jobs so they could be near to help. They sat up
> in shifts. They kept a cool damp cloth on her forehead and she got
> weaker and sicker. Finally, although they didn't want to, Hazel
> and Jones were chosen to call on Doc. [P. 154]

Because he is available, Doc becomes the pivot of Cannery Row, whether splinting a bone broken in a fight, half-
listening to Frankie, or treating Darling the pup; he is
there. This is a decisively naturalistic world, stripped of
the vertical dimension exercised freely if imaginatively in
Tortilla Flat, and peculiarly open in its non-teleological
being to the poison of civilization.

In a dramatic way, however, as exemplified in the two
chapters on Frankie, Doc is ineffectual as a redemptive
agent. Frankie's adoration of Doc is like Lennie's fawning
adulation of George in *Of Mice and Men.* In fact, Frankie is
like a small, stray dog as he crawls into the excelsior crate
to sleep or weep. And Doc can only treat Frankie with the
same objective care he shows to one of Dora's whores or
Mack's dog: "Doc clipped Frankie's hair and got rid of the
lice. At Lee Chong's he got him a new pair of overalls and a
striped sweater and Frankie became his slave" (p. 59). Before Frankie's terrible plea, "I love you," Doc is helpless
and cannot reciprocate or alleviate Frankie's pain when
he attempts to demonstrate his love by serving and spilling
the beer:

> The room was quiet. The could hear him run downstairs, and
> go into the cellar. They heard a hollow scrabbling sound—and
> then silence.

Doc walked quietly down the stairs and into the cellar. Frankie was in the excelsior box burrowed down clear to the bottom, with the pile of excelsior on top of him. Doc could hear him whimpering there. Doc waited for a moment and then he went quietly back upstairs.

There wasn't a thing in the world he could do. [p. 62]

In chapter 28, in which Frankie violates civilized law by stealing the clock, once again Doc is helpless:

"What did he take?" Doc asked.

"A great big clock and a bronze statue."

"I'll pay for it."

"Oh, we got it back. I don't think the judge will hear of it. It'll just happen again. You know that."

"Yes," said Doc softly, "I know. But maybe he had a reason. Frankie," he said, "why did you take it?"

Frankie looked a long time at him. "I love you," he said.

Doc ran out and got in his car and went collecting in the caves below Pt. Lobos. [P. 186]

Love is the spiritual bond in the comitatus of *Tortilla Flat;* here, among the animal drives that conflict with civilization, human love founders helplessly.

In such a world, with its humor increasingly dark and grim, as if one were sneering at the devil, what hope is there? The answer in this peculiarly bitter little novel is contained in the concluding poem that Doc reads, elevated on his table, a peanut-butter sandwich in one hand and a beer in the other, "cool, soft soothing music" in his head, while the party careens in near madness about him. The poem surfaces so lightly and quickly in the wild climax of the novel that a casual reader might miss reading it and thereby miss the point of the novel. The poet recalls a lost love, acknowledges the loss, but takes comfort in this fact at least:

> Even now,
> I know that I have savored the hot taste of life
> Lifting green cups and gold at the great feast.
> Just for a small and a forgotten time

I have had full in my eyes from off my girl
The whitest pouring of eternal light—[P. 208]

Here lies a thoroughly non-teleological resolution to a thoroughly non-teleological novel: while aware of the transitory nature of life, to glory in the fact of having lived one moment of it fully. Is it sufficient? I tend to agree with Richard Astro's assessment:

Ostensibly then, Steinbeck says in *Cannery Row* that man can savor "the hot taste of life" if he pursues a free and uninhibited existence. But there is some question whether Steinbeck regards this approach to life as a tenable solution to man's quest for meaning in an increasingly rapacious world. For while Cannery Row is a self-contained island populated by "saints and angels and martyrs and holy men," the type of behavior practiced by the Row's denizens would be inadmissable anywhere else in the world. And whenever one of the characters ventures beyond the Row's sheltered confines, he encounters suspicion and resentment.[34]

Although *Cannery Row* ends in festivity akin to *Tortilla Flat*, it is a festivity with a difference, ending here in the quiet wreckage of the day after, with the final image one of rattlesnakes that "lay still and stared into space with their dusty frowning eyes" (p. 208). A morose atmosphere lingers. The comedy of the novel is charged with human-animal energy and spirit but ultimately acquires a grim aspect. Civilization, a term Steinbeck uses freely for both a technological-materialistic society and for the darker side of man lurking along the ocean bottom of his spirit, always encroaches on human affairs. Steinbeck was to deal forthrightly with this threat in *East of Eden* but still had an ace up his tragicomic sleeve in the good-natured farce of *Sweet Thursday*.

Sweet Thursday

However one explains the poison invading *Cannery Row*, whether as an effect of World War II or as an effect of the author's personal problems, or simply as an effect of his always jaded view of civilization as a corrosive influence on the affairs of individuals, Steinbeck's tone shifts dramatically in the concluding novel of the trilogy. *Sweet Thursday* is a light and giddy book. While imperfect artistically, it soars on a series of delightful situations to high levels of farcical good humor. In his essay "The Meanings of Laughter," Wylie Sypher suggests that

At the radiant peak of 'high' comedy . . . laughter is qualified by tolerance, and criticism is modulated by a sympathy that comes only from wisdom. Just a few writers of comedy have gained this unflinching but generous perspective on life, which is a victory over our absurdities but a victory won at a cost of humility, and won in a spirit of charity and enlightenment.[35]

Sweet Thursday is one such "high" comedy.

As a novelistic structure the work has little compelling narrative order. The chapter sequences are arbitrary and fail to establish any firm intercalary and narrative sequence. Yet in its simple story woven around Doc and Suzy's falling in love, the novel has a sense of wholeness that transcends *Cannery Row*. Perhaps it fulfills Henri Bergson's injunction for comedy: "The first point to which attention should be called is that the comic does not exist outside the pale of what is strictly *human*."[36] For this is a strictly human novel, freed from the deadly poison of civilization as depicted in *Cannery Row*. The threat of civilization fails to gain any prominent place in the novel. It is alluded to overtly only in two instances: in chapter 8, on the Pacific Grove-Monterey feud, and in chapter 38, on the butterfly festival. In the plot narrative outside civilization is briefly present in Old Jingleballick's tempting offer to Doc of the sinecure in the California Institute of Technology, and in the faintly admonishing discourse in chapter 27: "If only people would give the thought, the care, the judgment to international affairs, to politics, even to their jobs, that they lavish on what to wear to a masquerade, the world would run in greased grooves" (p. 179). Even here, though, the direction quickly turns back to Cannery Row and its preparations for the great party. This high comedy is a thoroughly human one, residing finally in characters and their farcical human actions.

The intent to focus on the humanity of the Row is clear in the novel itself. The prologue establishes Mack's criteria for a good book, criteria to which the author assiduously adheres. But the counterpart is provided in the ludicrously nonhuman "work" of Joe Elegant. This late descendent of Henri, the faddish painter of *Cannery Row*, appears three times in the novel in the midst of artistic woe—roughly comparable to Doc's ambition to write a "highfalutin'" paper, precisely the kind of paper and kind of science that Steinbeck and Ricketts ridiculed in *The Log from The Sea of Cortez*. Joe affects the artistic role in kind of schizophrenic displacement between his human existence—"The girls said he made the best popovers in the world, and he could give a massage that would shake the kinks out of a Saturday night when the fleet was in" (p. 81)—and his artistic existence—"He sneered most of the time, and except at mealtime kept to himself in his little lean-to behind the Bear Flag, from which the rattle of his typewriter could be heard late at night" (p. 81). While rattling away on the typewriter, he tries his best to craft a novel no one will understand:

> After lunch Joe Elegant read Fauna his latest chapter. He explained the myth and the symbol. "You see," he said, "the grandmother stands for guilt."
> "Ain't she dead and buried?"
> "Yes."
> "That's a kind of a messy guilt."
> "It's the reality below reality," said Joe Elegant.
> "Balls!" said Fauna. "Listen, Joe, whyn't you write a story about something real?" [P. 133]

Many pages later Joe is well along in his masterpiece of meaninglessness:

> The book was going well. His hero had been born in a state of shock and nothing subsequent had reassured him. When a symbol wasn't slapping him in the mouth, a myth was kicking his feet

out from under him. It was a book of moods, of dank rooms with
cryptic wallpaper, of pale odors, of decaying dreams. There wasn't
a character in the whole of *The Pi Root of Oedipus* who wouldn't
have made the observation ward. [P. 240]

While Joe Elegant serves as an antithesis to the kind of
novel Steinbeck is writing in *Sweet Thursday,* he serves
also as an internal parallel to the kind of paper Doc is trying
to write, a paper absolutely removed from the real life of
the Row. In chapter 6, Doc is laboring at his paper when
suddenly

there was a flick of skirt and she was gone. But Doc could see in
his mind her swinging limbs, the melody of her lithe, swift movement. Probably ugly as a mud fence, he thought, and then he
laughed at himself. "That's full circle," he said, "Mind, I con-
gratulate you. You jumped me to sex, translated it to aesthetics,
and ended with sour grapes. How dishonest can I be?" [P. 44]

It is interesting that Doc accuses his human side of dishonesty and believes that the paper is the honest side of him,
all the while in his deepest being howling "Lonesome!
Lonesome!" Here lies a neat non-teleological–teleological
dilemma, and Doc has to resolve it (teleological) in the life
about him (non-teleological) to rediscover his humanity.
Richard Astro points out the further philosophical confusion of the Doc-Suzy relationship:

Interestingly, Steinbeck portrays Doc resolving his ambivalent
feelings about Suzy by means of the non-teleological method of
thinking. For just as he is about to conclude that Suzy is an illiter-
ate girl with a violent temper who "has all the convictions of the
uninformed" (155), his lower, deeper mind tells him that "Nothin's
bad. It's all part of one thing—the good and bad. Do you know
any man and woman—no matter how close—who don't have
good and bad?" (156). Indeed, Doc employs non-teleological
methodology to sanction his foray into romantic love—a strange
but certainly significant application of Ricketts' mode of seeing. [37]

Thematically the novel is one of discovering humanity
and discovering love, and the comic form of farce that

Steinbeck adapts is a thoroughly human one. It is also one of the oldest comic forms, considered by Plato in book 10 of the *Republic* and enduring in the modern period in vaudeville, cartoons, and slapstick movies. Farce is appropriate in the trilogy also as it moves from the tragicomedy of *Tortilla Flat* to the grim, black humor of *Cannery Row* to a rollicking good cheer that surely would have appealed to Jesus Maria Corcoran, that great-hearted man and "pathway for the humanities." The cliché one wants to avoid is "good-natured" farce, but that is a part of its definition; farce is good-natured in that it recognizes the limitations, foibles, and capacity for wrong in human nature but also the essential good.

Consider first how the tone of farce is established in the novel, and second how the story exhibits certain specific traits of farce. Successful farce depends on a light and detached authorial tone, which Steinbeck establishes in several ways. The author is present in the work, in a narrative tone that is faintly admonishing but never angry, like a realistic but loving and unpatronizing grandfather watching his slightly removed progeny from a distance. One observes this in the descriptions of setting. Cannery Row is in the afterglow of its heyday; the factories are largely silent, life has settled into a postwar slowness. This is an occasion not for a sense of loss but for fond realism:

> The canneries themselves fought the war by getting the limit taken off fish and catching them all. It was done for patriotic reasons, but that didn't bring the fish back. As with the oysters in *Alice*, "They'd eaten every one." It was the same noble impulse that stripped the forests of the West and right now is pumping water out of California's earth faster than it can rain back in. When the desert comes, people will be sad; just as Cannery Row was sad when all the pilchards were caught and canned and eaten. The pearl-grey canneries of corrugated iron were silent and a pacing watchman was their only life. The streets that once roared with trucks were quiet and empty. [P. 3]

In this setting, touched with nostalgia and candor, one finds characters clustered around a perpetually emptying quart of Old Tennis Shoes. The characters themselves are presented with light and humorous detachment. Most notable among them is Hazel, descriptions of whom are friendly if unflattering, in short, straightforward sentences like a comedian's one-liners: "Thinking is always painful, but in Hazel it was heroic. A picture of the process would make you seasick. A gray, whirling furor of images, memories, words, patterns. It was like a traffic jam at a big intersection with Hazel in the middle trying to get something to move somewhere" (p. 75). Yet there is an endearing quality to Hazel, manifested most openly in his confused love for life: "In the pleasures and passions of guilt, Hazel should have been voted the human least likely to succeed. Guilt is a selfish pastime and Hazel had never been aware enough of himself to indulge in it. He watched life as a small boy watches a train go by—mouth open, breathing high and light, pleased, astonished, and a little confused" (p. 211). More than this, Hazel epitomizes a common trait of the other characters. Like Danny and the boys from *Tortilla Flat*, characters here are unified in their quest to help their friends, particularly their friend Doc: "Doc was more than first citizen of Cannery Row. He was healer of the wounded soul and the cut finger. Strongly entrenched in legality though he was, he found himself constantly edged into infringements by the needs of his friends, and anyone could hustle him for a buck without half trying. When trouble came to Doc it was everybody's trouble" (p. 58). Doc's friends "sensed his pain and caught it and carried it away with them. They knew the time was coming when they would have to do something" (pp. 58–59). In a sense, the comitatus, disrupted in *Cannery Row*, is reestablished in *Sweet Thursday*.

A fulfilling quality in this novel is Steinbeck's light facility with language, which also made *Tortilla Flat* such an unmitigated pleasure. All three books are crafted in essentially the same rhetorical style: short sentences averaging approximately ten words each, relatively short paragraphs, and, save for occasional scientific discourses related to Doc's activities, a common diction. But in *Sweet Thursday*

the subtle twist of phrase and the juxtaposition of expectations once again breed an excitement and liveliness meant
to evoke the Row itself. That subtle twist can work as a mar-
velous deflation of character: "Eddie had stayed on his job
with Wide Ida at the Cafe La Ida. The medical examiner,
when he looked at his check sheet and saw what was wrong
with Eddie, came to the conclusion that Eddie had been
technically dead for twelve years" (p. 5). Or it can create a
certain liveliness of character, as in Joseph and Mary Rivas,
who replaces the almost mechanical Lee Chong of *Cannery
Row*. The descriptions of J&M are masterfully matched to
this man, who learns to his dismay that one cannot cheat at
chess: "At twelve he matriculated at reform school, and two
years later emerged with honors. He had learned nearly
every criminal technique in existence" (p. 14). The liveliness of language occurs also in the quick and light-hearted
repartee among characters, as in this dialogue when Fauna
receives the invitation from Mack:

"That Mack," she said. "What a gent! I guess he'd drain the em-
balming fluid off his dead grandma, but he'd do it nice."
    "Is his grandma dead?" Agnes asked.
    "Who knows?" said Fauna. "Listen to this, young ladies. 'Mack
and the boys request the pleasure of your company at their joint
tomorrow aft. to drink a slug of good stuff and talk about something important. Bring the girls. R.S.V.P.'" Fauna paused. "He
could of yelled outside the window, but not Mack—he requests
the pleasure of our company." She signed. "What a gent! If he
wasn't such a bum I'd aim one of you young ladies at him."
    Agnes asked, "What's the matter with Mack's grandma?" [P. 96]

The effect of such passages is to provide a liveliness and joy
to the novel and also to offset comically the potentially
tragic theme of Doc's loneliness. The tone informs the
reader that in this tragicomedy the comic will prevail. Instead of braving the dragon head of civilization as he did in
Cannery Row, Steinbeck here relaxes in the human comedy, perhaps recognizing the social effect of comedy as Wylie Sypher articulates it: "Comedy is a momentary and pub-

licly useful resistance to authority and an escape from its
pressures; and its mechanism is a free discharge of re-
pressed psychic energy or resentment through laughter."[38]

In yet another important way Steinbeck humanizes and
locates the comedy of *Sweet Thursday*—in religion. A
dominant motif in *Tortilla Flat* and a darkened absence in
Cannery Row, religion resurfaces in *Sweet Thursday* in a
farcical and human fashion. The farcical side occurs in
Fauna's flawed stargazing as the boys attempt to intercede
with some higher, magic power that will given them certainty in their uncertain lives. The prognostication in this
instance results in the humor of Hazel's predicted ascen-
dancy to the presidency of the United States:

> "I don't want to be President," Hazel said, and he didn't.
> "There is no choice," said Fauna. "The stars have spoke. You
> will go to Washington."
> "I don't want to!" Hazel cried. "I don't know nobody there."
> [P. 61]

The charts, it conveniently turns out, are ultimately manipulated by man. To save Hazel from the terror of loneliness in Washington, regardless of his obvious and unques-
tioned presidential stature, Fauna finds on the chart a
flyspeck that had thrown everything out of whack; but for a
brief and pleasant time pandemonium reigns as Hazel attempts mightily to prepare for his presidential role.

Despite the whimsicality of the stars, which ultimately
people manipulate to their own ends, there is in the novel a
religious creed that affects human actions—that is, the
creed of truth, particularly as articulated by Doc, the near-
est character to a deity in the novel:

> "I love true things," said Doc. "Even when they hurt. Isn't it
> better to know the truth about oneself?" And he asked it of him-
> self. "Yes, I think it is. I think it is. You're quite right, I've got
> nothing. That's why I built up the whole story about my paper
> until I believed it myself—a little man pretending to be a big
> man, a fool trying to be wise."

"Fauna will kill me," Suzy moaned. "She'll wring my neck. Say, Doc, you got no right to take mad talk from a two-bit hustler—you got no right."

"What's it matter where the truth comes from," he said, "if it's the truth." [P. 108]

As humankind tries to follow true things to the end, there is also at the close of the festivity (as in *Tortilla Flat*) a divine benefaction that seems to sanction their feeble efforts:

What a day it was! A day of purple and gold, the proud colors of the Salinas High School. A squadron of baby angels maneuvered at twelve hundred feet, holding a pink cloud on which the word J-O-Y flashed on and off. A seagull with a broken wing took off and flew straight up into the air, squawking, "Joy! Joy!" [P. 268]

In keeping with the tone of the farce, the divine appearance here is thoroughly naturalized: the colors of the Salinas High School, baby angels, and a squawking seagull.

Even more specifically, in the humanized religion of *Sweet Thursday*, we have the advent of the seer—the mystic who has appeared in other novels in different guises, but here is thoroughly humanized. Doc first meets him while collecting. He opens a new door on Doc's scientism, appearing to Doc as a motley figure somehow above and beyond common life. The initial description of the seer is a magnificent piece of writing, comparable to some of the best in *The Grapes of Wrath:*

Doc stood up from his squatting position. The tendons in back of his knees creaked with pain. The seer towered above him, and on closer inspection it was true that his blue eyes had the merry light of a wise baby. But his face was granitic—chiseled out of the material of prophets and patriarchs. Doc found himself wondering if some of the saints had not looked like this. From the ragged sleeves of the blue shirt wrists like big grapevines protruded, and hands sheathed in brown calluses crisscrossed with barnacle cuts. The seer carried a pair of ancient basketball shoes in his left hand, and, seeing Doc look that them, he said, "I only wear them in the sea. My feet aren't proof against urchins and barnacles." [P. 73]

This saint is fallen, however, and even perverse with his candy-bar kleptomania. Nonetheless, he opens a door for Doc, thematically the most important one in the novel, for he discloses to Doc the need for love that cannot be cast in any neat, scientific formula. Their discourse along the sunset bay is illuminating:

"There are some things a man can't do alone. I wouldn't think of trying anything so big without—" He stopped. The heavy waves beat the hard beach, and the yellow light of the setting sun illuminated a cloud to the eastward, a clot of gold.
"Without what?" Doc asked.
"Without love," said the seer. [P. 73]

Doc will come to see the seer again, physically to intercede with Joe Blaikey when the seer is jailed, but spiritually as he begins to accede to love. In *Cannery Row,* Frankie's offer of slavelike love represents a hideous threat before which Doc is rendered spiritually impotent. In *Sweet Thursday* he begins to assent to love's mystery. In defiance of his IQ, his Ph.D., and his unwritten paper, Doc crawls on his hands and knees to the door of Suzy's boiler.

The general tone of the novel, with its light and humanizing effect, sets up the dramatic apparatus for farce. As a type of comedy, farce is also a means of dealing with tragedy; it is a variation on the tragicomic pattern but with particular traits that distinguish it as a genre.[39]
Farce, curiously enough for a subgenre of comedy, is typified by violence, but the violence is cartoonlike and exaggerated. Violence is in *Cannery Row,* but it is dark and predatory: the young girl's dead body on the barrier reef. In *Sweet Thursday* violence emerges as an improbable solution to a quandary: Hazel's breaking Doc's arm with the bat. Here a bad thing (the broken arm) may lead to a good thing (Suzy caring for Doc). But the improbability of the whole situation is that it emanates from Hazel's poor, overloaded mind:

Hazel was approaching a state of collapse. In his whole life he had never sustained a thought for more than two minutes. Now

his resources reeled under the strain of four hours of concentration. And it was not yet over. He had to make two more visits,
and then he had to retire under the black cypress tree to sift his
findings. So far he could see no light anywhere. His mental pictures were like those children's kaleidoscopes that change color
and design as they are turned. It seemed to Hazel that a slight
zizzing sound came from his brain. [P. 229]

Coming from Hazel, the whole broken-arm scenario has
the quality of a slapstick cartoon rather than a back-street
mugging.

Laughter at certain "untouchables" such as marriage is
also a requirement of farce. Farce delves freely into areas
considered in genteel circles impolite—delves and finds itself comfortable there. Whorehouses, illicit bedrooms—
such are the homes of farce. Farce, unlike satire, does not
condemn such settings but finds human nature revealed
there. The very term "bedroom farce" is common critical
parlance in drama partly because, as *The Oxford Companion to the Theatre* notes in its definition of *farce*, extra-
marital affairs provide a setting for the often ludicrous chain
of events. In tragedy—*Othello*, for example—such settings
establish the tragic context for the terror of infidelity; in
farce they supply the arena for a high-spirited sexual romp.
The exuberant sexuality of *Sweet Thursday* humanizes the
novel and its characters.

Farce additionally is typified by having common people
as characters, often people with inordinately uncommon
aspirations and dreams. According to Wylie Sypher: "The
tragic hero, noble and magnified, can be of awesome stature. The comic hero refuses to wear the trappings of moral
or civil grandeur, usually preferring motley or the agility of
the clown."[40] At times such common characters can descend to simple buffoonery, as at the great, "tom-wallager"
party of *Sweet Thursday*. This in turn contributes to the
comedy of the sheerly ridiculous:

Hazel was a breathtaking sight. He did not glance around. He
knew he was right—he knew it by the silence. Smartly he turned

the saber to parade rest and crossed his hands on the hilt. His breath caught in his throat.

"I," he said huskily, "I am Prince Charming." And the company could see now that his cheeks were rouged and his eyelashes beaded. "I proteck dam—damsels," he announced. And only then did he turn his proud head for the applause and approval he knew he merited. [P. 193]

Sweet Thursday's tom-wallager represents one of the most explosive parties in literature, a virtual romp of farcical catastrophes.

And thus we come to the final trait of farce, and its most important. Aristotle insisted that tragedy provided a catharsis through pity and fear, but comedy achieves catharsis through the gaiety of festivity. Each of the works in the Cannery Row trilogy culminates in festivity, but none is so carefully or successfully arranged as the party in *Sweet Thursday*. Sypher comments on the general effect of the comic festivity: "If the authentic comic action is a sacrifice and a feast, debate and passion, it is by the same token a Saturnalia, an orgy, and assertion of the unruliness of the flesh and its vitality. Comedy is essentially a Carrying Away of Death, a triumph over mortality by some absurd faith in rebirth, restoration, and salvation."[41] He adds: "From the earliest time the comic ritual has been presided over by a Lord of Misrule, and the improvisations of comedy have the aspect of a Feast of Unreason, a Revel of Fools—a *Sottie*. Comedy is a release, a taking off the masks we have put on to deal with others who have put on decent masks to deal with us."[42] In farce man's greatest evil is folly, and this is cured by folly. Like the Aristotelian catharsis festivity cleans away resentment and bitterness, and it thereby initiates *renewal* and *return*. No matter how chaotic events may appear in life, the greater chaos of Festivity under the Lord of Misrule (here represented jointly by Mack and Hazel) undercuts everything so that life may begin again. Festivity is therefore both cleansing and consecration. The belly laugh restores clarity to human vision. The cleansing

in *Sweet Thursday* occurs both in the knowledge of owner-
ship of the Palace Flophouse and in Doc's renewed vision of
a life that includes Suzy's love for him. The return to life
and consecration occur with Doc and Suzy lurching wildly
up the street in Doc's old car. The farce is topped off by the
solemn presentation of the "microscope":

> Mack cleared his throat. "Friends," he said, "on behalf of I and
> the boys it gives me pleasure to present Doc with this here."
>
> Doc looked at the gift—a telescope strong enough to bring the
> moon to his lap. His mouth fell open. Then he smothered the
> laughter that rose in him. [Pp. 272–73]

With the telescope safely stored in the lab, "the old car deliberately climbed the curb, ripped off the stairs of Western
Biological, careened into the street, and crawled away,
scattering lumber as it went" (p. 273).

With the lightness of tone and in certain plot elements,
there exists a certain degree of parody in *Sweet Thursday*.
Jackson Benson commented of *Cannery Row:* "I can't help
but feel that we have been too literary, too ingenious in our
approach to this novel. The scholar, looking inward, steeped
in respectable literary tradition, finds Renaissance drama
rather than Zane Grey."[43] In a way it is preferable also to
take *Sweet Thursday* as a kind of Zane Grey western rather
than as a sophisticated literary effort. The book is enter-
taining and fun and shares similarities with the western
that might suggest a parody. While one would be hard
pressed to make a convincing case of deliberate design,
some fascinating parallels occur.

As a genre, westerns are so multifarious as to defy neat
categorization. Yet, regardless of aesthetic category, all
westerns share elements of a common myth, some with
startling parallels in *Sweet Thursday*. First, many westerns
have the theme of a return from the wars, either the Civil
War or the Indian wars. The counterpart in *Sweet Thursday* is the return from World War II in which Doc served
his time as a technical sergeant in a VD section, Whitey

No. 1 worked in a war plant in Oakland, Whitey No. 2
joined the Marine Corps, Joseph and Mary got a dishonor-
able discharge that was a "masterpiece of understatement,"
Hazel survived, and Gay died. Hazel, incidentally, rates
the one image in the novel that comes straight out of the B
western: "Hazel didn't even take off his clothes before
we went to bed, but he didn't sleep either; at least not until
the dawn crept out from Salinas. His brain was blistered
and his responsibility rode him with surcingle and spurs"
(pp. 234–35).

Other parallels emerge. Like the small town in the Old
West, Cannery Row has its café and whorehouse and its cul-
tured madam. It has its beautiful and mysterious stranger
in Suzy, a stock feature in every western. It has its good
sheriff in Joe Blaikey, a fairly slow but kindhearted sort
clearly modeled on the western type rather than on the
mean-spirited, paunch-bellied sheriffs that parade through
a great deal of popular southern literature. Further, there
is, in both the western and *Sweet Thursday,* a suspicion of
outside civilization as alien and corrupting and a concomitant sense that the home boys can take care of matters well
enough by themselves. In the same vein the people "outside" have money, while the boys on the home range are a
hardscrabble lot making do on less than little but happy
to do so. And, finally, after the showdown at the Palace
Flophouse and then outside Suzy's boiler, the good guy in
the white hat (slightly battered and gray in this case) rides
off into the sunset with the pretty girl.

Such parallels at best should be considered a pleasant diversion instigated by a pleasant novel. If such links do
exist, they only further the lighthearted tone of this charming farce. The final effect of the book, and consequently of
the Cannery Row trilogy, is appropriately summarized in
Wylie Sypher's comment on the effect of comedy in general:

At its most triumphant moments comic art frees us from peril
without destroying our ideals and without mustering the heavy
artillery of the puritan. Comedy can be a means of mastering our

disillusions when we are caught in a dishonest or stupid society. After we recognize the misdoings, the blunders, we can liberate ourselves by a confident, wise laughter that brings a catharsis of our discontent. We see the flaws in things, but we do not always need to concede the victory, even if we live in a human world. If we can laugh wisely enough at ourselves and others, the sense of guilt, dismay, anxiety, or fear can be lifted. Unflinching and undaunted we see *where we are*. This strengthens us as well as society.[44]

Beyond doubt, the Cannery Row novels, particularly with their triumphant conclusion in *Sweet Thursday*, help us know where we are and strengthen us in that knowledge.

Their Deeds Follow Them: The Fiction of the Forties

The Moon Is Down AND Burning Bright

THE YEARS BETWEEN *The Grapes of Wrath* and *East of Eden* were troubled ones for Steinbeck and for his writing. In *The Grapes of Wrath* he exhausted the fictional drama of the migrants as a means of exploring his two major early themes, the individual versus society and the threat of loneliness. Those themes turned grim and bitter in *Cannery Row*. *The Moon Is Down*, published in 1942, formed an almost mechanical attempt to apply the themes to world conditions.

In his study of Steinbeck published shortly after the publication of *The Grapes of Wrath*, Harry Moore wrote that Steinbeck "doesn't enjoy being a best-seller; the fact that he is one causes him to doubt his work, and to wonder if it is lacking in ideas, since it attracts so many readers."[1] Steinbeck never lacked ideas; in fact, both the pleasure of his work, which lies in its wide diversity, and the difficulty of his work, which lies in its abstraction, often rest in his pursuit of ideas like elusive will-o'-the-wisps. One can scarcely fault an author for his ideas; but one may legitimately fault him for failure to control and craft those ideas artistically, and the failure of of *The Moon Is Down* is finally artistic. The work, another variation in his novel-drama approach, was published in dramatic form less than a year after its publication as a novel in 1942. But the writing of the book was hasty and superficial, at best a mechanical hack work, and the weaknesses show everywhere.

The novel echoes Steinbeck's trenchant theme that a large social power cannot dominate the will of free men. Specifically its suggests world conditions during World War II in its focus on a democratic people in contention with an imperialist aggressor. Joseph Fontenrose suggests, however, that, if the aggressors are to be linked specifically with those of World War II, they are not particularly aggressive in light of the historical record: "They want Germany to win; they carry out orders; but they are not personally harsh, brutal, or ruthless. They are human, even kind, and take a good deal of insult and even injury rather meekly."[2] While it may be that Steinbeck wanted to show the individual humanity of aggressor soldiers, the passivity of these soldiers is surprising from an author who so poignantly depicted the brutalities and power mongering of the landowner-migrant wars. Fontenrose speculates further:

In his essay, "My Short Novels" (1953), Steinbeck says, "I had written of Germans as men, not supermen, and this was considered a very weak attitude to take," and he thought that events had justified him. The fault, however, does not lie in his attempt to reveal the humanity of German officers, but in the false humanity that he gave them. These men do not ring true; they are like sentimental Americans.[3]

The first evidence of a perfunctoriness in this novel is the simple failure to create a convincing setting and body of characters. At its best Steinbeck's fiction develops a threat that makes the audience discover the weakness and strength of characters—especially their strength in unexpected weakness and the weakness in expected strength. The occupied town and dominated people here suggest the makings of such a struggle, but in fact The Moon Is Down lacks the energy of character confrontation that would make such subtle tensions and complexities believable.

More significantly, however, the novel reveals for the first time in Steinbeck's fiction a failure of language and stylistic technique. Part of Steinbeck's artistic success, as has been observed, lies in his ability to craft complex and powerful sentences that appear deceptively simple. The reader is thus moved by the power of the rhetoric without being aware of the rhetoric. The situation is quite different, for example, in some of Faulkner's prose, where one is always aware of what the artist is doing rhetorically. Faulkner's sentences sometimes deliberately twist the reader into psychological and rhetorical knots—an effect Faulkner surely wanted—but the reader is aware of being so twisted. Even when he is working with sophisticated, complex structures, however, Steinbeck normally propels the reader along in the narrative. The writing in *The Moon Is Down* stands apart from the other works as comparatively wooden.

During the forties Steinbeck's sentence structures developed a very taut, short, almost journalistic form. This served him admirably in *Sweet Thursday*, where nearly every sentence seems charged by energetic verbs and contains a neat little linguistic surprise. But in *The Moon Is Down* the repetitively short sentences seem more like a recording from someone bored with his own work. Although it is a mechanical tool for measuring such weaknesses, a quantitative rhetorical analysis effectively reveals the difficulties in Steinbeck's prose in this novel. Selecting a chapter at random, in this instance chapter 5 and two paragraphs from that chapter—the first and second—we see in a quantitative rhetorical analysis the following patterns. The first paragraph has nine sentences; the second, twelve. The prose is cast in a fairly similar, repetitive pattern of sentence lengths averaging sixteen words each, or, with the exception of the one unusually long sentence (forty-eight words) in the first paragraph, fourteen words each. Moreover, in the compound and complex sentences the clauses average ten words. Five sentences or clauses are exactly ten words each, three of them sequentially in the second paragraph (and five additional sentences or clauses are within one digit of ten). Nearly half the rhetorical structures, then, are virtually the same in length and pattern. A second major pattern is the five-word sentence or clause, of which there are seven. Fully two-thirds of the sentences are simple declarative sentences.

A routine sameness of rhetorical method can be demonstrated by these statistics, but a second factor, word length, also influences the rhetorical structures. Here the analysis is applied only to the first paragraph, but the patterns hold true for much of the book. In the paragraph 125 words, or 81 percent of the total, are monosyllabic; 24 words, or 16 percent of the total, are disyllabic; only 5 words, or 3 percent, are polysyllabic. The few polysyllabic words are of the most perfunctory sort—adverbs and adjectives that Steinbeck would be hardpressed not to use.

Finally, a third factor in addition to sentence length and word selection contributes to the dullness and inefficiency of the prose to move the story along. The sentence and paragraph links themselves give the feeling that someone unwillingly and ploddingly is recording a story in which he has little real interest. In the first nine paragraphs of chapter 5, paragraphs nearly the same length and pattern as the first two analyzed above, only two paragraphs begin with an article and noun (paragraph 1, "The days," and paragraph 8, "The year"). All others begin with conjunctions or adverbs of time: "And," "Now," "And," "Then," "And," "Thus," "And." In addition, individual sentences within paragraphs adhere to the pattern. In paragraph 2, four sentences begin with "And."

But, one might object, did not Steinbeck make use of these same techniques—the short sentence, the conjunctive sentence openings, the repetition—in the intercalary chapters of his novels? He did, and in a sense the opening paragraphs in each chapter of *The Moon Is Down* strive toward an intercalary mood. But at their most successful in other works the intercalary chapter are marked by variety—absent here—by energy of language, particularly of verbs—absent here—and by surprising and subtle turns of phrase, raising expectations in the reader, then suddenly shifting direction—also absent here.

The failure of language also affects characterization. Doctor Winter, for example, seems one more character in the series patterned on Ed Ricketts—the man involved in the action but somehow apart from the action so that he can observe it with non-teleological vision.[4] But Doctor Winter seems almost apishly to mouth the words that come more forcefully from the lips of Doc Burton of *In Dubious Battle* or Doc of *Cannery Row* and *Sweet Thursday*. It is almost as if Steinbeck were parodying his own character. Dr. Winter often speaks the phrases so familiar to Ricketts-Burton-Doc: "'That is a great mystery,' said Doctor Winter. 'That is a mystery that has disturbed rulers all over the world— how the people know. It disturbs the invaders now, I am told, how news runs through censorships, how the truth of things fights free of control. It is a great mystery'" (p. 80). Here, because of their repetitiveness, the phrases seem hollow and scarcely applicable to the narrative plot.

Many of these same objections, the woodenness of plot and character, the failure of language and technique, could be raised with *Burning Bright*, another effort at the novel-play combination. In his preface to *Burning Bright*, Steinbeck defended the novel-play form:

> My reasons for wanting to write in this form are several and diverse. I find it difficult to read plays, and in this I do not find myself alone. The printed play is read almost exclusively by people closely associated with the theater, by students of the theater, and by the comparatively small group of readers who are passionately fond of the theater. The first reason for this form, then, is to provide a play that will be more widely read because it is presented as ordinary fiction, which is a more familiar medium.
>
> The second reason for the creation of the play-novelette is that it augments the play for the actor, the director, and the producer, as well as the reader. The usual description of a character in a play—"Businessman, aged forty"—gives them very little to go on.

After discussing the qualities of the genre he believes he is forging, Steinbeck confesses that "the difficulties of the technique are very great." Were it not for the success of his first effort in the form, *Of Mice and Men*, one would add— "insurmountable," for so they appear here.

Burning Bright represented a crisis in Steinbeck's artistic and personal life. As Jackson Benson points out: "It was a very dramatic story for him because it was based on his own story. He had taken Gwyn's unpleasant revelation, the divorce, and his own breakdown and spent the summer mentally transposing the elements in order to universalize his experience and create a modern allegory. It had been an expiation of pain and doubt and anger through daydream."[5] Benson adds a perceptive observation: "Indeed, such a play was the kind of thing a writer who didn't care whether he retained his popularity or not might do."[6]

But in *Burning Bright* we also see another tendency growing in Steinbeck: a reversion to and reliance on his earlier works and ideas. Peter Lisca has pointed out that in language and idea Steinbeck seems here to have reverted to *Cup of Gold:*

The real difficulty is not that the characters speak "a kind of universal language," as Steinbeck puts it (and whatever that may mean), but that this language is a kind of incredible hash of realism, coined archaisms, and poetic rhetoric. The closest thing to it in Steinbeck's works is found in the language of his first book, *Cup of Gold,* and indeed some of the images are taken right out of that early book—"the blackbirds flocked nervously a week and now they are gone"; "the steel winter lay on the land and crept to the door and windows and peered whitely in." The passages of simple conversation about daily affairs are studded with such synthetic gems as "wifeloss," "friend-right," "Friend Ed," and "very yes," which make the characters sound like nothing so much as members of an isolated and inbred religious group.[7]

In several instances this reversion would serve Steinbeck well; for example, in *East of Eden,* where he returned to his early dream of writing a novel of the Salinas Valley, or in *Sweet Thursday,* where he purged the bitterness of black humor through farce. In other instances, such as *The Moon Is Down* and *Burning Bright,* he attenuates an early technique or theme to the point of exhaustion. There are, however, two bright spots in Steinbeck's artistry during an otherwise dim decade: *The Wayward Bus* and *The Pearl.*

The Wayward Bus

The Wayward Bus achieves eminence in the grouping of this chapter by virtue of the fact that it contains Steinbeck's best writing of the forties and some of the best of his career. The work, as Antonia Seixus points out in her "John Steinbeck and the Non-Teleological Bus," is a model for a young writer: "An apprentice writer would do well to study the way, for example, in which the character and past life of Juan Chicoy is conveyed through Steinbeck's inventory of his clothes, his scars, the contents of his pockets, the way he handles a wrench."[8] Using a very narrow group of characters and a similarly narrow narrative framework modeled on the picaresque adventure, Steinbeck brings his specimens to a rare and abundant life. The reader gets to know these characters intimately—from Pimples' consuming concupiscence to Camille Oaks's worldly ennui—but gets to know them in a series of small disclosures that ultimately give one the feeling of having grown up with the characters. Moreover, the novel evidences again the simple eloquence and power in Steinbeck's language, as in this passage where Van Brunt feels his stroke coming on:

Van Brunt listened to age creeping in his veins. He could almost feel the rustle of blood in his papery arteries, and he could hear his heart beat with a creaking whistle in it. His right hand was going to sleep, but it was his left hand that worried him. There wasn't much feeling in his left hand. The skin was insensitive, as though it were a thick rubber. He rubbed and massaged his hand when he was alone to bring the circulation back, and he really knew what was the matter although he hardly admitted it even to himself. [P. 292]

Here are pleasing flashes of Steinbeck's best writing—terse understatement, twists in expectations ("Juan was clean-shaven, but not since yesterday"), energetic diction.

The ingenuity of language and liveliness of character in *The Wayward Bus* make the novel absorbing and pleasurable reading. But is there more to the novel than "a good read"? Is it an allegory of mankind, a modern Everyman, as some have suggested? Or is it in fact a non-teleological trip arriving at the place where one has always been but now knows it for the first time? I believe the latter case holds.

First, however, consider what kinds of things in the story might suggest allegory. The first item would include the group of allusions that, as I have argued earlier in this book, provide a religious or Christian "coloring" for the tale. There are several such items, beginning with those that are quite forced, such as the initials of Juan Chicoy representing the initials of Jesus Christ and thereby drawing a link to Juan as leader and savior of men in the little world of the wayward bus. Possibly Juan saves himself by his final decision to return to Alice. Possibly he saves Mildred Pritchard from futility and insignificance by their wild little romp in the hayloft. But that is it. Any salvation in this story is humanly centered—characters coming to grips with their own dreams and natures. The bus trip is accidental, not substantive. In the second grouping of suggestive elements the reader confronts a host of details that flesh out the characters and personality of the San Ysidro Valley. The original name of the bus, "El Gran Poder de Jesus," is just visible under its more recent, humanized name, "Sweetheart." "REPENT" is emblazoned on a cliffside, advice the characters do not heed: Pritchard rapes his wife, Mrs. Pritchard connives anew, and Pimples tries mightily to seduce Camille, then Norma, and finally attacks the bus itself in concupiscent rage. The characters to a degree come to grips with themselves: some come to self-understanding, but such awareness is hardly repentence. Finally, there is the popular religious apparatus pertaining to all of Steinbeck's common characters; for example, the Virgin of Guadalupe, of whom Juan asks a clear sign but follows his own will anyway. There are other details that an imaginative allegorist might seize on: the presence of the flies that plague Alice Chicoy and might suggest the Lord of the Flies, Beelzebub; the dangerous bridge to salvation; the detours that man selects; the slough of despond that mires the pilgrimage. But recalling the accoutrements that hang side by side with the Virgin—the baby's shoes, the tiny boxing glove, the plastic Kewpie doll—and also the contents of the glove compartment—pistol, bandages, iodine, smelling salts, and a pint of whiskey—one observes that religion is practical and earthly here. Above all, this pilgrimage is human and metaphorically arrives at a better understanding of human nature.

The second suggestive influence, however, derives from the epigraph from *Everyman*. Warren French writes, "It is obvious from the moment one reads the prefatory quotation from *Everyman* and learns on the first page that the novel concerns a journey from Rebel Corners to San Juan de la Cruz that the book is an allegory."[9] But if *Everyman* is the basis of the allegory, the allegory is badly flawed. Originally a Dutch play, but popular in fifteenth century England with its spate of moralities, and translated by, among others, Thomas à Kempis, *Everyman* personifies certain religious abstractions in a contest for man's soul. Central to the play in any of its forms is that God sends Death to summon Everyman and Death finds him walking alone. Everyman is a rather pathetic and lonely creature from the start. Fellowship, Kindred, Cousin, and Goods—each refuses to accompany Everyman on his pilgrimage. He is stripped down to the essentially human. In short order even his own nature fails to support his case as Good Deeds and Knowledge prove insufficient grounds for salvation, and Everyman is left with only the plea, "Our Lord Iesus helpe me." Needing grace, and having undergone a form of penance, Everyman is strengthened by four new virtues—Beauty, Strength, Discretion, and Five Wits—interior or spiritual virtues to replace the four friends that proved false. In sum, the story of *Everyman* is a story of discovering one's spiritual need through being stripped back, robbed of old assumptions and dependencies, and emerging fortified by inward spiritual strength as one begins to learn what one must do to be saved.

The Wayward Bus in no way approaches a close allegorical parallel to *Everyman*. The theological bias is missing, and to suggest that the summoning by Death is approximated in the lure of Hollywood or the arrival at San Juan at night is forced. Similarly, Joseph Fontenrose's suggestion that "Camille might be identified with Beauty and Pimples with Five Wits" [10] totally misconstrues the original *Everyman*. Everyman's four spiritual counselors "of grete myght" are nowhere allied with human or physical qualities, and if they were, they would be quite unlike Camille or Pimples (it is Five Wits who tells Everyman of the priests that "God hath to them more power gyuen / Than to ony aungell that is in heuen"—something Pimples might have said only in reference to Baby Ruths or carmel-cream pies). But in a general, nonallegorical way *The Wayward Bus* is comparable in that each character comes to Rebel Corners with worldly dreams, and each is stripped back to a new self-realization by the action of the journey. This is, in a sense, a teleological bus ride whose aim is to expose the non-teleological, the "what-is" of the human character. Each mile of going forth in the bus is also a stripping back of the masks of civilization and pretense, revealing the essential nature of the character.

Each character on the bus, from Juan Chicoy to Norma, has a dream of a better and richer life. Alice Chicoy dreams of a day-long drunk, but through the alcoholic mists she dreams also of a better love with Juan. Bernice Pritchard, a woman of displaced sexuality somewhat like Elisa Allen ("She loved flowers and planted and pinched and fertilized and cut them. She kept great bowls of flowers in her house always, so that her friends said it was like being in a florist's shop, and she arranged them herself so beautifully"), dreams desperately of an adventure that will rank above her cut flowers: "This will turn into an adventure when it's over. I can almost hear you telling it. It will be funny" (p. 65). Her real adventure occurs when all her social stratagems, her headaches, her cute letters home, are stripped away by her husband forcing sex on her.

Mildred Pritchard dreams of freedom that everyone but her seems to possess.

She envied Camille. Camille was a tramp, Mildred thought. And things were so much easier for a tramp. There was no conscience, no sense of loss, nothing but a wonderful, relaxed, stretching-cat selfishness. She could go to bed with anyone she wanted to and never see him again and have no feeling of loss or insecurity about it. That was the way Mildred thought it was with Camille. She wished she could be that way, and she knew she couldn't. Couldn't because of her mother. [P. 214]

Mildred finds her freedom in the barn loft. Mr. Pritchard dreams of a manhood he has lost in the managing of money, both loathing and envying Juan Chicoy for his unabashed sensuality and freedom, Ernest Horton for his war heroism, Camille for her unapproachability, and his wife for her docility. Ernest Horton, the salesman of gags and illusions, the Willie Loman of San Ysidro Valley, is the character with fewest dreams and fewest illusions. He refuses to test a dream, even to let it develop. He will not try to patent his inventions. Under his breezy exterior lies an acidic core of cynicism fostered by both war and life. Camille Oaks dreams of the domesticated normalcy denied her by her desirability:

What she really wanted was a nice house in a nice town, two children, and a stairway to stand on. She would be nicely dressed and people would be coming to dinner. She'd have a husband, of course, but she couldn't see him in her picture because the advertising in the women's magazines from which her dream came never included a man. [P. 110]

Ed "Pimples" "Kit" Carson dreams simply of acceptance, but for him it is impossibly clouded by an adolescent sexuality that might serve as a forceful example of what Aquinas called the "concupiscible tendency" and described amply in his discussion of Permanent Dispositions:

But to generate any quality in a passive power, the active principle must gain entire control over the passive principle. Thus we see that when a fire is unable immediately to consume a combustible object, it does not immediately cause it to burst into flames, but by gradually ridding it of contrary dispositions and thus completely gaining control over it, it imposes its likeness upon it.[11]

Pimples is like a combustible sexual machine, waiting to have his switch thrown. Like Pablo of *Tortilla Flat*, however, Pimples also has a "great-hearted" dream: "I thought maybe I'd be a missionary like Spencer Tracy and go to China and cure them of all those diseases" (p. 159). Finally, Norma dreams of Hollywood, lives in an imaginary world dominated by Clark Gable, and, after Camille brings reality slowly dawning to her, finds herself grappling in a bus seat with Pimples.

This action of revealing and unraveling individual dreams parallels the travel of Sweetheart deeper and deeper into the primitive, unmarked wasteland. The journeying of the novel is twofold: away from civilized customs that ensure little routines and desperate dreams and into paths as dangerous as head-on confrontation with those dreams.

Above all, however, *The Wayward Bus* is one of Steinbeck's superior entertainments. The characters supply enough individual delight and group friction to be worth paying attention to. The motif of the bus ride, although an old one in literature, is presented here with vigor and whimsy. The work is a pleasant alternative to the forced moralities in *The Moon Is Down* and *Burning Bright*, for in this unassuming tale, with little to prove or defend, Steinbeck performs wonderfully as entertainer.

The Pearl

Like *The Wayward Bus* an unpretentious little book, *The Pearl* is successful in its very simplicity. Steinbeck allows the folktale he encountered in La Paz to open discreetly but suggestively on the spiritual dimension. The spiritual significance rises from the story and extends beyond it rather than being imposed by the author.

Originally published in the *Woman's Home Companion*

as "The Pearl of La Paz," *The Pearl* contains a prefatory note in which Steinbeck describes the story as a parable. Through his boyhood training at Saint Paul's Episcopal Church, Steinbeck no doubt encountered the time-honored definition of a parable: an earthly story with a heavenly meaning. And that is an adequate definition since its emphasis on the suggestiveness of the story would have attracted Steinbeck. But suggestiveness opens a wide door.

At least one critic has argued a connection to the medieval *Pearl* manuscript on the basis that "Steinbeck's familiarity with medieval English literature is easy to document."[12] While it is true that Steinbeck, with his lifelong fascination with languages, had since boyhood been profoundly influenced by *Morte D'Arthur*, and that in the late fifties and early sixties had probably studied Anglo-Saxon as well as medieval French under the tutelage of the noted medievalist Eugene Vinaver in order to master sources for his Arthurian rendition, it is less certain that Steinbeck had any close attachment with medieval allegorical literature at the time he wrote *The Pearl*. Such a link is fetching because of the visionary and allegorical nature of the medieval *Pearl*, culminating as it does in the testimony that

> To please the Prince or be reconciled,
> It is quite easy for the good Christian
> For I have found Him both day and night
> A God, a Lord, a Friend most noble.
> Upon this hill this destiny I grasped,
> Prostrate in sorrow for my pearl.
> And afterward to God I gave it up
> In the dear blessing and memory of Christ.[13]

But the character, theme, and action of the medieval fragment have little or nothing to do with Steinbeck's novel. However intriguing the tenuous link by title, one must reject the fragment as having had any direct influence on Steinbeck.

Mention of the story first occurs in *The Sea of Cortez*, when the *Western Flyer* put in at La Paz—thus the original title. It is a long section in *The Sea of Cortez*, prefaced by a reflection on human greed, materialism, and the inherent worth of a thing. The particular local legend of the pearl is told on page 102, and Steinbeck observes of it:

This seems to be a true story, but it is so much like a parable that it almost can't be. This Indian boy is too heroic, too wise. He knows too much and acts on his knowledge. In every way, he goes contrary to human direction. The story is probably true, but we don't believe it; it is far too reasonable to be true. [P. 103]

The idea of a parable, a suggestive meaning couched in a story that is "reasonably true," was with Steinbeck from his earliest conception of the tale. The reasonable truth of the final novella is also reflected in Steinbeck's observation of the conflict of culture. In *The Sea of Cortez* he muses: "On the water's edge of La Paz a new hotel was going up, and it looked very expensive. Probably the airplanes will bring week-enders from Los Angeles before long, and the beautiful poor bedraggled old town will bloom with a Floridian ugliness" (p. 118). In *The Pearl* a similar conflict emerges between the old rituals of Kino's life—the song of the family—and the new culture that oppresses and destroys that ancient harmony.

Thus the origins and final significance of *The Pearl* seem to be largely cultural and spiritual. A possible analogue also resides in the biblical parable of "The Pearl of Great Price," recorded in Matthew 13:45–46. The biblical analogue would function ironically, for there the pearl represents the kingdom of heaven, for which the merchant gives all that he has. In Steinbeck's novel the pearl becomes an ulcerous thing that infects all that Kino has; it becomes, in effect, a hell—or, perhaps, a purgatory—for him.

To appreciate the suggestiveness and richness of the story, one must consider it as a literary type. *The Pearl*, while often and offhandedly referred to as an allegory (as is *The Wayward Bus*), is in fact not one. All great literature suggests meanings that lie beyond the immediate narrative level, but very few do so in a strictly allegorical fashion marked by the intensity and consistency of two separate levels of meaning—narrative and allegorical. In allegory the author deliberately patterns the fictional world to suggest specific meanings to the reader, and the author must pattern the work with hard rigidity. To be successful, the allegorical work must be self-restrictive; that is to say, a figure who on page one represents death may not on page ten represent life. Moving without variation from the plane of the narrative to the plane of the predetermined allegorical meaning, the story is essentially two-dimensional. In fact, any lessening or wavering in the two-dimensional unity, or any admission of more than one theme, lessens the worth of the work as allegory. The task of the reader upon considering allegory is to establish that two-dimensional interplay in his own mind. The matter is one of puzzle solving, of arranging the pieces within their narrative frame; and it is a matter of solving someone else's puzzle, not making and solving one's own.

The danger of allegory to many modern authors is that the characters in the narrative may become wooden signposts pointing toward their individual allegorical meanings. Freedom of artistic ingenuity is limited; freedom of character development and realism is truncated by the allegorical framework. Characters come to represent abstractions thereby losing some of their humanity. While Steinbeck did revert to his early mysticism at times during the forties, he had become too much of the non-teleological realist in the thirties to revert fully to allegorical role casting.

Although Harry Morris was correct in his judgment that "John Steinbeck has never been very far away from the allegorical method. Some of his earliest work—and among that, his best—shows involvement with elements of allegory," [14] one should not confuse involvement with allegory as the allegorical method itself. Steinbeck's involvement with allegory operates on the level of a rich suggestiveness in story, but with characters and thematic plot development coming first. Story, for Steinbeck, is never a handmaiden to meaning; rather the meanings that arise are constructed in suggestive analogues or symbols in the work, which may open different doors of signification for any individual reader, so that the reader apprehends spiritual patterns or abstractions that have been stimulated by certain literary figures, symbols, or devices. By repetition of pointing signals, or symbols, the author constructs a pattern that guides the interpretation. But in no sense does the writer force the patttern on the reader. *The Pearl* may be read first and foremost as a tragic tale of an impoverished fisherman consumed by internal and external greed. Such a reading is thoroughly consonant with Steinbeck's major theme throughout this period: that civilization represents a destructive force over the individual and his dreams. But the work also suggests a spiritual struggle and, finally, a tragic victory over civilization.

At its most immediate, narrative level, the book details the explosive conflict of the civilized world, as Steinbeck uses "civilized" in the Cannery Row trilogy to signify the aggressive power structure of society over an uncivilized, outcast minority. Kino and his small clan on the beach are roughly equivalent to the small clan on Cannery Row encroached upon by the civilized world. Typifying the beach group are family ties, poverty, dreams of a better life— qualities one observes in all of Steinbeck's outcast minority groups. Typifying the civilized world are hatred for the outcast, some degree of wealth and desire for more, and the ignoring of human need. Ever protective of its wealth and power, the civilized world becomes a devourer, a monstrous combine raking the lives of lesser creatures into its insatiable maw. After Coyotito is stung by the scorpion, the tiny beach group, seeking help, proceeds into town like a small morsel of food straying into the jaws of a predator. That is precisely the nature of civilization in Steinbeck's perception—it will devour all lesser objects. The town itself is presented in animalistic imagery: "A town is a thing like a colonial animal. A town has a nervous system and a head and shoulders and feet. A town is a thing separate from all other towns, so that there are no two towns alike. And a town has a whole emotion" (p. 32). Beyond the town,

moreover, lies an ever-larger chain of predatory civilization. Behind the many hands of the pearl buyers lies one
large hand that controls. While the doctor rejects the Indians, he dreams of Paris, which has rejected him. And beyond the sea, we are told, lie great cities that seem part of
an ever-enlarging sphere. The image arises of a huge biological chain, its larger members preying constantly upon
lesser members; the smallest unit is comprised of the Indian people of the Gulf. Their confined little world of traditional innocence and naïveté is fragile and susceptible. The
tidal-flat imagery of *The Log from the Sea of Cortez* and
the Cannery Row novels prevails here also: "Out in the estuary a tight woven school of small fishes glittered and
broke water to escape a school of great fishes that drove
in to eat them. And in the houses the people could hear
the swish of the small ones and the bouncing splash of the
great ones as the slaughter went on" (p. 47). The marine-
biological image typifies the social order of Kino's larger
community.

Not surprisingly, when Kino finds the pearl, he thinks of
it first and foremost as a means of access to things of the
civilized power structure; for just as the larger organism
preys upon the lesser, so the smaller organism aspires toward the larger in an evolutionary spiral. One notices this
tension particularly well in Kino's reaction to the doctor of
the village upon his first trip:

Kino felt weak and afraid and angry at the same time. Rage and
terror went together. He could kill the doctor more rapidly than
he could talk to him, for all the doctor's race spoke to all of Kino's
race as though they were simple animals. And as Kino raised his
right hand to the iron ring knocker in the gate, rage swelled in
him, and the pounding music of the enemy beat in his ears, and
his lips drew tight against his teeth—but with his left hand he
reached to take off his hat. [Pp. 15–16]

The clear contrast between the animalistic antagonism—
"his lips drew tight against his teeth"—and his trained def-
erence to civilized niceties—"with his left hand he reached

to take off his hat"—encapsulates the tension of the book.
Thus the pearl initially represents for Kino the ability to
aspire upward, to defeat the civilized power structure by
acquiring its properties. When asked what he will do now
that he is a rich man, Kino provides four responses, all of
which are steps in the upward cultural spiral. First, he and
Juana will be married in the church, thereby obtaining
civilized approbation. Second, they will buy new clothes,
thereby obtaining respectability. Third, Kino, will have a
rifle, thereby obtaining power over other men. Fourth,
Coyotito will go to school, thereby obtaining status in the
civilized order. With each step in the upward spiral the music of the pearl rises, but it also changes from "a chorus of
trumpets" to a "shrilling with triumph."

The essential outline of plot and theme is charged with
symbolism and suggestiveness. The symbols in the story
are not abrupt, sudden, or confusing; rather they emerge
naturally and powerfully from a carefully arranged symbolic
environment cast in the narrative framework. In its broad-
est pattern the novella is a kind of reversal of the biblical
Book of Job: the story of a man who has everything, then
loses everything, finally to gain back "twice as much as he
had before" (Job 42:10). Kino is the man who has nothing,
gains the pearl of the world, and ends with less than he began with, save for the knowledge that he now knows and
has experienced the lie of civilization's lures.

More specifically, however, the work is framed by several
kinds of patterned imagery, primary among which is that
referring to light. The novella begins in "near dark" that
washes into golden morning, "a morning like other mornings and yet perfect among mornings" (p. 3). The crystal
clarity is shattered when Coyotito is stung by the scorpion,
and the following morning dawns in a haze: "Although the
morning was young, the hazy mirage was up. The uncertain
air that magnified some things and blotted out others hung
over the whole Gulf so that all lights were unreal and vision
could not be trusted; so that sea and land had the sharp
clarities and vagueness of a dream" (p. 21). And through

this haze, appropriately, we catch a glimpse of the region of the town: "Across the estuary from the town one section of mangroves stood clear and telescopically defined, while another mangrove clump was a hazy black-green blob. Part of the far shore disappeared into a shimmer that looked like water. There was no certainty in seeing" (p. 21). By the time the villagers journey into the town itself, the light has faded, to be replaced by an oppressive blackness symbolic of the villagers' greed: "The news stirred up something infinitely black and evil in the town; the black distillate was like the scorpion" (pp. 34–35).

By chapter 5, after the open conflict in the town, the atmosphere has become opaque and dim. This time Kino "opened his eyes in the darkness." Only the pale light of the moon stabs the gloom. The shift from brightness to darkness and from clarity to obscurity is accompanied by a decisive shift in color emphasis, from the clear golds, yellows, and earth hues of green and brown that dominate the first chapter to more emotionally charged colors. In chapter 5, Kino's "brain was red with anger." Now the light that was formerly a source of joy becomes a threat: "Suddenly Kino was afraid. The light made him afraid. He remembered the man lying dead in the brush beside the path, and he took Juana by the arm and drew her into the shadow of a house away from the light, for light was danger to him" (p. 88). And the physical darkening in the novella is mirrored psychologically in Kino's own fear and uncertainty:

In a few moments Juan Tomás came back with her. He lighted a candle and came to them where they crouched in a corner and he said, "Apolonia, see to the door, and do not let anyone enter." He was older, Juan Tomás, and he assumed the authority. "Now, my brother," he said.

"I was attacked in the dark," said Kino. "And in the fight I have killed a man."

"Who?" asked Juan Tomás quickly.

"I do not know. It is all darkness—all darkness and the shape of darkness." [P. 89]

Such characters fumble in a morass of darkness. Kino, Juana, and Coyotito climb into the tenebrous and threatening mountains from which "the sun had passed." They head west, into the dying sunlight, and wander a maze of crooked chasms. Finally, it is "late in the golden afternoon" when Kino and Juana attempt to reclaim the light by hurling the pearl into the sea. As they walk toward the sea, "The sun was behind them and their long shadows stalked ahead, and they seemed to carry two towers of darkness with them" (p. 119). Only when the pearl disappears beneath the waves do we get a suggestion of renewed light:

And the pearl settled into the lovely green water and dropped toward the bottom. The waving branches of the algae called to it and beckoned to it. The lights on its surface were green and lovely. It settled down to the sand bottom among the fern-like plants. Above, the surface of the water was a green mirror. [P. 122]

The transition in light imagery from gentle familiarity to the fearsome dark is paralleled in the book through increasingly predatory animal imagery. The setting at large is carefully established in animal imagery—the colonial organism, the devouring power of civilization, the doctor's regard for the Indians as so many insects—but the progress of the pearl's influence on Kino is also measured by his devolution into the animalistic. His very finding of the pearl, in fact, announces the transformation: "Kino's fist closed over the pearl and his emotion broke over him. He put his head back and howled. His eyes rolled up and he screamed and his body was rigid" (pp. 30–31). From that point on, the animal imagery steadily becomes more grim and feral, as a primitive hatred rises in Kino.

It is impossible to list all the examples of animal imagery in the book, but the following illustrate the transformation of Kino revealed in animal imagery. When he goes to sell the pearl, "Kino had grown tight and hard. He felt the creeping of fate, the circling of wolves, the hover of vultures" (p. 69). When Juana attempts to throw the pearl

away, "Kino looked down at her and his teeth were bared.
He hissed at her like a snake, and Juana stared at him with
wide unfrightened eyes, like a sheep before the butcher"
(p. 80). When attacked by robbers, "Kino moved slug-
gishly, arms and legs stirred like those of crushed bug, and
a thick muttering came from his mouth" (p. 84). When his
canoe is destroyed, "He was an animal now, for hiding, for
attacking, and he lived only to preserve himself and his
family" (p. 86). When he flees the village, "Some ancient
thing stirred in Kino. Through his fear of dark and the dev-
ils that haunt the night, there came a rush of exhilaration;
some animal thing was moving in him so that he was cautious and wary and dangerous; some ancient thing out of
the past of his people was alive in him" (pp. 94–95). And
finally, when pursued, "Kino edged like a slow lizard down
the smooth rock shoulder," and "The Song of the Family
had become as fierce and sharp and feline as the snarl of a
female puma" (pp. 114–15). The steps trace the reversion
in Kino to the primitive and predatory. Touched by the malignancy of civilization, he has become one of the "tigers"
of Cannery Row.

Operating concomitantly with the darkening light imagery, intensifying color imagery, and increasingly predatory
animal imagery that mark Kino's dark night of the soul, is
the transformation in the quasi-symbolic Song of the Family. This fascinating structural device forms a part of the
realistic narrative level as an actual song of the Indian
families but assumes symbolic significance as the novella
progresses. Thus it operates at two levels—structural technique and symbol—and forms a transition to the larger
symbolism of the story.

As part of the native reality recounted in the narrative
plot, the Song of the Family is of a piece with the religious
fabric woven into the daily lives of the Indians, a fabric curiously steeped in Christianity and folk tradition: "The
scorpion moved delicately down the rope toward the box.
Under her breath Juana repeated an ancient magic to guard
against such evil, and on top of that she muttered a Hail

Mary between clenched teeth" (p. 10). The Song of the
Family is part of the daily structure, a melody of life in
order, and a life in harmony with God. But the song quickly
assumes symbolic significance as the tension between the
Song of the Family and the Song of Evil intensifies.[15]

The song established early in the story speaks to the
order of daily life, the history and unity of the people, and
all the small things that make life commonplace and good.
This virtue of the commonplace, this natural rhythm of
life, are what greed and civilization destroy; and once destroyed they are impossible to recover. There is no going
back, no going home again. But for a time the people live in
the midst of the measured harmony that emanates from nature and the people themselves:

> Kino heard the little splash of morning waves on the beach. It
> was very good—Kino closed his eyes again to listen to his music.
> Perhaps he alone did this, and perhaps all of his people did it. His
> people had once been great makers of songs so that everything
> they saw or thought or did or heard became a song. That was very
> long ago. The songs remained; Kino knew them, but no new
> songs were added. That does not mean that there were no per-
> sonal songs. In Kino's head there was a song now, clear and soft,
> and if he had been able to speak of it, he would have called it the
> Song of the Family. [Pp. 3-4]

While the making of songs roots the people in a tradition,
each small task of daily life participates in an ongoing rhythm
and melody. While Juana was grinding corn, "the rhythm of
the family song was the grinding stone where Juana worked
the corn for the morning cakes" (p. 5). While she was rock-
ing Coyotito, she "sang softly an ancient song that had only
three notes and yet endless variety of interval. And this
was part of the family song too. It was all part. Sometimes it
rose to an aching chord that caught the throat, saying this is
safety, this is warmth, this is the *Whole*" (p. 6).

The song begins to change with the first minute movements of the scorpion on the crib ropes: "In his mind a new
song had come, the Song of Evil, the music of the enemy,
of any foe of the family, a savage, secret, dangerous melody,

and underneath, the Song of the Family cried plaintively"
(pp. 9–10). The scorpion is prefigurative of the internal
"sting of evil" that the pearl poses. One is outward and
physical, the other inward and spiritual. Each is equally
malevolent and heralded by the Song of Evil before which
the Song of the Family quails.

Into this dialectic of the family song and the evil song,
one symbolizing order and harmony, the other disorder and
destruction, enters the Music of the Pearl. There is a curious neutrality of the theme here. The pearl song in and of
itself is not evil; it is merely music. How people play the
music, one might say, constitutes the good or evil. The Music of the Pearl is first introduced as possibility, a "counter-
melody" within the Song of the Family, a part of its harmony yet somehow counter to it: "But in the song there was
a secret little inner song, hardly perceptible, but always
there, sweet and secret and clinging, almost hiding in the
counter-melody, and this was the Song of the Pearl That
Might Be" (p. 27). In fact, once the pearl is found, the Song
of the Family runs apace in its natural rhythm; the Music of
the Pearl even seems to strengthen and solidify the family
song: "And the music of the pearl had merged with the music of the family so that one beautified the other" (p. 35).

But possibility is always attended by ambiguity. For Kino
the pearl opens the door on the possibility of owning the
power tools of civilization. For the doctor, the merchants,
and others, it opens on greed. As Kino's own dreams are
consumed by greed, the Song of the Family grows uncertain and disturbed: "Now uncertainty was in Kino, and the
music of evil throbbed in his head and nearly drove out
Juana's song" (p. 48). And the music, with uncertainty,
changes dramatically to a dark, pulsing beat of evil.

With the attempt to sell the pearl and the open exposure
of human greed, the Song of Evil rises and drowns out
that of the family. Juana notes this most perceptively and
struggles to retain the natural rhythms:

Juana watched him with worry, but she knew him and she
knew she could help him best by being silent and by being near.

And as though she too could hear the Song of Evil, she fought it, singing softly the melody of the family, of the safety and warmth and wholeness of the family. She held Coyotito in her arms and sang the song to him, to keep the evil out, and her voice was brave against the threat of the dark music. [P. 75]

In her effort to preserve the natural harmony and to secure the Song of the Family, Juana tries to throw the pearl away. This in itself exposes a terrible breach in the family, for it pits one member of the family against another. But from the start Juana has recognized the terror represented by the pearl and its dark, threatening music: "'This thing is evil,' she cries harshly. 'This pearl is like a sin! It will destroy us,' and her voice rose shrilly" (p. 54). Not until the end does Kino recognize her wisdom, which he sanctions by handing her the pearl to throw away. In this crucial scene Kino acknowledges Juana as the victor over evil and her essential rightness in spiritual perception. Until that time the Song of Evil rises to a shrill, howling pitch. All melody and harmony seem lost: "Now the darkness was closing in on his family; now the evil music filled the night, hung over the mangroves, skirled in the wave beat" (pp. 85–86). Finally, in this battle of songs the Song of the Family must itself become fierce and predatory, something eminently dear and worth battling for. When Kino and Juana battle the trackers in the mountains, the Song of the Family rises like the fierce cry of the female puma, and as they walk back through the town, "in Kino's ears the Song of the Family was as fierce as a cry" (p. 121).

The final sentence in the book notes the dissipation of threat: "The music of the pearl drifted to a whisper and disappeared." One assumes that order has been restored, and in a way it has been. Even though the price has been paid, the pearl tossed into the sea, and the priceless pearl of Coyotito offered like a propitiation to human greed, the Song of the Family has emerged stronger, victorious.

This major thematic pattern of the dialectic of songs is sustained by degrees of symbolic significance in the story, chief of which is the pearl itself. Although like its music the pearl is simply an object and therefore neutral, achieving symbolic significance in how it is used, the pearl has the possibility of transforming the human spirit. The obvious symbolism, of course, is that the pearl represents Kino's dreams of social aspiration and achievement. In chapter 3 at each stage of his dreaming of things that the pearl will make possible, he sees the fulfillment of the dream mirrored in the pearl. For example, the final dream is for Coyotito's education, which will ensure social position: "In the pearl Kino saw himself and Juana squatting by the little fire in the brush hut while Coyotito read from a great book" (p. 38). Thus the pearl represents a dream and a hope for the future, but the dream turns nightmare. One often observes this theme in Steinbeck's earlier work, always with the effect that dreams will be dashed against the monolithic shores of civilization's greed.

On a second level of meaning the pearl reflects the mutations of Kino's own soul. After his dreaming, Kino closed his fist on the pearl "and cut the light away from it." At the same time he closed the light on his own soul, a fact that he openly confesses as he flees the village: "'This pearl has become my soul,' said Kino. 'If I give it up I shall lose my soul'" (p. 93). It is true that the pearl is by now an inward thing, the physical object simply a symbol of the spiritual struggle between the Song of the Family and the Song of Evil at war within Kino. Only when the Song of the Family begins to emerge victoriously in the mountains can Kino see the hideousness of greed, a third level of meaning represented in the pearl: "He looked into its surface and it was gray and ulcerous. Evil faces peered from it into his eyes, and he saw the light of burning" (p. 121). Finally, the pearl represents liberation for Kino, at first from the old family structures as he dreams of his wealth, but ultimately and ironically from the lures of civilization and wealth themselves as he is liberated to throw away the pearl and to return to the Song of the Family.

Other minor symbols work quietly in the novella. The

Indian boats represent to the people a heritage and tradition, a way of life and a part of the Song of the Family. Such is also the case with Kino's canoe, inherited from his father and emblematic of long tradition:

Kino and Juana came slowly to down to the beach and to Kino's canoe, which was the one thing of value he owned in the world. It was very old, Kino's grandfather had brought it from Nayarit, and he had given it to Kino's father, and so it had come to Kino. It was at once property and source of food, for a man with a boat can guarantee a woman that she will eat something. It is the bulwark against starvation. And every year Kino refinished his canoe with the hard shell-like plaster by the secret method that had also come to him from his father. [Pp. 21–22]

The destruction of the canoe thus represents a destruction of one's most sacred treasure, as if the altar of a temple were defiled and something beyond price, beyond even the pearl of the world, were lost: "The canoe of his grandfather, plastered over and over, and a splintered hole broken in it. This was an evil beyond thinking. The killing of a man was not so evil as the killing of a boat" (p. 86).

Another minor symbol is the rifle, which appears in the story twice, first in Kino's dream of a Winchester in which it represents an unattainable dream of power, freedom, and wealth, and then as the actual rifle used during the manhunt, in which it represents only death, terror, and fear. It is significant that Kino returns to the shore carrying the rifle; the Song of the Family will be protected by its power, but also the only dream Kino has realized from his early list is the rifle with its death-bringing power.

Finally, as in so many of his other novels, one should include the mountains as symbolic of the escalating series of obstacles, and the hard, mounting urgency of confrontation in the novel. As with Pepe in the short story "Flight," the mountains also represent self-discovery and ultimately death.

One might charge that Steinbeck has written a story only to sustain a pattern of symbolism. But there is a kind of deft artistic simplicity in the novella that counters the charge. Technically this derives from a narrative objectivity with, save for the prefatory note, little authorial intrusion. There is very little dialogue in the tale, with concentration chiefly upon Kino's character as it is presented in a documentary fashion. The action is direct, and the plot is perfectly developed. In sum, *The Pearl* is a simple, unpretentious, and successful work in which Steinbeck seems to have worked out and settled his theme of nearly two decades, pitting the individual and his dreams against the threat of social power structures.

8

Harvest of the Earth: *East of Eden*

IN PUBLIC and critical perception, *The Grapes of Wrath* has always been Steinbeck's "big" novel; for Steinbeck it was *East of Eden*. While the former was a novel that nearly possessed him, and sucked him physically and emotionally dry in the fevered writing, the latter was a novel that he nurtured, in his own words, all of his life and that seemed to grow with him until the time of writing was at hand.

BACKGROUND TO THE WRITING

The seeds of the novel were in Steinbeck's mind as early as 1933, when he wrote to George Albee: "I think I would like to write the story of this whole valley, of all the little towns and all the farms and the ranches in the wilder hills. I can see how I would like to do it so that it would be in the valley of the world. But that will have to be sometime in the future. I would take so very long" (*LL*, p. 73–74). While he took a step toward this in *The Pastures of Heaven*, that "sometime in the future" did not arrive until November 17, 1947, when Steinbeck began to contemplate the actual writing:

I have a great deal of work to do this year and I would like to get it all done by this summer because then I would like to stop everything to do a long novel that I have been working on the notes of for a long time. It seems to me that for the last few years I have been working on bits and pieces of things without much continuity and I want to get back to a long slow piece of work. I need to go out there for a lot of research so I may be out in California this summer. [*LL*, p. 301]

To Ed Ricketts a few months later Steinbeck wrote again of his novel-to-be, projecting it at "nearly half a million words" and reminding himself of the need for careful deliberation to get all the words right (*LL*, p. 309). Finally, in August, 1950, he announced to Webster ("Toby") Street that he was nearly ready: "I want to start on my long novel—the one I have been practicing for all my life. It is the Salinas Valley one. I think that if I am not ready to write it now, I never will be. I am nearly fifty and I've been practicing for about 33 years" (*LL*, p. 408). And the feeling did not relent as he engaged the work. In July, 1952, when he was nearly finished with the manuscript, Steinbeck noted: "That earlier work was practice for this, I am sure. The rest was practice" (*JN*, p. 117).

Of no other work had Steinbeck spoken with such persistent fondness, and several factors account for his feeling. Nearly all of Steinbeck's work arises out of his own peculiar experience, and the stories are of people and places Steinbeck knew. The further Steinbeck moved from this spring of personal experience that nourished his work, the less successful his work was. The strictly cerebral works such as *The Short Reign of Pippin IV* lack the compelling quality that fascinates a reader. *East of Eden* is unique among the works based on Steinbeck's life experience because it is, in part, the story closest to him—his own. And it is the only story in which he enters directly as a character.

Furthermore, its vastness was compelling to him. Instead of being a small slice of life like *Tortilla Flat, Cannery Row*, or *Sweet Thursday*, this work took on the whole life. It contained in practice the theory of *The Log from the Sea of Cortez*—that all life must be seen whole in its environment, in relation to the all. It would bring all the threads together for him. It is no accident that over and over in *Journal of a Novel* he concludes a letter to Covici with this phrase: "I will get to my knitting."

One observes also that the work represented, in moral theme, an answer to and fulfillment of all his other work. For such reasons Steinbeck took an unrelenting, pure joy in the writing:

I have never enjoyed my own work as I have this book. I am as excited about it now as on the day I started it. There is no let down in my energy. I still think it is The Book, as far as I am concerned. Always before I have held something back for later. Nothing is held back here. This is not practice for a future. This is what I have practiced for." [*JN*, p. 124]

East of Eden was to be the focal point for the moral views about humankind and human relationships that he had been developing since the early thirties.

A fourth reason must be added. The late forties was a discouraging time for Steinbeck, fully as depressing as his very early disillusionment about getting published and establishing himself as a writer. The discouragement here was for different reasons. His health for the last half-dozen years had not been good. While living in Mexico, he and Gwyn both suffered from food poisoning, and its effects had lingered in a susceptibility to various ailments. The physical debilitation was matched by psychological problems; frequently he notes in his letters of this period of being afflicted by a "blue despair." Furthermore, his marriage with Gwyn had deteriorated. While pregnant with their son John in 1946, Gwyn stayed in bed often and late, complaining of numerous maladies, real or imagined. Jackson Benson describes the situation:

But then staying in bed seemed to become more and more combined with the symptoms of various illnesses—a cold, the flu, and allergy of one sort or another, and, most violently, asthma. John became suspicious of these recurring illnesses, and having little patience with the illness of others anyway, was half convinced that they were largely psychosomatic, possibly even voluntarily self-induced. It seemed to him as if his wife was sick all the time, lacking energy, and always unwilling to go anywhere or do anything without extensive urging on his part. As her lethargy increased, so did questions regarding the genuineness of her suffering—and when John was in a black mood, not an infrequent phenomenon, there were bitter words exchanged. [1]

Steinbeck was also concerned by national and international affairs. Once admitted to the charmed power circles of high political officials, Steinbeck relished the privilege and was deeply affected by political events. The close of the war, the death of the president, the national change: all gave him a sense of displacement and a longing for his California roots.

Finally, there was his own sense that his work had become thin and inconsequential. *Cannery Row* received many negative reviews. *The Wayward Bus,* whatever its merits as a literary work, had been dashed off quickly. Too much of his time was spent cranking out Hollywood fare. Covici was encouraging him to write a truly substantial work:

Covici was concerned, just as were Steinbeck's agents, that the author had not tackled anything really substantial in years. They wouldn't say anything directly, but in their hearts they felt that the movie [*Zapata*] was just another perverse detour from the real use of his talent. And with yet another small book following two that had been criticized for their slightness, they would have to brace themselves for a real onslaught of negative criticism.[2]

With the dissolution of his marriage to Gwyn his artistic and emotional security seemed to cave in. Feeling the pressure of critics to write a substantial work, Steinbeck turned to the only place he knew where he could find the roots for such a work—California. Gwyn, having just endured Steinbeck's absence during his several months abroad, rufused to accompany him, and Steinbeck went alone. He plotted with Ed Ricketts to do a kind of northern *Log*, to be called "The Outer Shores," a plan destroyed on May 7, 1948, when Ed drove his noisy old Packard into the path of the Del Monte Express. Upon his return from the funeral Steinbeck was notified by Gwyn that she wanted a divorce. A gray and desolate period followed, and the only thing that filled the hollow were the whispers of Gwyn's infidelities and the growing awareness that she had stopped loving him years before. Steinbeck entered a bizarre psychological period in his life, having retreated into his Pacific Grove cottage with its blackened room holding Ed Ricketts' enshrined microscope, like a hermit dredging the depths of an irrecoverable past.

The presence of Elaine Scott burst upon that grayness like a sun. Benson writes:

Now, as he emerged from a long night filled with nightmares of self-doubt and self-deprecation, both of his own worth and the value of his work, he was determined to be strong, and he rededicated himself to defining himself. He would insist on his own beliefs and maintain them regardless of the many pressures to conform and compare within the arena of the tastes, values, and modes of thinking and expression set up for him by others.[3]

In attaining this position, and in his reemergence as a writer, the influence of Elaine is enormous. She provided him solace and direction, which pointed now to the writing of his "big" novel, *East of Eden*. To Covici he reflected: "I did not expect to survive then and I don't think I would have. Every life force was shriveling. . . . Now two years later I have a new life and a direction" (*JN*, p. 95). He set about the writing with the methodical, exacting care of an architect, and slowly the book took over his life. "Never," he wrote Elizabeth Otis, "has a book so intrigued me." Benson gives an illuminating portrait of the writer at this time:

For a man who while writing could have a very short temper (in his journal he confessed, "Pat, there is so much violence in me. Sometimes I am horrified at the amount of it"), he could show extraordinary patience with cuttings, bulbs, seedlings, and unseasonable frosts. He could also become totally absorbed by some project, sitting for hours carving on a piece of wood or fashioning some new convenience for himself or the household. If what he was working on fell apart, one might hear "Nuts!" or "Rats!" or some other strangely innocuous expletive. Then, he would usually pick up the pieces, and quietly try again.[4]

And also:

As he grew older he became increasingly more absent-minded and inadvertently sloppy, although consciously he wanted to be neat and organized. He liked to have everything in its place, particularly his writing materials and his tools, and it drove him crazy when he couldn't find something. His tendency to lose things was a major impetus toward invention, so that it seemed as if he was forever thinking up various kinds of organizers, brackets, holders, and straps, so that he could find things when he needed them.[5]

Despite the careful structuring and labor Steinbeck gave this work, it has met with little critical respect. Critics have objected to the presence of the first-person narrator as an intrusion. They have condemned the sprawling nature of the narrative. Perhaps the most detailed such criticism is given by Peter Lisca, who calls into question everything from the novel's structure to the author's confusion on the question of free will. But Lisca's deepest criticism is reserved for the rhetoric: "The scrambled syntax and awkward expression are evident everywhere,"[6] and "Steinbeck's prose is not so much casual or careless as affected."[7] The redeeming quality of the novel for Lisca is the successful presentation of the

minor characters and of his maternal family—excepting Samuel Hamilton, who is nevertheless more credible and effective than any of the other major characters. These are successful because they are drawn from memory, with no attempt to make them fit into a myth or illustrate a type. Unfortunately, these warm, credible human beings are in no way involved in the novel's narrative.[8]

In the twenty years between the publication of his *The Wide World of John Steinbeck* and his later study *John Steinbeck: Nature and Myth*, Lisca moderated neither his views nor his tone toward *East of Eden*. The work remains for him a failure.

Lisca's concern is chiefly for structural technique and unity; Joseph Fontenrose is similarly disappointed in the work because of what he considers an obfuscation of good and evil in the novel. "The reader is never clear about the relation of good to evil in the novel," he argues, "for it is presented in four inconsistent ways."[9] These Fontenrose details as: (1) good is opposed to evil, (2) good and evil are complementary, (3) evil is the source of good and may even be necessary to good, and (4) good and evil are relative terms. "For a novel on good and evil," he concludes, "*East of Eden* strangely lacks ethical insight." [10]

In *The Novels of John Steinbeck*, Howard Levant strikes a more moderate position. Levant notes structural flaws, "a strangely unblended novel, an impressive, greatly flawed work," [11] but he also observes that the novel works thematically with tensions and themes that endure from Steinbeck's earliest work. Levant provides a valuable insight into the novel by his careful relation of its themes to earlier work and by his careful examination of the structural impact and philosophical significance of the *timshel* doctrine:

Still, a peculiar impressiveness survives the organizational failure of the manipulated superficial devices and parallels. To understand this survival is to comprehend a crucial aspect of the art of fiction.

The *timshel* doctrine enables Steinbeck to broaden an autobiographical kernel into the spiritual autobiography of mankind, of life itself, since all ideas, characters, and events can suggest the vast confusion of life. This is the lasting impression of *East of Eden*. [12]

Finally, though, for Levant the work remains flawed by "disregard for a harmonious relationship between structure and materials." [13]

Some praise has been offered, of course, particularly by early reviewers including, for example, Joseph Wood Krutch, who observed that not even in *The Grapes of Wrath* has Steinbeck "exhibited such a grasp upon himself and his materials," [14] and Mark Schorer, who particularly appreciated the presence of the first-person narrator. [15] In his *Thematic Design in the Novels of John Steinbeck*, Lester Marks provides a carefully reasoned rebuttal to Peter Lisca, arguing that "Steinbeck invests the novel with its dominant motif out of which emanate several subsidiary but linking themes." [16] That primary motif, for Marks, resides in the *timshel* doctrine of Lee. Finally, a more recent collection of essays on *East of Eden*, published by the John Steinbeck Society, gives almost unwavering praise to the novel.[17]

The negative comments about stylistic lapses and ethical confusion, have been persistent and significant in any critical consideration of the novel. Yet aside from what the novel may fail to do, there is considerable value in what it does—its response to earlier themes, its grappling with the problem of good and evil, its profound insights into human nature and human aspirations, and its potent character portraits. In his introduction to Levant's *The Novels of John Steinbeck*, Warren French provides an excellent introductory appraisal of Steinbeck criticism. In his call to see the fiction as a whole, to see its structural patterns linked decisively with the narrative event of plot and character, French encourages scholars to what he calls "constructionist criticism"—"an examination of the adequacy of the novels' blueprints to the embodiment of their vision,"[18] as opposed to mere appreciations, theme discussions, or stylistic analyses. While he marshals support from different areas, including Northrop Frye's *The Critical Path*, surprisingly French finds his most compelling support in a study of popular western fiction by John Cawelti, *The Six-Gun Mystique*. Cawelti's work provides valuable insights into the method of fiction and critical treatment of it, particularly in his caution against analysis that extrapolates theme out of context and ignores the total structure of the work. The following statement by Cawelti particularly guides French's thinking and provides an adequate statement of constructionist criticism as French uses the term:

A good plot model should provide a basis for explaining why each event and character is present in the work, and why these events and characters are placed in the setting they occupy. If some element remains unexplained, it is clear that the organizing principles have not been adequately stated.[19]

The question remains, then, in critical appraisal of *East of Eden:* Is there a structural and thematic core to the novel that roots the whole in the groundwork of the artist's technique and vision? The response lies in the very character whom critics fault as the most flawed, thematically ambiguous, and structurally unassembled in the novel, Cathy Ames. My first intention in this chapter is to examine Cathy Ames's role as thematic and structural center of the novel. The novel is also, however, Steinbeck's rendition of a contemporary *Paradise Lost,* one in which Cathy is the seducer east of Eden. My second intention is to examine the relationship of several other characters to Cathy on the issue of good and evil. The result, I believe, is to demonstrate that Steinbeck possessed a far clearer perception of structural unity and of moral theme in this novel than has been commonly assumed.

CATHY AMES AS CENTRAL CHARACTER

It is doubtful whether Cathy was complete in Steinbeck's mind at the outset of the writing. His expressed intention was to write a narrative history for his sons, coupled with the theme he announced in a March 7 entry in the *Journal* as "the symbolic killing of brother by brother" (*JN*, p. 25). From his earliest work Steinbeck had been intrigued by the love-hate relationship, how closely the two stand side by side. While he wrote the first lines of *East of Eden* and pondered the many lines before him, Steinbeck noted:

I will tell them [his sons] one of the greatest, perhaps the greatest story of all—the story of good and evil, of strength and weakness, of love and hate, of beauty and ugliness. I shall try to demonstrate to them how these doubles are inseparable—how neither can exist without the other and how out of their groupings creativeness is born" [*JN*, p. 4]

While surely not as radical as Freud in his perception, Steinbeck often probed the violence that seemed poised just on the other side of love. Early examples may be Elisa of "The Chrysanthemums," Peter Randall of "The Harness," Tularecito of *The Pastures of Heaven,* and George and Lennie in *Of Mice and Men.* Cathy is a focus in the same way. From his earliest conception of her Cathy was a figure of evil to Steinbeck, but one in relation to whom other characters find their own good or evil. I believe this also explains the ambiguity of good and evil which Fontenrose finds in the novel, for the fact is that everyone reacts to evil in a different way and with varying degrees of attraction or repulsion.

As Steinbeck describes her, Cathy is a monster, devoid of moral sensibility, and a woman, as he noted in his *Journal*, who "is going to worry a lot of children and a lot of parents about their children" (*JN*, p. 46). While it is questionable how and when Cathy's role developed in the novel, it is clear that from the earliest stages Steinbeck conceived of the novel as a moral statement, and Cathy came to serve as the pivot around which other characters discover their own "story of good and evil, of strength and weakness, of love and hate, of beauty and ugliness." Cathy provides a kind of diabolical backdrop for all such discoveries, and if these discoveries are not clearly categorical, as Fontenrose suggests, it is simply because for Steinbeck there are few such clear categories in anyone's life. Yet he works from this fundamental premise: evil is an inward force that sucks all things into itself in order to feed and perpetuate itself, and therefore evil is essentially destructive; good, on the other hand, is always open to life, is outwardly directed and altruistic.

In *East of Eden*, Steinbeck states the premise thus: "We have only one story. All novels, all poetry, are built on the never-ending contest in ourselves of good and evil. And it occurs to me that evil must constantly respawn, while good, while virtue, is immortal. Vice has always a fresh young face, while virtue is venerable as nothing else in the world is" (p. 415). Rather than a focus of good in relation to which one can measure his failures, Steinbeck has provided in this novel a focus of evil in relation to which one can measure small advances from the abject lovelessness that Cathy represents.

Cathy's essential evil is indeed the evil of lovelessness: instead of affirming life, she perverts and bends life to her darkness. Steinbeck introduces Cathy as a monster (chap-

ter 8), a statement he partly retracts later in the novel
(chapter 17). Yet she is and remains a monster for two reasons. First, she bends and twists life: "Some balance wheel
was misweighted, some gear out of ratio." Second, she debases sexuality, and in Steinbeck's fiction human sexuality is
always a sign of robust vigor and energetic life. Fontenrose
observes of this second point: "We should notice that in
contrast to Steinbeck's treatment of sex in earlier novels,
there is no good or healthy or lusty sexual intercourse in
East of Eden. It is always sordid, joyless, depraved, or mer-
cenary."[20] The sexual weapon that Cathy wields wounds
everyone in the novel.

Cathy's moral monstrousness is enforced consistently in
two important stylistic ways throughout the novel. In keeping with Steinbeck's biblical use of the Eden story, Cathy is
consistently presented in the serpent imagery of Satan who
lured Adam and Eve into the transgression that drove
them out of Eden. She is attractive, and the lure of the serpent in Genesis is attractiveness—the fruit of the tree "was
a delight to the eyes, and that the tree was to be desired."
She is subtle, described when she takes over Faye's whorehouse as knowing the secrets of men. The serpent is described as "more subtle than any other wild creature that
the Lord God had made." Cathy is subtly adept, Adam
Trask discovers, in using "all the sad, weak parts of a man."

Other such analogies with Satan can be made. For example, Satan cannot create but can only destroy materials
already given. So too Cathy uses people as things and destroys them for her own malevolent end. She never acts
positively or creatively out of love, but only negatively and
out of fear. When Charles, who is perhaps best qualified to
know, says to her, "You know what I think? I don't think I'm
half as mean as you are under that nice skin. I think you're a
devil," Cathy responds with a laugh, "That makes two of
us" (p. 117).

The analogy of Cathy to Satan is sustained through the
physical imagery of the serpent. Cathy's twisted spirit is
disguised in "a face of innocence," but the closer details of

that face are revealing. Her eyes are hazel and wide-set, and the upper lids droop to make her appear "mysteriously sleepy." The serpent imagery of her eyes is repeated in the novel; sometimes they are described as "nearly lidless." She has a heart-shaped face, at once attractive but resembling a snake as well. Most telling, perhaps, are the very tiny ears, "thin flaps sealed against her head." Her body, moreover, carries out the imagery, thin and narrow-hipped, down to the "round and stubby" feet.

The snake imagery never relaxes in the novel; Cathy's diabolical nature, if anything, intensifies or becomes more openly manifested along with the progress of the imagery. When Samuel Hamilton first meets Cathy, he observes that "when she had swallowed, her little tongue flicked around her lips," and immediately he intuits: "Something—something—can't find what it is. Something wrong" (p. 173). When he glances at her again, he finds that "the eyes were flat and the mouth with its small up-curve at the corners was carven" (p. 173). Cathy, as inscrutable as a mask, stirs a profound sadness in Samuel. On the way back to his arid ranch from the lushness of Adam's Eden, he reflects on her peculiar eyes: "Were they cold? Was it her eyes? He was circling to the point. The eyes of Cathy had no message, no communication of any kind. There was nothing recognizable behind them. They were not human eyes" (p. 177). Somehow, in Samuel's mind Cathy forms the antithesis to joy itself. It is not surprising that Lee forms similar opinions. In dialogue with Samuel, Lee says:

> "Since I've come here I find myself thinking of Chinese fairy tales my father told me. We Chinese have a well-developed demonology."
> "You think she is a demon?"
> "Of course not," said Lee. "I hope I'm a little beyond such silliness." [P. 189]

The snake-Satanic imagery intensifies each time we see Cathy. When Adam goes to see her after Samuel's funeral, he observes that "her little teeth showed, the long canines sharp and white" (p. 318). As Cathy reveals to him the monstrosity of evil in man, the evil she uses and exploits in her wretched whorehouse, her "rage congealed to poison," but "her eyes were flat and cold." The scar on Cathy's forehead, which suggests the curse on the serpent in Genesis 3 ("he shall bruise your head"), is ironic in that it is administered by the whoremaster, Mr. Edwards. After her beating Cathy fulfills the rest of the Edenic curse as she crawls on her belly to the Trask ranch and has dirt in her broken mouth (Genesis 3:14, "upon your belly you shall go, and dust you shall eat"). Furthermore, there are two marks on the forehead in the Genesis account, as there are in *East of Eden*. The first is the promise of the bruised head represented here in Cathy; the second is the seal on Cain represented here in Charles. The mark on Cain was in fact not a physical mark but a mark of protection.[21] Charles may be mean, vicious, and violent, but he is not of the same nature as Cathy regardless of her assertion to that effect. Charles recognizes the evil that he does for what it is, and he is in fact regretful if not repentant. This is not true of Cathy, whose evil is an undiluted, consuming rage in her.

Complementary to the distinguishing snake imagery, Steinbeck develops a second pattern of light and dark imagery, employed often in his fiction with both psychological and spiritual significance. In the opening chapter of *East of Eden* the Salinas Valley is depicted as a place caught tensely between light and dark, life and death, good and evil:

I remember that the Gabilan Mountains to the east of the valley were light gay mountains full of sun and loveliness and a kind of invitation, so that you wanted to climb into their warm foothills almost as you want to climb into the lap of a beloved mother. They were beckoning mountains with a brown grass love. The Santa Lucias stood up against the sky to the west and kept the valley from the open sea, and they were dark and brooding—unfriendly and dangerous. I always found in myself a dread of west and a love of east. [P. 3]

It is in keeping with Cathy's character that she retreats to the dark. Her excursions into light become more infrequent. At Adam's ranch she already huddles in the deep shadows as if afraid of the light, and Adam, tragically, believes that all his labor is for her: "I'm going to make a garden so good, so beautiful, that it will be a proper place for her to live and a fitting place for her light to shine on" (pp. 170–71). Instead, Cathy brings darkness like a storm of night upon the ranch. As the time time of her birthing approaches, Cathy retreats into a house "very quiet, almost broodingly quiet, and the shades were pulled down." Adam says: "She doesn't want the light. It hurts her eyes" (p. 191).

Cathy's retreat into darkness accompanies her retreat into evil. This narrowing isolation is the curse of evil, a violation of every life-loving principle of Steinbeck's from the relational vision of *The Sea of Cortez*, the "fambly of man" theme of *The Grapes of Wrath*, and the "song of the family" of *The Pearl*. "Cathy had the one quality required of a great and successful criminal: she trusted no one, confided in no one. Her self was an island" (p. 159).

The pattern of isolation, darkness, and evil intensifies when Cathy takes over Faye's whorehouse. At first she incubates her evil from Faye's old room, and then, as if narrowing and hardening, or, perhaps, as if slinking into her serpent's den, she has a small, windowless lean-to attached to the room. The room is decorated in gray, as if a miasmal cloud hung there: "Indeed the gray walls seemed to suck up the light and destroy it" (P. 462). "The light hurts my eyes," Cathy says. And repeats it as if by affirmation. She is a thing of abject and thorough darkness now, reduced to a predatory animal lurking in her den:

She believed that the light pained her eyes, and also that the gray room was a cave to hide in, a dark burrow in the earth, a place where no eyes could stare at her. Once, sitting in her pillowed chair, she considered having a secret door built so that she would have an avenue of escape. And then a feeling rather than a thought threw out the plan. She would not be protected then. If

she could get out, something could get in—that something which
had begun to crouch outside the house, to crawl close to the walls
at night, and to rise silently, trying to look through the windows.
[p. 474]

Steinbeck further reinforces her warped nature by her
arthritic hands, which are gnarled claws, bent inward,
incapable of reaching out any more, and symbolic of the
crookedness of her spiritual nature. The metaphorical equation is made clear: ". . . her hands and her mind grew more
crooked" (p. 504).

In artistic terms Cathy Ames is a compellingly complex
character who goes beyond the biblical Satan archetype
and the respawning evil associated with light and dark imagery. She also clearly resembles the *belle dame sans merci.*
Given Steinbeck's strong and lifelong attraction to medieval
literature, it is not particularly surprising to find the *belle
dame* here in relation to Cathy Ames, and also the Morgan
Le Fay figure from Arthurian literature.[22] But the Romantic
counterpart of the Lamia figure, the dream goddess who
destroys those who dare dream of her, also figures prominently in the character of Cathy Ames. One finds the clearest parallel in Keats's work, where the Lamia figure is depicted in snake imagery and functions symbolically as the
dream goddess, the deluder, and the sexual tormentor.
In each of Keats's three *belle dame* poems, "The Eve of
St. Agnes," "Lamia," and "Isabella," the parallelism holds.
It is interesting, furthermore, how Keats frames the figure
in light-dark imagery as Steinbeck does Cathy's figure in
East of Eden. In "Isabella" Keats writes:

> In the mid days of autumn, on their eves
>   The breath of Winter comes from far away,
> And the sick west continually bereaves
>   Of some gold tinge, and plays a roundelay
> Of death among the bushes and the leaves.[23]

Keats's "Lamia" focuses almost exclusively on the delusive
dream in which the serpent is perceived as the lovely god-

dess. Here too is a parallel to *East of Eden*. As Keats's Lycius suddenly fears his master Apollonius, "my trusty guide / And good instructor; but to-night he seems / The ghost of folly haunting my sweet dreams," Adam Trask's dream is "haunted" by the clear realism of Samuel Hamilton. Samuel points out to Adam that he has only worshiped a dream Cathy and has never seen the reality of the destroyer behind her fair appearance:

How we do defend a wrongness! Shall I tell you what you do, so you will not think you invented it? When you go to bed and blow out the lamp—then she stands in the doorway with a little light behind her, and you can see her nightgown stir. And she comes sweetly to your bed, and you, hardly breathing, turn back the covers to receive her and move your head over on the pillow to make room for her head beside yours. You can smell the sweetness of her skin, and it smells like no other skin in the world. [P. 296]

Cathy's mythic trappings are intertwined with the biblical serpent in such a way as to form a figure of unmitigated evil and spiritual brutality. If one recalls Steinbeck's idea that evil must always respawn, it is absolutely fitting that Cathy becomes herself the sacrifice to her own evil. Her diabolical plots outstrip her. Threatened by Ethel, then by Joe Valery, she retreats finally to the dim hole of her lean-to and finally to the black night of her suicide:

When the forest of her enemies surrounded her she was prepared. In her pocket she had a bottle of sugar water and on its red-framed label she had written, "Drink me." She would take a sip from the bottle and she would grow smaller and smaller. Let her enemies look for her then! Cathy would be under a leaf or looking out of an anthole, laughing. They couldn't find her then. No door could close her out and no door could close her in. She could walk upright under a door. [P. 552]

The allusion to *Alice in Wonderland* is fitting: Cathy has shrunk under her own evil until it has consumed her.[24]

The figure of Cathy also leaves room for fascinating speculation, although direct influence is questionable, on the influence of Milton's portrayal of Satan and evil in *Paradise
Lost*. It is certain that Steinbeck read Milton early and
often; the epigraph to *In Dubious Battle* is taken from the
epic, and Milton, as Jackson Benson points out in his biography *The True Adventures of John Steinbeck, Writer*, was
a part of Steinbeck's regularly used library. There may be
an arguable case for influence in the *timshel* doctrine of
free will, as John L. Gribben has demonstrated in his essay
on that relation.[25] But there are, at least, fascinating parallels between the representative evil of Cathy Ames in *East
of Eden* and the representative evil of Satan in *Paradise
Lost*. Milton argues that one of the immediate effects of the
Fall was psychological chaos caused by the "sensual appetite" overruling will and reason:

> They sat them down to weep; nor only tears
> Rained at their eyes, but high winds worse within
> Began to rise, high passions, anger, hate,
> Mistrust, suspicion, discord, and shook sore
> Their inward state of mind, calm region once
> And full of peace, now tossed and turbulent;
> For understanding ruled not, and the will
> Heard not her lore, both in subjection, now
> To sensual appetite, who from beneath
> Usurping over sovran reason claimed
> Superior sway.
>
> [9.1121–31][26]

Such is surely the case with Cathy, whose will is wholly
subservient to her "sensual appetite." As such she moves
closer to the mind of Satan himself. In book 1, Milton's
Satan says:

> "The mind is its own place, and in itself
> Can make a heav'n of hell, a hell of heav'n."
>
> [1.254–55]

And

> "Here we may reign secure, and in my choice
> To reign is worth ambition, though in hell:
> Better to reign in hell than serve in heav'n."
>
> [1.261–63]

Cathy's "hell" is finally the twisted malevolence of her mind, which has bent to it and blackened all things. The fallen Satan of *Paradise Lost* curses heaven and himself when he realizes this:

> Be then his love accurst, since love or hate,
> To me alike, it deals eternal woe.
> Nay cursed be thou, since against his thy will
> Chose freely what it now so justly rues.
> Me miserable! which way shall I fly
> Infinite wrath, and infinite despair?
> Which way I fly is hell; myself am hell;
> And in the lowest deep a lower deep
> Still threat'ning to devour me opens wide,
> To which the hell I suffer seems a heav'n.
> O then at last relent: is there no place
> Left for repentance, none for pardon left?
> None left but by submission; and that word
> Disdain forbids me . . . .
>
> [4.69–82]

Finally Cathy's inward devolution to this abyss of evil leads to the "magic pill" that makes her hell irrevocable. Only death and darkness lie at the end of her path.

While it is the case that Cathy Ames's self-destructive and all-consuming evil is the negative pole in relation to which we understand the good and evil of other characters, Steinbeck provides a context for this understanding in the changes in modern civilization itelf. This is the external backdrop that also structures the novel. Steinbeck believed that modern civilization was in a process of devolution fairly similar to the narrowing of Cathy Ames. It is impos-

sible to say when civilization reached an apex for Steinbeck—probably in the legendary court of Camelot, certainly sometime in the medieval era—but it is clear that he
saw modern civilization as threatening the spirit of man
and the individual creative consciousness. The intercalary
chapters of the novel evoke that threat as surely as they did
in *The Grapes of Wrath*, with the exception that here they
are general and wide-ranging, like a vast curtain of events
against which the Trasks and Hamiltons work out their particular story, while in *The Grapes of Wrath* the intercalary
chapters always focus sharply and urgently on the narration
and the immediacy of the Okie migration. That external
world of *East of Eden* is vast and fairly amorphous in its
generalized threat, yet it parallels the narrower struggle
captured in the narrative. In part two of the novel Steinbeck introduces the movement from the narrative world of
the Salinas Valley to the world at large: "For the world was
changing, and sweetness was gone, and virtue too. Worry
had crept on a corroding world, and what was lost—good
manners, ease and beauty?" (p. 129). Like the press and
urgency of the narrative struggle with good and evil, that
larger external world explodes from a general moral malaise
to the viciousness of world war. When Steinbeck introduces
part four with his reflection that "humans are caught—in
their lives, in their thoughts, in their hungers and ambi-
tions, in their avarice and cruelty, and in their kindness and
generosity too—in a net of good and evil" (p. 413), the two
stories, narrative and intercalary, have merged. The diabolical nature of Cathy is counterpart to the diabolism of
world war. Aron flees one for the other but is destroyed by
both, psychologically in the Salinas Valley and physically in
combat.

CHARACTERS IN PROCESS OF SELF-DISCOVERY

Within the narrative account Cathy is the pivot of the other
characters' lives, for there is a part of Cathy—or her essentially evil nature—in every man, according to Steinbeck: "Nearly everyone in the world has appetites and im-

pulses, trigger emotions, islands of selfishness, lusts just beneath the surface. . . . Everyone concealed that little hell in himself, while publicly pretending it did not exist" (p. 75). The narrative plot is the process of characters discovering that nature and dealing with it. This may be made clear by considering five of the principle characters and how they deal with this evil nature, which is manifested openly in Cathy: Horace Quinn deals with it socially, Charles and Caleb in differing psychological orders, Lee philosophically, and Samuel spiritually.

Horace Quinn: Social Order

Horace Quinn is an intriguing but overlooked figure in *East of Eden*. By and large Steinbeck deals casually and sympathetically with law officers in his fiction. Certain men in *Tortilla Flat* and *In Dubious Battle* are clearly pawns of the large landholders, but often law officers are a natural piece of the human landscape. Someone has to book Joe Portagee when he has one of his peculiar longings for the comfort of the jail cell. Some law officers, like Joe Blaikley of *Sweet Thursday*, combine native good sense with sensitivity and compassion. Joe steers Suzy in the direction she should go and keeps an eye on her to make sure she gets there. If her way points toward the city limits, Joe will give her a buck to see that she gets beyond them. But the most important thing about the small-town law officer is that he knows the people of that community. In *Sweet Thursday* the narrator reflects:

It is popular to picture a small town constable as dumb and clumsy. In the books he plays the stock bumpkin part. And people retain this attitude even when they know it's not true. We have so many beliefs we know are not true.

A constable, if he has served for a few years, knows more about his town than anyone else and on all levels. He is aware of the delicate political balance between mayor and councilmen, Fire Department and insurance companies. . . . He is aware of every

ripple on the town's surface. If there is a crime the constable
usually knows who didn't do it and often who did. With a good
constable on duty a hundred things don't happen that might.
[*ST*, p. 34]

That opinion is restated in *East of Eden:* "Only when everything else failed did a good sheriff make an arrest. The best
sheriff was not the best fighter but the best diplomat. And
Monterey County had a good one. He had a brilliant gift for
minding his own business" (p. 212).

Horace Quinn is one such law officer. He knows the
people, their efforts to do good and their achievements in
evil, and knows how to keep the good and evil in a delicate
balance so that the town may survive. For a town is a curious social animal, as Steinbeck describes it in *East of Eden*,
given to spasms of rectitude that will threaten the moral
balance, or given to such depravity that good hardly stands
a chance. The sheriff who precedes Horace Quinn speculates to him: "Now there's one thing a good quiet whorehouse is more scared of than anything else. Take a flighty
randy girl runs off from home and goes in a house. Her old
man finds her and he begins to shovel up hell. Then the
churches get into it, and the women, and pretty soon that
whorehouse has got a bad name and we've got to close it
up" (p. 214). The sheriff walks a daily tightwire as the conscience of his community. Like Steinbeck, speaking as the
narrator of the novel, so too Horace Quinn, both as a deputy and as sheriff after his election in 1903, believes that
extremism of any sort is dangerous, that a community is an
organism of individuals whose freedom must be protected:

And this I believe: that the free, exploring mind of the individual human is the most valuable thing in the world. And this
I would fight for: the freedom of the mind to take any direction it wishes, undirected. And this I must fight against: any idea,
religion, or government which limits or destroys the individual. [P. 132]

Above all, the good Steinbeckian law officer values honesty. Suzy's honesty makes her a favored ward of Joe Blaikley.

Adam's apparent dishonesty and masquerade cause a deep resentment in Horace Quinn; only years later does he realize that Adam was too pure to be dishonest, but also too pure to see the truth: "Adam could do no dishonesty. He didn't want anything. You had to crave something to be dishonest" (p. 562). After his election to the office of sheriff Horace perseveres in his sense of keeping a social balance: "When Faye died, he knew instinctively that Kate was probably responsible, but he also knew he hadn't much chance of convicting her, and a wise sheriff doesn't butt his head against the impossible" (p. 558). When the devastating photographic evidence of the sins of Salinas Valley are found on Joe Valery's body, Horace does precisely what a peace officer should do. He provides peace:

> Quinn took the picture from his hand.
> "Horace, what are you going to do with it?"
> "Burn it." The sheriff ruffled the edges of the envelopes with his thumb. "Here's a deck of hell," he said. "These could tear the county to pieces." [P. 560]

It is a painful decision, for Horace realizes that each man to whom he has provided peace will hate him for the knowledge that he brings as peace bringer. That is the difficult and terrible task: to see the truth and to act on it in such a way—without moral outrage and without prurient delight—that the social order may be restored. Perhaps better than anyone else, Horace Quinn would understand the narrative speculation Steinbeck set forth years before in *Tortilla Flat*:

> It is astounding to find that the belly of every black and evil thing is as white as snow. And it is saddening to discover how the concealed parts of angels are leprous. Honor and peace to Pilon, for he had discovered how to uncover and to disclose to the world the good that lay in every evil thing. Nor was he blind, as so many saints are, to the evil of the good things. [*TF*, p. 99]

Insert Horace Quinn in place of Pilon, and the statement still holds true. He knows the evil that stands just on the other side of goodness; his response is to hold it communally in the delicate balance that brings peace.

Charles: Psychological Balance

In many ways, surely more than the mere structural link of the twice-rejected offering, Caleb's character runs parallel to Charles's character. Both feel some inward alliance with Cathy. Both confront their own inward evil. But their responses to that confrontation differ. To appreciate fully Caleb's ability to achieve psychological balance in relation to Cathy, consider first the effort of Charles.

When Cathy crawls up to the Trask farm after her beating by Edwards, she immediately recognizes Adam as the one she can manipulate—"She had not only made up her mind to marry Adam but she had so decided before he had asked her"—but she is fearful of Charles. Why? When Charles calls her a devil, Cathy says to him in sardonic rejoinder, "That makes two of us." But she is also frightened of Charles because, as she believes, "If he had recognized her, so had she recognized him. He was the only person she had ever met who played it her way" (p. 118). Without exception, reactions of fear govern Cathy's actions; she is a predatory animal in that sense, always conniving and striking out when threatened. But this is not the case with Charles. Something of Cathy is indeed recognizable in him; but his violence is of a different nature and gains definition and clarity in relation to her.

Charles's violence is triggered by jealousy, evidenced most clearly in the gift his father rejects. In reaction Charles beats Adam and later returns with an ax to kill him. Charles is a violent person; he would have killed Adam had he found him. But he did not, and he does feel remorse for his act. When Adam leaves for his enlistment, Charles writes him several pained letters desperately striving to understand himself and his life. It's a psychological maelstrom that he cannot fathom:

It's like the whole house was alive and had eyes everywhere, and like there was people behind the door just ready to come in if you looked away. It kind of makes my skin crawl. I want to say—I want to say—I mean, why didn't he like that knife I bought for him on his birthday. Why didn't he? It was a good knife and he needed a good knife. . . . If he'd liked it I wouldn't have took out after you. I had to take out after you. [P. 37]

When Adam returns, Charles tries to establish some reconciliation. But it proves impossible; he is a man set apart by his own psychological horror, and the Cain scar that he receives sets him apart. The biblical mark of Cain, however, functions not so much as a mark of sin as a mark of protection. When Cain was filled with remorse upon slaying Abel (as Charles feels remorse at being rejected by his father and beating Adam), he is driven from the company of men, and the Lord lays the mark of protection upon him: "And the Lord said unto him, Therefore whosoever slayeth Cain, vengeance shall be taken on him sevenfold. And the Lord set a mark upon Cain, lest any finding him should kill him. And Cain went out from the presence of the Lord, and dwelt in the land of Nod, on the east of Eden" (Gen. 4:15–16). Charles also lives in isolation on his land of Nod, tilling the earth alone, protected by his alien status against his own violent nature.

Clearly, Charles's violent nature is qualitatively different from Cathy's. Charles feels remorse, while Cathy never does. Charles is able to control his violent nature by his separation, while Cathy deliberately inflicts her evil on the men she lures to her whorehouse. An ironic parallel prevails here: Charles regularly visits a whorehouse to "relieve" himself—but this Steinbeck accepts as a normal and even healthy thing. Cathy, on the other hand, runs a whorehouse that debases and perverts man's sexual urge. The essential difference between Charles and Cathy is expressed in Steinbeck's own note on Cathy: "This is probably why Kate is so frightening. She has no conscience" (*JN*, p. 96). But while Cathy becomes the monstrous, conscienceless animal Kate, Charles sets himself apart from humanity because of the pain of his conscience. There is some of Kate in him, surely—as Steinbeck said, "She is a little piece of the monster in all of us" (*JN*, p. 97)—but what we do with the monster in all of us, whether we attempt to order it as Charles does, or whether we allow it to devour us as Kate does, is the essential tension of *East of Eden*.

Caleb: Psychological Balance

While Charles orders his psychological nature to a certain degree, he does so in an artificial world apart from human relationships. The lonely existence in Nod would not represent a genuine psychological ordering for Steinbeck, who would insist upon an ordering in relation to an environment of fellow human beings. Caleb's effort to achieve this brings him much closer to Steinbeck's ideal.

With Caleb it seems that the Edenic cycle is revisited, but Adam's ranch is a devastated Eden in which his Eve is in fact the destructive serpent. The lush land lies fallow as the sons grow nameless. Yet Steinbeck reminded himself while writing these passages that "although East of Eden is not Eden, it is not insuperably far away" (*JN*, p. 116). The story of Caleb is the story of this discovery, a story of reclamation by discovery both of what he is and what he is not. Caleb forms a new principle, a psychological and social ordering principle as opposed to Charles's isolation. Caleb is, of course, helped immeasurably in this by the presence of Abra, whom Steinbeck described as "the strong female principle of good as opposed to Cathy. Her strength will not be soft. Abra is a fighter and an effective human being. She will take active part in the battle" (*JN*, p. 146). But before she can do this, Caleb must also achieve his own psychological order in relation to the novel's pivotal figure—Cathy.

Caleb's struggle to achieve psychological balance occurs in two phases: the first in his relation to Aron and Adam, the second in relation to his mother, Cathy, and his biological father, Charles. The first phase seems a near repetition of Charles's uncontrollable anger, as the boys grow up in a devastated and disordered Eden in which "laid-out vegetable gardens rioted with weeds" (p. 252). When Caleb receives his first knowledge of Cathy, he wields it insinuatingly like thrusts of a weapon to hurt Aron, but always his cruelty is followed by remorse: "Cal came close to him and hugged him and kissed him on the cheek. 'I won't do it any more,' he said" (p. 339). Again, when Caleb discovers himself with a power to cause confusion and helplessness—the same power that Cathy so malevolently uses—Aron says to him: "I'd like to know *why* you do it. You're always at something. I just wonder why you do it. I wonder what's it good for" (pp. 374–75). Flayed by Aron's simple bewilderment, Cal intuitively feels sullied, and he loathes it: "A pain pierced Cal's heart. His planning suddenly seemed mean and dirty to him. He knew that his brother had found him out. And he felt a longing for Aron to love him. He felt lost and hungry and he didn't know what to do" (p. 375).

In discovering what to do, Caleb is granted the benefactor that Charles never had, the patient servant, Lee. Lee teaches him that the first step toward controlling evil is to confront it and control it within oneself. This lesson evokes Caleb's desperate prayer:

"Dear Lord," he said, "let me be like Aron. Don't make me mean. I don't want to be. If you will let everybody like me, why, I'll give you anything in the world, and if I haven't got it, why, I'll go for to get it. I don't want to be mean. I don't want to be lonely. For Jesus' sake, Amen." Slow warm tears were running down his cheeks. His muscles were tight and he fought against making any crying sound or sniffle. [P. 379]

To the psychologist and to the theologian, no doubt the childish bargaining in the prayer renders it insufficient. And for Steinbeck also this plea is insufficient; one must also know oneself by openly and honestly confronting the truth. This belief, which Steinbeck held throughout his career, at once forms both the thematic foundation and also the psychological foundation of the novel. Steinbeck may well have been articulating his own artistic belief when Samuel says to Tom: "Thank you for wanting to honor me with the truth, my son. It's not clever but it's more permanent" (p. 291). Steinbeck's view of the task of the artist is, above all, to honor the reader with the truth.

This belief in seeing the true thing as it is, and seeing it whole in its life environment also undergirds Lee's *timshel* doctrine, for there is no "thou mayest" unless the truth is first confronted. Guided by that premise, Samuel dares to tell Adam the truth about Cathy; and also by that premise, stumbled on in his own way, Caleb dares to confront the truth about his mother. Only at that point can he begin to dominate and order his own psychological nature.

While discussing Cathy with Caleb, Lee observes:

"She is a mystery. It seems to me that she is not like other people. There is something she lacks. Kindness maybe, or conscience. You can only understand people if you feel them in yourself. And I can't feel her. The moment I think about her my feeling goes into darkness. I don't know what she wanted or what she was after. She was full of hatred, but why or toward what I don't know. It's a mystery. And her hatred wasn't healthy. It wasn't angry. It was heartless. I don't know that it is good to talk to you like this." [P. 448]

In response Caleb murmurs, "I hate her because I know why she went away. I know—because I've got her in me" (p. 449). But Caleb's claim thoroughly controverts Lee's *timshel* doctrine: each person is his own person; only the free, independent individual is also free to exercise choice. This, finally, Caleb also realizes when he confronts his mother:

Cal spoke happily. "I'm going," he said. "I'm going now. It's all right. What Lee said was true."
"What did Lee say?"
Cal said, "I was afraid I had you in me."
"You have," said Kate.
"No, I haven't. I'm my own. I don't have to be you." [P. 466]

Having confronted the truth about Cathy, and thereby also having discovered the truth about himself, Caleb tries to order the devastated Eden about him. He speculates in the bean crop, is successful, and gives his father the offering that Adam so brutally rejects. For a time hatred descends in a blind rage; Caleb's world narrows: "His hand went to a pencil and he drew tight little spirals one after another on his blotting pad. When Lee came in an hour later there were hundreds of spirals, and they had become smaller and smaller" (p. 544). The symbolic parallel to Cathy's inward devolution is clear. In his lust to hurt, Caleb takes Aron to the source of hurt, his whore-mother Kate.

The violence remains in Caleb, as it always will and as it always did with Charles, standing side by side with bitter remorse. There is no purgation for that violence, but one may learn, as Horace Quinn learned to establish social equilibrium, to hold good and evil in social balance, to confront the truth of evil's presence and control it by choices. Caleb burns the $15,000 as testimony to his freedom to choose, a sacrifice that frees the power of his psychological control. This is not a desperate act but a controlled and freely chosen one granting him psychological serenity. In a sense, he has grown up. Abra points out to him that "when you're a child you're the center of everything. Everything happens for you. Other people? They're only ghosts furnished for you to talk to. But when you grow up you take your place and you're your own size and shape. Things go out of you to others and come in from other people. It's worse, but it's much better too" (p. 577). The passage contrasts the childlike self-appeasement of Cathy's sensual appetite to Caleb's newly won adulthood. The truth of her words is confirmed this time by the accepted offering, which is nothing less than Caleb's confession to his dying father: "'I did it,' Cal cried. 'I'm responsible for Aron's death and your sickness. I took him to Kate's. I showed him his mother. That's why he went away. I don't want to do bad things—but I do them'" (p. 595). Only the truth can set him free, and this truth, this recognition of his own capacity for evil, his confrontation with it, and his willingness to master it by free choices, does set Caleb free.

Lee: Philosophical Order

While Horace Quinn deals with the evil represented by Cathy socially, attempting an equilibrium that recognizes the necessary tension between good and evil, Charles deals with it by a psychological distancing, and Caleb deals with it by confronting the truth and thereby ordering the internal battle of good and evil, Lee deals with it philosophically. This is not to say that Lee's world is abstracted from and devoid of the presence of evil, for his personal story is a cloak of anguish, frayed and tattered. Moreover, it is the world of dreams of his own kind of Eden that he envisions in the bookstore, a dream world he eventually forsakes. But Lee, as Caleb strives to do and as Samuel Hamilton intuitively does, is determined to face life truthfully.

In developing his doctrine of *timshel*,[27] Lee relates the scarcely believable story of the three old men constructing the Hebrew verb form since, as Lee tells Adam and Samuel, the story of Cain and Abel "is the symbol story of the human soul." The fruit of their years of study is to construe the verb as "thou mayest," a construction that bears profound significance for Lee since "that says the way is open. That throws it right back on a man" (p. 303). This is the way Lee would have it, since for him man is the measure of all things. The first task of man is to confront the truth, and his second task is to make his own deliberate choices in relation to it. Lee's confidence and order rest finally on human will.

Lester Jay Marks settles on Lee as a kind of idealization of Steinbeck's non-teleological thinker: "Co-existent with their roles as Steinbeck's heroes, Lee and Samuel see men and events from a non-teleological point of view. Lee, in fact, drops his pidgin and admits Samuel into his confidence because he recognizes that Samuel, like him, cannot tolerate illusion and insists upon seeing things as they are."[28]

On that basis Marks finds the entire novel an exploration into non-teleological thinking:

> *East of Eden* is also the fictional illustration of what Steinbeck meant when, in *Sea of Cortez*, he declared that only by non-teleological methods could man ever really progress. Both Samuel and Lee realize, for example, that intelligent action can be taken by men only after they dispel their illusions. Hence, Lee insists that Caleb face the fact of his guilt in order that he might contend with it."[29]

The germ of "thou mayest" does exist in non-teleological thinking, for such thinking emphasizes the necessity to confront the total reality of life and to make personal choices in the context of that reality. Non-teleological thinking, however, as discussed in the first chapter of this book, is an ethically flawed and truncated philosophy. It has in it, in fact, the possibility of choice by a Cathy Ames and makes little distinction between her choice and, for example, that of Caleb. The *timshel* doctrine is rooted more deeply in an ethical "ought" than Marks admits. In *East of Eden* the premise is more nearly this: one may choose to do or not to do evil, but evil is a very real thing, and one "ought" not to choose it. Steinbeck's ethically mature theory of choice here seems more closely related to Milton's doctrine of good and evil than to non-teleological thinking.

The subject of free will is explored by Milton particularly in books 3 and 5 of *Paradise Lost*, the first a discourse between God and the Son and the second between Raphael and Adam. This order in itself sets a pattern: knowledge of free will flows from knowledge of God, not from oneself, as in the rebellious choice of Satan or of Cathy Ames. In *Paradise Lost*, Satan does not so much choose as act on an obsession fomented by "sensual appetite"; and acting in such a way, Milton demonstrates, he carries within himself the germ of his own destruction.

In the first relevant passage on free will in *Paradise Lost*, God foresees the expense of granting human freedom—that man can choose not to obey him:

"Not free, what proof could they have giv'n sincere
Of true allegiance, constant faith or love,
Where only what they needs must do, appeared,
Not what they would? What praise could they receive?
What pleasure I from such obedience paid,
When will and reason (reason also is choice)
Useless and vain, of freedom both despoiled,
Made passive both, had served necessity,
Not me. They therefore as to right belonged,
So were created, nor can justly accuse
Their maker, or their making, or their fate,
As if predestination overruled
Their will . . . ."

[3.104–11]

Only free choice, guided by right reason as opposed to
"sensual appetite," makes praise and obedience worthy.
The Son responds to the Father's foreknowledge by insisting that this free will in man will continue to have value,
since the Son will give to man as a guide to right choices

"My umpire Conscience, whom if they will hear,
Light after light well used they shall attain,
And to the end persisting, safe arrive."

[3.195–97]

And, further, he will give himself as the propitiation for
wrong choices.

On the basis of this divine discourse the angel Raphael
discusses free will with Adam in book 5. Adam inquires:

"What meant that caution joined, *If ye be found
Obedient?* Can we want obedience then
To him, or possibly his love desert
Who formed us from the dust, and placed us here . . . ?"

[5.513–16]

To which Raphael responds:

"God made thee perfect, not immutable;
And good he made thee, but to persevere

> He left it in thy power, ordained thy will
> By nature free, not overruled by fate
> Inextricable, or strict necessity.
> Our voluntary service he requires,
> Not our necessitated. . . .
>
> [5.524–30]

The point of free will here is that man is free to do wrong but is also free to do good, free to be obedient. By so doing, he may, as Lee says, "rule over sin."

Milton was, of course, influenced by Augustine's *City of God*, particularly book 14, chapters 11–28, in his view of the fall of man, and he was strongly guided by Aristotle's *Nicomachean Ethics* in his view of free will. While Aristotle may seem to move us further from the world of *East of Eden* for a moment, he does help us understand this crucial doctrine of Lee and its role in the novel. In book 3, section 2, chapters 1–17 of the *Nicomachean Ethics*, Aristotle discusses virtue as a state of character concerned with choice. For Lee, too, virtue derives from the choices one makes. Aristotle admires choice because it is a voluntary act, although he cautions that not all voluntary acts are choice (we might include Cathy's actions). Choice is not constituted of desire—irrational animals desire but do not exercise choice, and desire can run counter to choice (which is precisely the tension Caleb feels: the good that he would do he does not; what he would not do he does). Nor is choice passion, wish, or opinion. Rather, for Aristotle, choice is an act of voluntary will preceded by deliberation and involving reasoning through alternatives and relative consequences. This is the free will that Milton celebrated and Lee counsels, and it stands over against "sensual appetite." It is standing for something rather than being consumed by something.

The influence of Milton on Steinbeck may be arguable, but the distinction made here is germane to the novel. Opposed to the consuming and self-destructive passion of a Cathy, Lee counsels intelligent, deliberate choice that ultimately confirms the individual who chooses.

Lee resides in the novel as an even center to the emotions reeling about him. He has robed his life in equanimity, preferring to see the large patterns of life in a balance of choices rather than to be overridden by the exigencies of the moment. Thus, while recounting the horror of his own birth to Adam ("My father clawed me out of the tattered meat of my mother with his fingernails"), Lee concludes that even out of such horror beauty may arise: "Before you hate those men you must know this. My father always told it at the last: No child ever had such care as I. The whole camp became my mother. It is a beauty—a dreadful kind of beauty" (p. 360). But neither is Lee's life as unemotional as he would sometimes pretend. Lee too has his offering, his carved wooden box, and this offering is received by Abra as testimony to a loving-kindness that somehow endures evil and finally trimphs over it.

Samuel Hamilton: Spiritual Order

To Cathy's symbolic heart of darkness we see approaches of social equilibrium represented by Horace Quinn, of psychological equilibrium represented by Charles and Caleb, and of philosophical equilibrium represented by Lee. Each of these recognizes Cathy for what she is, recognizes her diabolical presence to a certain extent in his own life as well as in the lives of all other human beings, and is able to order his life in relation to that recognition. Samuel Hamilton, however, seems to represent a life that lies in direct opposition to Cathy. While her world devolves inward in a hideous cyclone, Samuel's life always radiates outward. If he has a fault—and Samuel himself would list many—it is that he thinks too seldom of himself. Yet he is thoroughly human and not to be confused with Aron's inhuman goodness: "Aron had reached a point of passionate purity that made everyone else foul" (p. 451). Because he has steeped himself in humanity, Samuel ranks as one of Steinbeck's most eminent heroes. Although his narrative presence in *East of Eden* is relatively brief, that presence hovers like a

benedictory spirit over all the action. He shows a way a
person might go, and be the better for having gone that
way. He is, as Lee says, a man who "loved a celebration of
the human soul" (p. 359).

In chapter 1 the narrative overvoice speaks of rain as a
metaphor for human life. It was Samuel Hamilton's misfor-
tune to settle on a large, sprawling stretch of land virtually
untouched by rain. But in a positive reversal of the mis-
guided Joseph Wayne in *To a God Unknown*, Samuel Hamilton is the rain. Not only does his household literally burst
with the fruition of his loins, but he figuratively brings life
to others: "Samuel had no equal for soothing hysteria and
bringing quiet to a frightened child. It was the sweetness of
his tongue and the tenderness of his soul. And just as there
was a cleanness about his body, so there was a cleanness in
his thinking" (p. 11). It is no accident that Samuel, as life
bringer, delivers Cathy's twins. He brings them into the
world, and he designates their place in the world by forcing
Adam to name them. He effectively brings them to life.
When Steinbeck describes the impoverished immigrant
settlers of the Salinas Valley, he is also describing Samuel:

They had a tool or a weapon that is also nearly gone, or perhaps it
is only dormant for a while. It is argued that because they believed thoroughly in a just, moral God they could put their faith
there and let the smaller securities take care of themselves. But I
think that because they trusted themselves and respected themselves as individuals, because they knew beyond doubt that they
were valuable and potentially moral units—because of this they
could give God their own courage and dignity and then receive it
back. [P. 12]

Samuel Hamilton is one man remaining, at least, who trusts
himself, who is a "strong sure man," who brings to others
something that is beyond society, psychology, or philosophy, but is rooted in a life-bringing spirit.

The first time Adam meets him, Samuel is described as a
"patriarch," but perhaps it would be more accurate to call
him a prophet. As a lover of light and goodness and natural

urges, he divides the valley into the high, arid, sun-washed
hills, and the verdant lushness below. But Samuel feels a
darkness descending upon that valley as he says:

"There's one thing I don't understand. There's a blackness on
this valley. I don't know what it is, but I can feel it. Sometimes on
a white blinding day I can feel it cutting off the sun and squeezing
the light out of it like a sponge. . . . There's a black violence on
this valley. I don't know—I don't know. It's as though some old
ghost haunted it out of the dead ocean below and troubled the air
with unhappiness. It's as secret as hidden sorrow." [P. 146]

The feeling is made specific and concrete when he first
meets Cathy: as if they were antipodes of each other, each
intuits the spiritual chasm between them. While in Cathy
this intuition stirs a kind of predatory withdrawal, in Samuel it evokes a profound sadness.

Samuel functions thematically in the novel as a life bringer,
an antithesis to Cathy, and one who immediately intuits her
diabolical otherness. Because of the strong spiritual nature
of Samuel, there is a temptation, as there was with Doc
of the Cannery Row trilogy, to apotheosize him. Joseph
Wayne made that mistake about himself; Samuel clearly
does not, and it is not fitting in his case. Samuel is human—
subject to fear when he enter's Cathy's den to deliver her
babies; subject to emotions when he tells her bluntly, "I
don't like you"; subject to pain when he suffers the sting of
her evil; subject to hard anger when he threatens Adam at
the naming of the twins. He knows himself to be only human: "When the Lord God did not call my name, I might
have called His name—but did not. There you have the
difference between greatness and mediocrity. It's not an uncommon disease. But it's nice for a mediocre man to know
that greatness must be the loneliest state in the world"
(p. 264). Yet somehow in his very humanity, full and over-
flowing, he represents a presence that gives guidance and
direction. He calls others to be human, as when he charges
Adam to reconstruct his dream of a garden east of Eden:
"'Don't think it will ever die,' he cried. 'Don't expect it. Are

you better than other men? I tell you it won't ever die until you do'" (p. 272).

Called not to be superhuman but to be fully human, led to lead others to a fuller understanding of their humanity, keenly aware of spiritual presence in such leading, Samuel bears strong spiritual kinship with Milton's fallen man making the best of it in a fallen world. Like Milton's Adam, Samuel defeats death by grace:

> "Adam, Heav'n's high behest no preface needs:
> Sufficient that thy prayers are heard, and Death,
> Then due by sentence when thou didst transgress,
> Defeated of his seizure many days
> Giv'n thee of grace, wherein thou may'st repent,
> And one bad act with many deeds well done
> May'st cover. . . ."
>
> [11.251–57]

Moreover, Samuel fulfills Michael's injunction:

> "Nor love thy life, nor hate; but what thou liv'st
> Live well, how long or short permit to Heav'n. . . ."
>
> [11.553–54]

As he stands on the fallen side of paradise, Adam realizes in words that may well have been spoken also by Samuel:

> " . . . with good
> Still overcoming evil, and by small
> Accomplishing great things, by things deemed weak
> Subverting worldly strong, and worldly wise
> By simply meek; that suffering for truth's sake
> Is fortitude to highest victory. . . ."
>
> [12.565–70]

In the first portrait the reader sees of Samuel, he is pictured as the gray-bearded patriarch, full of humor, yet a leader of the people; in the final portrait he is imaged as the prophet. Lee sees "old Samuel against the sky, his white hair shining with starlight," while Doxology stumbles over the ridge of a hill. It is an overt but apt image and thoroughly consistent with Steinbeck's design for the character. If Cathy is the measure of man's capacity for evil, Samuel is the measure of man's spirit to endure and to work a good work. If Steinbeck saw a bit of Cathy in all human beings, it is clear that he also sees the possibility of Samuel in all humans. While writing the final scenes of Samuel's life, Steinbeck noted this in his journal:

I want Samuel to go out with wonder and interest. This man must not be defeated even though he may feel defeat all around him. It is the fashion now in writing to have every man defeated and destroyed. And I do not believe all men are destroyed. I can name a dozen who were not and they are the ones the world lives by. It is true of the spirit as it is with battles—the defeated are forgotten, only the winners come themselves into the race. And Samuel I am going to try to make into one of those pillars of fire by whom little and frightened men are guided through the darkness. [*JN*, p. 115]

That pillar of fire never entirely dies out in the novel; its flame burns in the people whose lives Samuel has touched. But it is also a larger flame that Steinbeck envisioned rising above the desolation of the modern world, the hope of man's spiritual aspiration and rejuvenation through the leadership of the one individual who is fully human and at work among humankind.

In *Little Gidding*, T. S. Eliot distinguished between the flame of the fire of lust that burns in the modern wasteland and the fire of the spirit that purifies the age. Like Steinbeck, Eliot recognized that "Sin is Behovely," inescapable and even, perhaps, necessary insofar as we define our spiritual place in relation to it. As Eliot wrote, echoing the words of Dame Julian of Norwich,

> All shall be well, and
> All manner of thing shall be well,[30]

so too Steinbeck believed that people can order their lives in such a way that the necessary sin is also ordered and held in dominion. Still, people have a choice. Lee argues that "Thou mayest" rule over sin. Eliot too emphasized the choice:

> The only hope, or else despair
> Lies in the choice of pyre or pyre—
> To be redeemed from fire by fire.

To choose the fire of the spirit over the fire of lust is also to redeem the wasteland that lies east of Eden. At the heart of the choice as its motivation, says Eliot, lies the familiar yet seldom known name: Love. Such also is the testimony of Samuel Hamilton. Human beings can ascend above the destructive fire of lust that rages in a Cathy and burns in the heart of every person to a love that is a spiritual force to transform the wasteland. Cathy has debased all love—the outward-reaching spirit—to lust—the inward whirlpool of sensual appetite. Over against Cathy stands the spirit of Samuel, reaching out, believing earnestly that despite the presence of sin in our fallen world east of Eden all shall be well, and all manner of things shall be well.

The heart of *East of Eden,* and it is a black and perverse heart, is Cathy Ames. She represents a dark force unleashed in the world, a dark principle in relation to which other characters must order their lives. There are many small stories—that of Olive Hamilton; that of Tom and Dessie, which Steinbeck described as a "dreadful and beautiful story"; those of Aron Trask, Will Hamilton, Joe Valery, Ethel, Abra Bacon. But none of these, finally, are separable from Cathy, and each attains thematic clarity when understood in relation to her. She is the pivot for Steinbeck's moral vision; the actions of the characters in relation to her represent his answers to her and the articulation of his moral vision.

9

Voice from Heaven:
The Winter of Our Discontent

FROM THE MID-FIFTIES until his death in 1968, Steinbeck worked chiefly on his research into and translation of *Morte D'Arthur*. The task varied, from periods of solid work to long stretches when family and social concerns usurped his attention. He approached the work with the avidity of a scholar and with the undisguised pleasure of the young boy he had been upon first reading Malory:

> I can tell you one thing I have finally faced though—the Arthurian cycle and indeed practically all lasting and deepseated folklore is a mixture of profundity and childish nonsense. If you keep the profundity and throw out the nonsense, some essence is lost. These are dream stories, fixed and universal dreams, and they have the inconsistency of dreams. Very well, says I—if they are dreams, I will put in some of my own, and I did. [*LL*, p. 640]

For nearly a decade his letters burst with arcane tidbits of information on word lore, medieval history, or small discoveries he made abroad, the latter often only tangentially related to Arthur.

BACKGROUND TO THE WRITING

The Winter of Our Discontent popped out of his labors almost accidentally. Perhaps Steinbeck's physical collapse on the Sunday after Thanksgiving, 1959, forced a hiatus in his preoccupation with Arthur into which Hawley crept like a twentieth-century Mordred. The illness receded, and a wave of artistic anxiety washed up. In March, 1960, Steinbeck hinted at that anxiety to Elizabeth Otis:

248

I remember once, long ago, I wrote you ten titles for unwritten stories and asked which one I should write, and you replied— "Write all of them." And that was correct. What's to stop me except the traffic officers of criticism and I don't mean only the external ones. I should have written everything—absolutely everything. And it's back to that I must go. What have I to lose except sadness, and anger and frustration. [*LL*, p. 662]

By the end of the month he announced to James S. Pope that he was "in the middle of a book"—*The Winter of Our Discontent*. If he was in the middle of it then, the actual writing of the book broke nearly all of Steinbeck's records for speed, for it was nearly done by early May. In a letter of May 25 he reported:

My new book is known to no one except Elaine. I have told only the title, a great one, I think. The Winter of Our Discontent. It's a strange book that is taking its own pace—part Kafka and part Booth Tarkington with a soup-song of me. It's writing along and I am following mostly amazed. I hope to finish it this summer. [*LL*, p. 666]

But by the date of this letter he was already planning his trip across America with Charley. It was almost as if *The Winter of Our Discontent*, like a dream, had come and gone in a few nights.

Certain signs always accompanied Steinbeck's sense of difficulty in writing ficlton, the chief of which was the need to explain or justify the work to his agent or editor. Unlike his early work, which was written with an exuberant devil-may-care attitude, his post-thirties fiction shows this hesitation more frequently. In *Burning Bright* he made the rare move of actually defending the work to the reader in the prefatory note

With *Winter*, Steinbeck made the same kind of overture to Covici:

This is an egocentric letter but I thought you might like to know these things. You say it isn't a novel. Maybe you're right. It's not a novel like any I have seen or read or heard of, but as far as I know a novel is a long piece of fiction having form direction and rhythm as well as intent. At worst it should amuse, at half-staff move to emotion and at best illuminate. And I can't know whether this will do any of those things but its intention is the third. [*LL*, pp. 676–77]

Since uncertainty and defensiveness about his work were rare for Steinbeck, they signal his own difficulties with the work at hand.

By the later 1950s, furthermore, the demands on Steinbeck's time had become tremendous. His lively interest in dozens of little affairs that piqued his curiosity—whether personalities, politics, or small diversions—could easily rob hours from a day. For almost a year while he was writing *East of Eden,* he walled himself off from the world; it was not so easy with *Winter,* and his effort at the sustained concentration and patterned writing habits so essential to his work now seemed haphazard at best. Jackson Benson describes Steinbeck's daily routine at this time and his effort to carve out time for work on the novel:

His habit in Sag Harbor . . . was to get up in the morning, have coffee, drive into the village with Charley, have breakfast and buy the papers, and then come back home and read them before going to work. Now, having moved to the country house in mid-April, he got up at six, listened to fifteen minutes of news on the radio while he drank his coffee, filled a Thermos, and went out to Joyous Garde [his writing quarters] and began work very early. Furthermore, the long period of warmup—the letters, the journal, or the articles—was largely eliminated. Elaine felt that he was pushing himself to write, that the novel was forced out of a need to prove himself to himself.[1]

Elaine Steinbeck's observation here is telling; few good novels get written out of a need to prove anything.

From his approach to the composition of the novel it is clear that Steinbeck had no conception of writing another "big" book to rank alongside *The Grapes of Wrath* and *East of Eden.* When he said that *East of Eden* was his big book, the one he had prepared all his life to write, Steinbeck was nothing less than honest. With that book he had, in a sense, accomplished his lifework and achieved his artistic aims. The motivations and artistic urgings that spawned *Winter* derive from quite another source, a response to what Steinbeck perceived as a peculiar moral darkening of the age. He wanted to reveal that and react to it. While nearly all his prior work had recreated personal experience in story, *Winter* probes a contemporary moral ailment and attempts a remedy. Here Steinbeck functions less as storyteller and more as philosopher. He is less the intercessory priest of fiction, mediating audience and truth by story, and more the schooled pastor, arguing the way one should not go.

Similarly, all of Steinbeck's earlier work is western American in orientation and setting, whereas *Winter* focuses closely on a small eastern town, with his own Sag Harbor as prototype. In fact, one of his fears in writing the book was that he would make of Sag Harbor another Cannery Row: "He was afraid people might come to seek him out there (apparently forgetting that he had already described where he lived in several magazine pieces), and he was worried about inadvertently creating a monster, turning the village into another Cannery Row."[2] The fear went unfulfilled, but its existence suggests that Steinbeck had removed himself from the sources that had always nurtured his art.

Winter differs in several other ways from his earlier work, notably in artistic design and technique. While his predominant mode of narrative had nearly always been objective, with some use of the omniscient point of view in the intercalary overvoice, in *Winter* there are several shifts in point of view. The primary mode is third-person objective, but this varies, nearly at random, with both a first-person point of view (in which the "I" tells his own story) and a first-person narrative point of view (in which the "I" tells the story of others). If there is a systematic narrative pattern, it seems adapted from stage directions, and the novel poses a difficulty in distinguishing who is thinking what and when.

More immediately noticeable as a change in artistic tech-

nique, however, is the startling difference in dialogue. In
no other novel had Steinbeck relied so extensively on dialogue to form character and develop plot. He seems to be
writing consciously in the modern trend toward quicker action punctuated by dialogue and a dramatic sense of character, a trend patterned more on television than on the stage.
While Steinbeck had a fine-tuned ear for both colloquial-
ism and the rhythm of human speech, revealed at its best
in *The Grapes of Wrath* and the Cannery Row trilogy, he is
less successful in imitating the dialogue of the faster-paced,
rather flippant characters of the eastern community. These
were never really the characters Steinbeck knew well, the
kinds of characters an artist hears whispering at the back of
his mind when he sits down to work. They always seem
to be strangers to Steinbeck, and while he imitates their
slightly foreign speech fairly well, it always bears the mark
of the stranger—the one who has to hold up a tape recorder to get it right.

Two specific problems emerge as a result of this heavy
emphasis on a dialogue with which Steinbeck was neither
wholly at ease nor wholly familiar. First, too often the characters merely pose; they make stage talk to fill lapses in action. They seem to be under the floodlights without a well-
rehearsed script, wondering, "Now, what shall we say to fill
in two blank pages and make people listen?" Thus we get
scenes in which Hawley talks to his vegetable cans or tries
hard to make witty remarks that might lift a listener's eye-
brow. The second problem arises from the idiosyncratic
language Steinbeck uses to distinguish his characters as
personalities. Strange little phrases come from the actors'
tongues, phrases that emanate from Steinbeck's mind and
not from any dramatic necessity of scene or conflict. Many
of these are the unusual little endearments that also flawed
Burning Bright: "Good stuff, fern tip"; "Okay, bugflower";
"Yes dearling"; "I won't, my fair, my lovely"; "I bring you
tidings of great joy, my flying squirrel"; "I think I'll burn
him up, heaven wife"; "They're the first—the very first, my
creamy fowl"; "Pigeonflake, I'm going to be a little late."

These phrases are Pollyanna in a way Steinbeck, with the exception of *Burning Bright*, had never been before, ironically on the lips of characters protrayed as fast-paced, contemporary realists. The effect of such pet names and endearments is maudlin. Elaine Steinbeck pointed out that in his personal life her husband was quite sparing of traditional endearments such as "honey," or "sweetheart" but that these curiously forced endearments appeared in his writings:

John was very sparing in his use of such words. When he said—very often to a child—"Dear, I want you to do such and such," it absolutely, always, broke my heart. "Dear" shouldn't be that passionate. He would say it to Gadg [Elia Kazan] in a moment of excitement or of argument, and he'd say, "Now look, dear, I think you are terribly wrong about that" or something like that. And he said it to me, and it always touched me tremendously. But on the other hand, he used all kinds of funny endearments, constantly, and he thought that was his way of showing affection, light affection. So he used it in his books, and it is cloying to most people.[3]

Other examples of idiosyncratic language in the novel range from some affected colloquialisms ("You seem to have got over your mullygrubs") to a kind of precious formality ("'I wish Margie would turn the cards,' said Mary. 'I would dearly love that'"). The examples could be multiplied, but suffice it to say that in a work relying so heavily and dramatically on dialogue this repeated artificiality of language seriously damages its effectiveness.

The artificiality of language poses the largest artistic problem in the novel simply because the book relies so heavily on dialogue, but other artistic flaws also mar the work. It is neither necessary nor pleasant to belabor such flaws, but the weakness in description and imagery should be mentioned, largely because it departs so far from Steinbeck's norm of excellence in these techniques. The power of his artistry always inhered in the hard, quick, almost impressionistic image that could seize whole and entire a per-

sonality, condition, or event. When Steinbeck writes here
of Margie that "her hands were like living things as they
shuffled and cut and shuffled and cut again" one wants to
exclaim, "Well, what else are hands like than living things?"
One does not find an artistic faux pas like this in the early
work. Again, far too many images are simply trite: "She was
laughing her lovely trill, something that raises goose bumps
of pleasure on my soul" (p. 146), or "My Mary was just
beautiful, just beautiful and shining. A light from inside her
oozed out of her pores."

Why then did Steinbeck write it? What did he have to
say? If, as Benson says, "he was so filled with the excitement of ideas, their implications and connections, and so
filled with the emotions that had generated the ideas, he
would virtually explode,"[4] what were those ideas?

They can be summarized by glancing through Steinbeck's
letters of the years preceding *Winter* and discerning a
thread woven through all of them: a deep sense of loss—of
moral fiber, of battling (Like Kino and Juana?) for a way of
life, even of a loss of moral fortitude. Shortly after Christmas, 1959, while he was recovering from his apparent coronary attack at Sag Harbor, Steinbeck wrote Elizabeth Otis:

> True things gradually disappeared and shiny easy things took
> their place. I brought the writing outside, like a cook flipping hot
> cakes in a window. And it should never have come outside. The
> fact that I had encouragement is no excuse. That same cook in a
> window can draw a crowd too but he is still making hotcakes. I
> tell you this because if I am able to go back, the first efforts will
> be as painful as those of a child learning to balance one block on
> top of another. I'll have to learn all over again about true things.
> [*LL*, p. 657]

The reference to "true things" certainly refers here to
Steinbeck's artistic belief in writing from the true-life event,
but the same term appears more often in the letters and
then in reference to a personal sense of loss and growing
incapacity. By the time he wrote *Travels with Charley* the
concern had become a preoccupation. Steinbeck openly
confessed in the book:

Who doesn't like to be a center for concern? A kind of second childhood falls on so many men. They trade their violence for the promise of a small increase of life span. In effect, the head of the house becomes the youngest child. And I have searched myself for this possibility with a kind of horror. For I have always lived violently, drunk hugely, eaten too much or not at all, slept around the clock or missed nights of sleeping, worked too hard and too long in glory, or slobbed for a time in utter laziness. . . . My wife married a man; I saw no reason why she should inherit a baby. . . . And in my own life I am not willing to trade quality for quantity. If this projected journey should prove too much then it was time to go anyway. I see too many men delay their exits with a sickly, slow reluctance to leave the stage. It's bad theater as well as bad living. [*TWC*, pp. 19–20]

While a concern for artistic and physical manhood pervades Steinbeck's writing during the period he worked on *Winter*, an equally strong concern for what we might call "moral manhood" also developed. For Steinbeck, moral manhood meant the strength to stand by convictions and to act according to them. His frustration with what he perceived as a moral torpor and spiritual flabbiness in Americans appears often in his letters of the late fifties and early sixties, and seems fomented by two separate experiences. First, the long labor over Malory always held before him the mystique of knightly actions to right the wrongs by direct and potent deeds. The glory of Camelot as a shimmering beacon of moral rectitude in a world blasted and darkened by moral perfidy grew in his mind as an analogy to America. At times it seemed as though he wished Arthur would ride the halls of Washington, D.C., and congressmen come forth on white chargers. Reflecting on Malory, Steinbeck wrote:

But the writer of the Morte did not know what had happened, what was happening, not what was going to happen. He was caught as we are now. In forlornness. . . . And out of this devilish welter of change—so like the one today—he tried to create a world of order, a world of virtue governed by forces familiar to him. [*LL*, p. 576]

Although he recognized the tragedy of Arthur, Steinbeck was keenly aware of Arthur's resilient nobility, and this he contrasted also to the present age:

The values have got crossed up. Courtesy is confused with weakness and emotion with sentimentality. We want to be tough guys and forget that the toughest guys were always the wholest guys. Achilles wept like a baby over Patroclus and Hector's guts turned to water with fear. But cleverness has taken the place of feeling, and cleverness is nearly always an evasion. [LL, p. 631]

He also recognized that heroism in the present age, unless offered as a sop to feelings in romantic novels, had become simply anachronistic:

The hero is almost bad form unless he is in a western. Tragedy— true tragedy—is laughable unless it happens in a flat in Brooklyn. Kings, Gods and Heroes—Maybe their day is over, but I can't believe it. Maybe because I don't want to believe it. In this country [England] I am surrounded by the works of heroes right back to man's first entrance. And if all of this is gone, I've missed the boat somewhere. And that could easily be. [LL, p. 635]

Finally, the link between *Morte D'Arthur* and *Winter* is made clear in a letter to Joseph Bryan of September 28, 1959:

This has been a good time—maybe the best we have ever had— not wasted at all. But my subject gets huger and more difficult all the time. It isn't fairy stories. It has to do with morals. Arthur must awaken not by any means only to repel the enemy from without, but particularly the enemy inside. Immorality is what is destroying us, public immorality. The failure of man toward men, the selfishness that puts making a buck more important than the common weal.

Now, next to our own time the 15th century was the most immoral time we know. Authority was gone. The church split, the monarchy without authority and manorial order disappearing. It is my theory that Malory was deploring this by bringing back Arthur and a time when such things were not so. A man must write about his *own* time no matter what symbols he uses. And I

have not found my symbols nor my form. And there's the rub.
[*LL*, pp. 649–50]

In this, perhaps one of the most specific letters Steinbeck
ever wrote about the motivation and meaning of his work—
although *Winter* was not even conceptualized at that time—
Steinbeck sees himself as a twentieth-century Malory crafting new symbols to address the moral nature of his age.

Coupled with his work on the Arthurian translation and
the inevitable moral parallels he discerned between the
lost glory of Camelot and the present-day darkness was a
second impulse deriving from his extensive travel abroad.
His relentless traveling in the late fifties seemed to distance
him from America and to make objective his vision of its
people. What he saw from abroad he did not always like
or admire. This culminated in his infamous letter to Adlai
Stevenson on November 5, 1959, in which he excoriated
American greed and moral torpor in much the same voice
he used to chastise the "tigers" of civilization lurking outside Cannery Row. Distinguishing between two kinds of
Christmases, the one filled with love and sacrifice and the
other addled with greed, Steinbeck wrote:

Well, it seems to me that America now is like that second kind of
Christmas. Having too many THINGS they spend their hours
and money on the couch searching for a soul. A strange species
we are. We can stand anything God and Nature can throw at us
save only plenty. If I wanted to destroy a nation, I would give it
too much and I would have it on its knees, miserable, greedy and
sick. [*LL*, p. 652]

This is the spirit that lies behind *Winter*, that in fact motivated the book personally and in narrative theme.

THE NOVEL: STRUCTURE AND THEME

Providing an artistic structure for that conflict, for this "excitement of ideas" as Benson called it, gave Steinbeck some
difficulties precisely because he was first of all writing
about ideas and then trying to craft a story structure that

would sustain those ideas. The primary theme of the novel focuses on moral revelation, which here parallels a kind of Jungian confrontation with one's self. The confrontation is structured between the two poles of spiritual festivity in the Easter weekend and political festivity in the Fourth of July weekend. Between these two poles lies the terrifying descent into moral self-confrontation.

Increasingly in his later years one finds Steinbeck reverting to early interests or themes as his dissatisfaction with the modern temperament grew. In and of itself this is not unusual for a writer. Personal experience always provides the best subject matter for the novelist, and in *East of Eden* it had served the author well. It served him less well when he mimicked early mannerisms—as opposed to subject matter or story—as in *Burning Bright*. In much the same vein the consensus about *The Short Reign of Pippin IV*, a work of this period which Steinbeck himself knew to be weak, is that Steinbeck was trying to recover an irretrievable past. Thomas Kiernan makes the point forcefully, almost mercilessly:

In achieving financial security, in aspiring to wide social and political personal acceptance and achieving it, in settling comfortably into the sophisticated and often artificial living environment that was New York—all things that he had formerly professed little interest in—he had betrayed his own fiery artistic principles. The original fire had been reduced to barely glowing embers. As in a self-fulfilling prophecy, the world had forced him, like the Henry Morgan of his first book, to compromise his youthful ideas in order to live comfortably in it. But he was unable to accept the fact that he had unwittingly sold out, that the world had humbled him. Instead he turned his vision of the world around. It was now possible to live in the world and still retain the ideals and hope of childhood.[6]

Aside from its interest to a psychologist, this tendency of Steinbeck's bears important significance for *The Winter of Our Discontent*, for one finds a curious series of circumstances growing out of this reversion. Thematically, as we have observed, Steinbeck wishes to recover the simpler nobility of character that he discovered in Malory. Yet in setting and tone *Winter* is his closest attempt at "modern" writing—an effort at slick, fast-paced motion relying heavily on dialogue, and a probing of a character's angst before the power of modern civilization. It is Cannery Row grown up to television and tranquilizers. Further, to write this "modern" story, he reverted in part to his earlier short story, "How Mr. Hogan Robbed a Bank," which appeared, shortly after he composed it, in *The Atlantic Monthly* of March, 1956. The specific qualities retained in *Winter* from the short story are discussed by Warren French in his essay "Steinbeck's Winter's Tale," but the sum of the borrowing, according to French, is that "a delightful comic fantasy has been turned into a contrived melodrama."[7]

The framing mechanism for the theme and events of the plot is fairly overt. Hawley, the swaggering blasphemer who delivers his lurid Good Friday monologue to the canned peaches, is about to undergo his own trial in faith on the Easter weekend. Although two-thirds of the book focuses on the Passion Week, the events of Christ's Passion do not correspond closely to the narrative plot. Peter Lisca details some of the overt similarities:

Good Friday becomes the day of Ethan's "temptation": Pride (Baker's appeals to his ancestral heritage), the Flesh (Margie's proposition) and the World (Bigger's bribe). The last of these is offered between noon and three o'clock in the afternoon (the sixth and ninth hours after sunrise) while Ethan is in his closed, darkened store commemorating Christ's three hours on the cross.[8]

It seems, however, that Steinbeck is random in his choice of elements and how he orders them. The dissimilarities between the plot and the biblical Easter weekend are more striking and reinforce the focus on man-centered conniving rather than Christ-centered salvation:

Easter Sunday morning begins with Ethan patting his wife's "silk-covered fanny" and saying, "Kyrie eleison!" They go to church and hear "the news announced that Christ was risen indeed." That day the ironically arisen Ethan confers shrewdly with Baker, high priest of business, about his financial future and decides definitely to rob the bank, get Marullo deported, and take possession of Danny's valuable property by providing him with the means of suicide—money for alcohol. Part One ends on the Monday after Easter with Ethan furthering all his plans for gaining the world he has bought with his soul.[9]

If anything, and in keeping with Steinbeck's general perception of the moral climate of his age, the Easter weekend represents a moral center from which man has strayed. Salvation by chicanery replaces salvation by propitiation. As in T. S. Eliot's *The Waste Land,* religion has been debased to human seeking for a sign, for some immediate assurance of a way out rather than for salvation. While Eliot's Madame Sosostris shuffles her "wicked pack of cards" and does not "find The Hanged Man," Margie Young-Hunt "had formed a cross of cards on the table. Then rapidly she turned up four in a line to the left of the cross, saying 'Yourself, your house, your hopes, your future.' The last card was the man hanged upside down, le pendu, but from where I sat across the table he was right side up" (pp. 82–83). Ironically, the Hanged Man, inverted on the Tarot deck, appears to Ethan right side up. But religion itself is turned on its head in this world, in which traditional moral norms for value are replaced by commerical ones. The inversion is clear in the image used when Ethan enters Baker's Bank: "Joey dialed the mystic numbers and turned the wheel that drew the bolts. The holy of holies swung stately open and Mr. Baker took the salute of the assembled money. I stood outside the rail like a humble communicant waiting for the sacrament" (p. 195).

In another sense, however, Ethan has already begun his descent into hell. The novel is rife with Jungian imagery typifying the descent into the subconscious—and the fearful meeting with the Shadow of one's inner self.[10] "What a frightening thing is the human," reflects Ethan, "a mass of gauges and dials and registers, and we can read only a few of those and perhaps not accurately" (p. 77). His own spiritual journey becomes a voyage into that frightening thing, imaged specifically in Jungian figures of the cave: "It's as though, in the dark and desolate caves of the mind, a faceless jury had met and decided. This secret and sleepless area in me I have always thought of as a black, deep, waveless water, a spawning place from which only a few forms ever rise to the surface" (p. 86).[11] The process of digging into that cave begins on Saturday, the presumed time of Jesus' descent into hell. Time itself seems to focus in on Ethan, force him to the inward journey: "It's always some kind of time. So far I have avoided my own time" (p. 102). Ethan reflects: "I think I believe that a man is changing all the time. But there are certain moments when the change becomes noticeable. If I wanted to dig deep enough, I could probably trace the seeds of my change right back to my birth or before. Recently many little things had begun to form a pattern of larger things" (p. 87).

In the western literary tradition such a descent as Hawley's becomes a mythic, archetypal pattern of rebirth. One must go down to be reborn. In his discussion of the *regressus ad uteram*, or the death-and-rebirth archetype, Mircea Eliade remarks that there is always "the initiatory passage through a *vagina dentata*, or the dangerous descent into a cave or crevice assimilated to the mouth or uterus of Mother Earth. All these adventures are in fact initiatory ordeals, after accomplishing which the victorious hero acquires a new mode of being."[12] The instances in western literature of a character going "under earth" to emerge reborn are numerous. On a spiritual plane, the archetype suggests a dying to this world in order to regain clear insight of an absolute reality that will give new direction and patterns for growth in the temporal world. By undergoing the mythic rebirth, the individual is radically changed or reborn.

The pattern culminates in Ethan in the second pole, the Fourth of July weekend, in which Steinbeck demonstrates how far we have fallen away from traditional patriotism. In

this instance, at the narrative level, Marullo, as a threat to
the nation is plotted against—quite the opposite of the
Fourth of July celebration of a nation that welcomes the
dispossessed with open arms. Marullo has to learn a new
code; the old verities no longer work. Richard Walker, a
kind of grand inquisitor, ironically from the Department of
Justice, explains to Ethan:

Before he came over he knew the words on the bottom of the
Statue of Liberty. He'd memorized the Declaration of Indepen-
dence in dialect. The Bill of Rights was words of fire. And then he
couldn't get in. So he came anyway. A nice man helped him—
took everything he had and dropped him in the surf to wade
ashore. It was quite a while before he understood the American
way, but he learned—he learned. "A guy got to make a buck!
Look out for number one!" But he learned. He's not dumb. He
took care of number one. [P. 226]

Further, the scandal of the plagiarized patriotic essay
emerges with young Allen's utter lack of remorse, his denigration of that "patriotic jazz," and his typically contemporary and ethically relativistic rebuff, "Everybody does it."
And Ethan himself is plunged deeper into the alien country
of his own soul: "In the strange, uncharted country I had
entered, perhaps I had no choice" (p. 185).

The external world becomes more pressing, shoving
Ethan to the exigency of his inner confrontation. Jungian
imagery intensifies and enforces the pattern. At one point,
"I walked in the cavern of the elms" (p. 202), and later,
"The night closed thick and damp about me, humid air
about the consistency of chicken broth" (p. 267). And in his
inward journey Ethan begins to understand how much he
has lost:

Once long ago when I lived in a daylight world, the world
being too much with me, I would have gone to grass. Face downward and very close to the green stems, I became one with ants
and aphids and sow bugs, no longer a colossus. And in a ferocious
jungle of the grass I found the distraction that meant peace.

Now in the night I wanted Old Harbor and the Place, where an inevitable world of cycles of life and time and of tide could smooth my raggedness. [P. 267]

At last events force him to the cave he calls simply "the Place," which is described in the Jungian terms reminiscent of certain passages from *The Log from the Sea of Cortez:* "I came to the Old Harbor. . . . I think I wanted to go to the Place, but man commensal with the sea would know that the tide was at flood and the Place under dark water. Last night I saw the moon only four days grown like a thickened, curved surgeon's needle, but strong enough to pull the tide into the cave mouth of the Place" (pp. 202–203). This is the pit that Ethan enters during his dark night of the soul, his descent into hell that began during Passion Week:

My light is out. There's nothing blacker than a wick.

Inward I said, I want to go home—no not home, to the other side of home where the lights are given.

It's so much darker when a light goes out than it would have been if it had never shone. The world is full of dark derelicts. The better way—Marulli of that old Rome would have known it— there comes a time for decent, honorable retirement, not dramatic, not punishment of self or family—just good-by, a warm bath and an opened vein, a warm sea and a razor blade. [P. 281]

And this time too the sea, like a warm bath, washes over Ethan. Rather than a sense of peace, however, one recalls the frightening imagery of the ocean bottom in *Cannery Row* and thinks of a trap with no way out.

Conceptually, *Winter* represents a culmination in Steinbeck's development as a moralist, in which he asserts that the abolition of moral norms for action is ultimately an abolition of man. In this sense Steinbeck echoes Herman Melville's belief posited eighty years earlier in his poem "The House-Top: A Night Piece," from *Battle-Pieces,* in which Melville describes the draft riots of 1863 as the unleashing of irrational evil and calls the scene "the Atheist roar of riot." As dyspeptic as Melville may have been about Christianity, finding it in evidence of all kinds of foolishness, pride, smugness, and intolerance, he recognized that it was a powerful force for the just ordering of society. Steinbeck shared none of Melville's vocal disdain for Christianity; in fact, he took pains to avoid vilifying a religion in which he himself did not believe, but he did share Melville's yearning for the "forms, measured forms" that Christianity provides and that make society both orderly and worthwhile. Rowland Sherrill's assessment of Melville bears curious applicability to Steinbeck also. In *The Prophetic Melville*, Sherrill writes, with an eye to the title of his own book:

At last, then, the image has its tragic aspect—the Melville who wanted to act on behalf of his fellows, who wanted to chart for his age a renewed idea of its deepest possibilities of being, but who finally thinks that he must fail as reformed of life and find himself left only to record its dangerous trend or else to cry in the wilderness, like the prophet, with the frail hope that someone would hear. [13]

Ethan Hawley, however, does not seem the right character through which to express such views as Steinbeck holds forth in this novel, for the simple reason that from the start he evidences little inherent nobility, no point of moral or spiritual promise from which to fall and which would artistically enrich the essentially tragic tenor of the novel. From the start Hawley is insipid—cute, perhaps, at times, maybe even witty—but not possessed of the stature to make the reader really care what happens to him or be interested in his moral pathos. However significant the moral revelation in the novel, it fails to take root in character.

The Winter of Our Discontent is indeed significant for its representation of Steinbeck's moral concerns. Steinbeck had achieved international attention, and it may have been tempting to use the fiction that had merited that attention as a podium. The things Steinbeck had to say in addressing the modern moral temper, while not startling in perspicuity, were nonetheless trenchant concerns worth articulating. The moral dereliction of an age is a timeless issue for discussion. It is, furthermore, a worthy theme for an artistic undertaking. Indeed, the failure in this instance was the inability of the artistic craft to match the moral concern. More clearly than anything else (and sadly for admirers) Steinbeck demonstrated that in his call to moral reason he had forsaken reasonableness of artistry. His masterpieces, from *In Dubious Battle* through *East of Eden,* were indubitably also moral explorations, but always guided in their exploration by the sure and shining genius of his literary artistry. In no work is the moral concern more clear and the artistry more shadowed than in *The Winter of Our Discontent.*

"That They May Rest from Their Labors"

The Winter of Our Discontent was Steinbeck's own winter of the moral spirit, poised as he was on the cold edge of the 1960s. The last years of Steinbeck's life were lived in a time of harsh and jarring impressions, a discordant age in which even the good times seemed hard-edged. Jack Kerouac was on the road and off the wall. Ken Kesey probed the black heart of the insane asylum and found us all inmates. The inmates howl with laughter for there is no other way out. Norman Mailer threw a sizable talent across far too many pages, too many issues, and people bought the books because he was also a media celebrity. Some of them even read the books. Ernest Hemingway, faced with the demise of heroism, took the coward's way out. Beat poets contemplated their own excellence in the navel of self-indulgence, and coffeehouses overflowed with people who came to watch their psychological striptease.

But the old, stern warfare of the migrants and landowners of the 1930s only seemed anachronistic. In fact, the lessons Steinbeck had disclosed then were never more exigent: lessons of the family of man, of shattered dreams, of the threat of a monolithic power structure.

For the sixties, no less than the thirties, were also a litany of broken dreams and the corrosive effects of power abuse. Martin Luther King walked in the ruins of burned cities, exhorting humankind to new visions, new dreams. He was slain in Memphis, and with him the spark flickered from the dream. Robert Kennedy walked through a campus still smoldering from fire bombing. He called for peace and was answered with a bullet. The memory of students at

Kent State University, huddled in the rain, holding gutter-
ing candles over the place where their classmates were
slain, is ineradicable.

In the sixties war seemed also to rage out of all control, as
the hawklike television cameras caught and thrust war into
the violated nests of our homes. The old battling corre-
spondent John Steinbeck, whose *Once There Was a War*
forms a brief masterpiece of World War II journalism,
packed his rickety, pained body in jungle fatigues, flak
jacket, and a steel pot and jumped flights in Hueys and
C-130s around Vietnam with the First Cavalry. This was a
different kind of war, a dirty, nasty war, and Steinbeck was
one of the few newsmen in 1966 who reported on the atroc-
ities that seemed to turn up in each small village. Never
would he have been able to write about this war a suave,
distanced book like *The Moon Is Down* with its polite military gentlemen. The barrels of the miniguns spitting red
tracers like quiet, deadly rain from the C-47, the earth-
shaking loads from the B-52s, the brilliant wash of fire from
napalm: these were the reality and the agony of war in the
sixties. But in that peculiar little horror of Vietnam, where
once there was a war in which brave men and women served
and anguished and died and dishonest people fought over
the war, Steinbeck found once again a certain nobility in
humanity. This is curious because, while Steinbeck went to
that war ambivalent about its worth and aims, he returned
from it with the sad realization that even in defeat ("We
seem to be sinking deeper and deeper into the mire. . . . I
know we cannot win this war, nor any war for that matter.")[1]
something noble in man's spirit, Steinbeck was convinced,
would endure. It was a small victory of faith for Steinbeck.
It took a war to bring it home to him, and also to bring him
to some of his best writing in his last years in the dispatches
from Vietnam.

It is curious, furthermore, how he went into that war
with his own death hovering before him, as if he wanted to
look at the final darkness full in the face. Steinbeck did not
go gentle into that good night; his work raged against the

dying of the light. There was always one more project to do. He just ran out of time.

Steinbeck's dying was painful, the coronary arteries clogged and the beginnings of emphysema constricting the lungs. His condition was judged too risky for the revascularization procedure that was just emerging at the time and is now so commonplace, performed every day on men much older and in much poorer condition than Steinbeck was. His trenchant realism, so often touched with cynicism that rose to the surface in humor, brought him a measure of calm. On one visit by his doctor, Denton Cox, Steinbeck advised him to read Ecclesiastes. Which chapter and verse, Cox wondered. "The whole thing," replied Steinbeck. "It's not very long." Nor, as Ecclesiastes points out, is life. After several days of intense pain, Steinbeck died on December 20, 1968, a few hours before winter began.

Few American authors have left so rich and diverse a legacy. And that diversity, in part, has led to misunderstanding and critical slighting. While Steinbeck's great novels are still regular fare in college courses, his masterly short stories are routinely ignored in college anthologies; one or two will include "Chrysanthemums," another "Flight," and that is about it. When lecturers refer to American Nobel Prize winners, they sometimes forget to include Steinbeck's name. Why is this?

For one thing, throughout his career Steinbeck's reviewers and critics were too quick to put a face on him that they had designed. Unable to see through the face they had fabricated, they ignored the real artist. Several such masks (or faces) they fabricated are notorious. Jackson Benson has observed:

One thing that stands out to anyone who examines Steinbeck's life in detail is how much abuse he suffered at the hands of political zealots, both within the public at large and within the ranks of literary critics. He was denounced by the right because he was on the left, by the left because he was not left enough, and, on occasions, by the right and the left at the same time.[2]

Moreover, adds Benson, "In reviewing the literary criticism of Steinbeck's work, one is struck by the frequent, gratuitous nastiness expressed in much of it."[3]

The reasons for this are ambiguous and puzzling. I believe that they reside chiefly in the very fact that reviewers and critics often did not bother to understand Steinbeck. They approached him too often with preconceptions. When his work failed to fit their personal hermeneutical theories, they judged him a failure. Nowhere is this clearer, for example, than in the early conception of Steinbeck as a Marxist.[4]

That image was carefully fabricated by several reviewers during the thirties, and when Steinbeck refused to fit the image, critics on both the political right and the left excoriated him. For some, like Mary McCarthy, reviewing in the *Nation*, Steinbeck had abdicated the struggle and was a fit subject for critical scorn. That McCarthy never grasped Steinbeck's aim and artistry did not in the least deter her or similarly minded cohorts.[5] At the opposite pole conservative critics quickly wrote Steinbeck off as a thoroughgoing Marxist and were bothered only that, despite their maledictions, Steinbeck would not go away. Both camps disregarded the fact that Steinbeck never was a Marxist. Both thoroughly ignored, or perhaps never understood, his aims as an artist. Yet the contention survived and marked critical consideration of Steinbeck's work for years. In an essay about that controversy and how it shaped critical views, Jackson Benson comments:

He had been called a Marxist so repeatedly that even the Marxists began to believe it, and he began to get appeals for money from Communist and Communist-associated organizations, as well as requests that his name be used for this "liberal" cause and that. Like the hate mail, this mail in all its insistence and presumptuousness was not only irritating but somewhat frightening—it was like being adopted without one's consent.[6]

The Marxist controversy, which persisted for years, was only the eye of the critical tempest. Steinbeck never did

the expected thing and that in itself was unsettling to reviewers and some early critics. Just when he told a story of
chilling realism, he gave a strange novel-play; just when he
told stories steeped in regionalism, he gave a scientific
travelogue; just when he told a rollicking tale of the paisanos, he revisited Monterey with grim, dark humor; just
when he told a story of a wayward bus with pretense toward an allegory that never quite arrives at the terminal of
fixed meaning, he gave a story of superbly crafted symbolism. And so it went. This fact many reviewers forgot:
Steinbeck never depended on them. He never wanted to
be a popular writer—although of course he wanted admiration and appreciated acclaim. Above all he wanted the freedom to pursue the peregrinations of his remarkably diverse
mind. He was as adaptable as an eagle to a pigeonhole. He
held his artistic vision wide open to life, and his work is as
varied as the life he observed. By his own confession Steinbeck wrote first about people, and his topics, themes, characters, and works are only as diverse as human nature
itself. If one were to call Steinbeck anything—always a
dangerous activity with any author—one must admit to
little more and no less than this: Steinbeck was a realist
who was also a speculative and daring symbolist. He was a
philosopher who listened to ditch-diggers, and he was a
ditch-digger who thought philosophically. He was, moreover, an unbeliever who took belief seriously. As such, he
had perhaps the best credentials available to write about
his own stated subject—people.

While Steinbeck's work is diverse, the candid critic must
also admit that it is uneven. To judge on artistic and technical terms, as this book has tried to do, Steinbeck at times
squandered a brilliant talent, and at other times readers
have not recognized half the talent he possessed. His chief
fault was his own inability to distinguish fault from virtue;
he did what he had to do, which was write, and sometimes
he did it better than others. It is possible, however, if one
judges the canon according to artistic criteria, to observe

certain patterns of faults and certain artistic achievements in Steinbeck's work.

Above all, I believe, one recognizes Steinbeck's genius for characterization, the ability to perceive a character in life, conceive the character in a fictional environment, and surely and steadily shape that character. When one recollects Steinbeck's fiction, it is often first of all a recollection of characters: Doc blasting off into the sunset with Suzy at the wheel of the old car; Ma Joad's heavy body and farseeing eyes envisioning the fambly of man; Cathy Ames's ineradicable evil; Samuel Hamilton's gentle toughness. They form a vast canvas, and the canvas is always full of motion, life, laughter, and tears. Possibly because of the fullness of memorable characters, the weakness of the more wooden characters—Joseph Wayne, Mayor Orden, Ethan Hawley—is accentuated. Steinbeck's characters seem to fail when they become mental constructs, figures used to demonstrate an idea rather than people drawn from life.

Steinbeck's fiction should be seen first of all not as exposition of ideas, which is the prevailing critical view of his work, but as revelation about human nature through character. In his *Poetics*, Aristotle implies that character is subordinate to idea. This remained the prevailing view throughout must of Western tradition, at least until the Romantic revolution in the nineteenth century. The Aristotelian tendency continues to mark Steinbeck criticism with its emphasis on plot and idea before story and character. Steinbeck is concerned first of all with character and what we can learn about humankind by observing that character in a living environment. Nearly all his major works focus on such epiphanies by characterization. Only through character relationships to a central figure, be it Ma Joad, Cathy Ames, Doc, Doc Burton, Kino, or Ethan Hawley, do we approach theme.

Second, Steinbeck's literary excellence rises from his genius for story. Compared to the more cerebral literature of the European continent, American literature has been more solidly rooted in the tradition of storytelling. Stein-

beck participates in that tradition thoroughly and forcefully. From his youth he knew that a reader wants a story,
and he learned how to provide it in the most appealing fashion. The stories are historically rooted in life itself—they
are of people and places. At his best, Steinbeck allows
theme and symbolic content to grow naturally from story.

Furthermore, Steinbeck's use of the Bible should be
seen as an integrative technique that forms the warp and
woof of plot and character development in many of his
major works. It is not simply a stylistic technique imposed
on the work for aesthetic enhancement, as some have considered the use of the Bible in *The Grapes of Wrath;* rather
the Bible serves as a moral and thematic foundation for
nearly all the work and the actions of the characters.

Steinbeck's weakness as an artist emerges, on the other
hand, when he allows the theme to dominate the story or
allows the story to grow mystical and confusing. While
some critics find this to be the case in *East of Eden,* I dis-
agree. The novel, conceptually and artistically, I believe is
among Steinbeck's best. I do observe the weakness, however, in some of the very early work—*Cup of Gold* and *To
a God Unknown* serving as the best examples, and in several
of the late works—*The Moon Is Down, Burning Bright,* and
The Winter of Our Discontent, where Steinbeck seems
more concerned about writing another book than telling
another story. If such works fail, it is inevitably due to the
failure of the narrative framework and the development of
the story: the theme dominates and overshadows the story.

Third, Steinbeck's artistic excellence resides in his genius
for language. Although he wrote in self-deprecation to the
Wallstens on December 20, 1961, that "I have whomped a
small talent into a large volume of work" (*LL,* p. 730), that
talent was neither small nor "whomped." Steinbeck's artistic talent is apparent at several levels having to do with language. Observed in the course of this book have been techniques of imagery, linguistic surprise in understatement
and juxtaposition, and rhetorical complexity and variation.
Although Steinbeck is capable of sophisticated and com-

plex structures and stirring rhetorical patterns, his linguistic skill does not match, for example, the dazzling intricacies of Faulkner, a page of whose prose can leave a reader breathless, with the feeling of having attended a performance orchestrated by one of the world's great composers. Yet there is a certain rhetorical self-consciousness in Faulkner that one never finds in Steinbeck. In the naturalness of his rhetoric Steinbeck surpasses many of his contemporaries. That naturalness is evident in the pacing of language to character and allowing language to define character by tone and implications of words and sounds. In the lesser works Steinbeck sometimes spun pretty words in lifeless grotesqueries. The language became forced and artificial, devoid of roots in the living person of his character, the character mouthing words like a puppet.

These three elements—his genius for character, story, and language—I take to be areas of Steinbeck's greatest strength and, when they fall short, his greatest weakness. Such categories hardly distinguish him from any other major author; they merely suggest that Steinbeck did well in what we would expect any major author to do well. Surely, as this book has explored, he took his own aesthetic road in achieving these categorical excellences. Unique to Steinbeck is his persistent belief in disclosing the nonteleological nature of a character, his careful crafting of biblical allusion and symbolism, his understanding of human nature in terms of supernatural naturalism. These marked the literary path as his own. The characters and stories he found along that road could belong to no other.

Beyond these, however, there is something unique to Steinbeck's work that one begins to appreciate after long and careful study. It does not derive from the work itself so much as from a sense of the author behind the work, that is, Steinbeck's lifelong insistence on doing his art his way. One's interest lies as much in the author who walked the road as in the road he took. Something noble—if a bit hardheaded—underlies his refusal to pander to the expected. Even his failed work is often notable for the experiment

undertaken. His writing career is marked, more than anything else, by versatility and an impressively broad range
of themes, attitudes, techniques, characters, and stories.
Steinbeck frequently took reviewers by surprise, and reviewers seldom appreciate that. Yet, as a complete canon,
the very liveliness and diversity of Steinbeck's art contribute to his permanence and value in the American literary
tradition.

Notes

1. An amusing account of Steinbeck's avowed seriousness is revealed in a letter to Carl Wilhelmson from the late 1930s in which Steinbeck recollects attending a party of young literati:

They don't even pretend there is any dignity in craftsmanship. A conversation with them sounds like an afternoon spent with a pawnbroker. Says John Calvin, "I long ago ceased to take anything I write seriously." I retorted, "I take *everything* I write seriously; unless one does take his work seriously there is very little chance of its ever being good work." And the whole company was a little ashamed of me as though I had three legs or was an albino. [*LL*, p. 30]

2. Nelson Valjean, *John Steinbeck, the Errant Knight: An Intimate Biography of His California Years*, p. 83.

3. John Steinbeck, "Critics—From a Writer's Viewpoint," *Saturday Review* 38 (August 27, 1955): 20–28.

4. Thomas Fensch, *Steinbeck and Covici: The Story of a Friendship*, p. 43. Consider also Steinbeck's comment to Carlton Sheffield: "With the exception of extreme invention in method or idea (generally disliked by critics because nothing to measure them against) the critic can tell a writer what *not* to do. If he could tell him what *to* do, he'd be a writer himself. What *to* do is the soul and heart of the book. What *not* to do is how well or badly you did it" (*LL*, p. 458).

5. Thomas Kiernan, *The Intricate Music: A Biography of John Steinbeck*, pp. 62–63.

6. The comment on *The Red Pony* is interesting because the precursor of Jody Tiflin's red pony was Steinbeck's own red pony, Jill.

7. Kiernan, *The Intricate Music*, p. 215.

8. Fensch, *Steinbeck and Covici*, p. 229.

9. Steinbeck's own attitude toward journalism (which he practiced often and well, particularly in his reporting on the California migrant camps of the 1930s and again late in his career) is summarized in a letter of 1956 to John P. McKnight, of the U.S. Information Service in Rome:

What can I say about journalism? It has the greatest virtue and the greatest evil. It is the first thing the dictator controls. It is the mother of literature and the perpetrator of crap. In many cases it is the only history we have and yet it is the tool of the worst men. But over a long period of time and because it is the product of so many men, it is perhaps the purest thing we have. Honesty has a way of creeping in even when it was not intended. [*LL*, p. 526]

10. In an earlier letter to Peter Benchley, Steinbeck had written: "Of course a writer rearranges life, shortens time intervals, sharpens events, and devises beginnings, middles and ends and this is arbitrary because there are no beginnings nor any ends" (*LL*, p. 523). And in a letter to Professor and Mrs. Eugène Vinaver, Steinbeck states: "A novelist is a kind of flypaper to which everything adheres. His job then is to try to reassemble life into some kind of order" (*LL*, pp. 591–92).

11. Kiernan, *The Intricate Music*, p. 162.

12. Two of the better stylistic studies of *The Grapes of Wrath* are Peter Lisca, "*The Grapes of Wrath* as Fiction," *PMLA* 72 (March, 1957): 296–309; and Mary Ellen Caldwell, "A New Consideration of the Intercalary Chapters in *The Grapes of Wrath*," *Markam Review* 3 (May, 1973): 115–19.

13. John M. Nagle, "A View of Literature Too Often Neglected," *English Journal* 58 (March, 1969): 405.

14. See Francis Christensen, *Notes Toward a New Rhetoric: Nine Essays for Teachers*. The cumulative sentence, Christensen argues, is "generative" because the form itself inspires the writer to generate ideas: "It serves the needs of both the writer and the reader, the writer by compelling him to examine his thought, the reader by letting him into the writer's thought."

15. Jackson J. Benson, *The True Adventures of John Steinbeck, Writer*, p. 480.

16. Ibid., p. 481.

17. Peter Lisca, *John Steinbeck: Nature and Myth*, p. 216.

18. Joseph Fontenrose, *John Steinbeck: An Introduction and Interpretation*, p. 90.

19. In language ("group psyche-memory which is the foundation of the whole unconscious," *LSC*, p. 32), as well as in idea, Steinbeck's theory of the "sea-memory . . . which lives deep in the mind" sounds particularly Jungian. Lester Jay Marks speculates on these echoes of Jung in his *Thematic Design in the Novels of John Steinbeck*, as do Robert DeMott at some length in "Steinbeck's *To a God Unknown*," in Tetsumaro Hayashi, ed., *A Study of John Steinbeck*, Chap. 12; and Clifford Lewis, in "Jungian Psychology and the Artistic

Design of John Steinbeck," *Steinbeck Quarterly* (Summer–Fall, 1977): 89–97. In his reminiscence on Ed Ricketts, "Philosophy on Cannery Row," Joel W. Hedgpeth makes it clear that Ricketts, at least, was influenced by Jung: "In his philosophy, Ed was obviously seeking a "holistic" blend of his diverse reading and thinking, that would lead to a 'breaking through' into a more peaceful and positively acquiescent perception of the nature of things. Among his sources were C. G. Jung, whose writings he abstracted in some detail, the Tao, Conrad, Whitman, and Robinson Jeffers. Hedgpeth's essay appears in Richard Astro and Tetsumaro Hayashi, eds., *Steinbeck: The Man and His Work*, pp. 89–129; quotation cited from p. 119. While there are possible echoes of a dozen or more thinkers, writers, sages, in Steinbeck's work, and while the echoes from Jung are perhaps clearest in *The Winter of Our Discontent*, his work is particularly dangerous ground for so-called influence studies. He was omnivorous and eclectic in his learning; his mind was a sponge soaking up all life and learning had to offer, finally to set it forth in a manner that was uniquely Steinbeck.

20. Benson, *The True Adventures*, pp. 2–3.

21. Joseph Fontenrose has briefly but ably pointed out the evident superficiality of Ricketts' and Steinbeck's "straw man" models, but also that "they have confused final cause, against which their case is good, with efficient cause, which we cannot eliminate from our thinking (nor did they)" (*John Steinbeck*, p. 92). Freeman Champney finds a "moral fatalism" in Steinbeck's theory:

If the height of wisdom is "things are because they are" and thinking in terms of cause and effect and of changes for the better are Sunday-school fatuities, we come to an attitude towards life remarkably oriental and passive. It is not the attitude with which we normally contemplate our house catching fire—nor our world catching fire. For that matter, it is not an attitude which would lead anyone to build a house in the first place—or to do any other creative job based on "what might be." Nor will observation which shuns the "why" of things see very much in the long run. Its only logical end is pure mysticism—a search for objectivity winding up in the absolute subjective.

Freeman Champney, "John Steinbeck, Californian," *Antioch Review* 7 (Fall, 1947): 345–62; reprinted in E. W. Tedlock, Jr., and C. V. Wicker, eds., *Steinbeck and His Critics: A Record of Twenty-five Years*.

22. Steinbeck may properly be located in the mainstream of naturalistic thinking as it developed from the middle of the nineteenth century, usually dated for the sake of convenience to 1860, a year

after the publication of Darwin's *On the Origin of Species*. To many thinkers in the nineteenth century it seemed that the ivory towers constructed with such pride and care during the Enlightenment were merely hollow shells on footings of clay. In place of feelings, emotions, and the subjective experience, eighteenth-century thinkers had aggrandized the conceptual, the formulaic, and the objective. And the nineteenth century found humanity reduced to a thing. As in Hawthorne's "Ethan Brand," the unpardonable sin had become the burial of the heart. In naturalistic philosophy humankind had become the victim of forces that had gone out of control and that no system could adequately explain.

Naturalism should not be understood first of all as a radical movement designed to change events. Rather, Naturalism may be defined as a way of looking at life that seems disordered, fragmented, and with no holding center for meaning. If the Naturalist vision seems bleak, it is because life itself seemed bleak.

But Naturalism is also a formal philosophy assuming that there is no God in the world and that humanity is subject to natural laws. Naturalists assume the right, therefore, to determine one's own meaning, to assert that knowledge autonomously discovered (rather than revealed by God) is certain, that there is in fact no sovereign God. Thus Naturalism is a crossroads in modern thought—humanity's striking out from the center of religious tradition to probe for meaning and knowledge apart from God. Naturalism, moreover, has a scientific basis, which makes it more significant to Steinbeck's philosophy.

Although such leading scholars as Parrington, Ahnebrink, Walcutt, Pizer, and Cowley have contributed studies of literary Naturalism, one of the clearest summaries of the philosophy is provided by Arthur C. Danto under the entry "Naturalism" in *The Encyclopedia of Philosophy*, 5:448–50.

23. Woodburn O. Ross, "John Steinbeck: Naturalism's Priest," *College English* 10 (May, 1949): 433–34.

24. Ibid., p. 434.

25. Ibid.

26. Ibid., p. 437.

27. Cf. M. H. Abrams, *Natural Supernaturalism: Tradition and Revolution in Romantic Literature*. In his preface Abrams states:

Despite their [Romantics'] displacement from a supernatural to a natural frame of reference, however, the ancient problems, terminology, and ways of thinking about human nature and history survived, as the implicit distinctions and categories through which even radically secular writers saw themselves and their world, and as the presuppositions and forms of their thinking about the condition, the milieu, the essential values and aspirations, and the history and destiny of the individual and of mankind.

28. See *LL*, p. 343.

29. The idea of this letter curiously echoes the sentiments of *To a God Unknown*, written thirty years before. After his marriage to Elizabeth, Joseph Wayne reflects: "Christ in His little time on the nails carried within His body all the suffering that ever was, and in Him it was undistorted."

30. Quoted by permission of the Stanford University Libraries and the John Steinbeck estate. The letter is in the John Steinbeck Collection, M263, box 1, folder 2.

31. In a letter of October 26, 1948, to Mr. and Mrs. Joseph Henry Jackson, there is an interesting account of Steinbeck's having burned a story which he felt was too evil to publish: "I wrote a little story that was so evil, so completely evil that when I finished it I burned it. It was effective, horribly effective. It would have made anyone who read it completely miserable. I don't mind evil if anything else is accomplished but this was unqualifiedly murderous and terrible" (*LL*, pp. 336–37).

32. The notorious political use Stevenson made of the letter if, as it appears, he passed the letter on to *Newsday* without Steinbeck's knowledge, is detailed by Jackson Benson in *The True Adventures of John Steinbeck, Writer*, pp. 876–77.

33. Mason I. Lowance, Jr., *The Language of Canaan: Metaphor and Symbol in New England from the Puritans to the Transcendentalists*, p. 4

34. Ibid.

35. Maud Bodkin, *Archetypal Patterns in Poetry*, p. 4.

36. Northrop Frye, *Anatomy of Criticism*, pp. 99–112. Cf. Steinbeck's statement in *LSC*: "The harvest of symbols in our minds seems to have been planted in the soft rich soil of our prehumanity" (p. 34).

37. The term "coloring" is ably defined and explored by Earl J. Wilcox, "Christian Coloring in Faulkner's *The Old Man*," *Christianity and Literature* (Winter, 1980). Wilcox defines his term "Christian coloring" thus: "The expression is used here to mean that as a frame of reference—seen through allusion, imagery, gesture, descriptive and narrative texture, and thematic implications—the Christian motifs sustain and integrate the story" (p. 63).

38. Unless otherwise noted, biblical quotations are taken from the King James Version.

39. H. Kelly Crockett, "The Bible and *The Grapes of Wrath*," *College English* 24 (December, 1962): 193.

40. There were similar title changes in the short stories; for example, "The Fool" became "The Harness"; "Manhunt" became "Flight"; and "The Sisters" became "Johnny Bear."

CHAPTER 2

1. Quoted by permission of Stanford University Libraries and the John Steinbeck estate. The letter is in the John Steinbeck Collection, M263, box 1, folder 2.

2. In a letter to Katherine Beswick, posted February 27, 1928, Steinbeck commented on the dialect used in *Cup of Gold:*

Now let me speak of the dialect used in the first chapter. A certain method of word sequences has been called Byrnian. Before Byrnne lived, Synge did it far better, far more beautifully. And before Synge, my grandfather spoke it to my mind more beautifully than either. Would you believe it, I spoke it myself when I was little, but of course, the public schools laughed it out of me.

Quoted by permission of Stanford University Libraries and the John Steinbeck estate. The letter is in the John Steinbeck Collection, M263, box 1, folder 2.

3. Willa Cather, "My First Novels," in *On Writing*, p. 97.

4. Harry Thornton Moore, *The Novels of John Steinbeck: A First Critical Study*, p. 12.

5. The story was at least fascinating enough that it was plagiarized by one Berton Braley in his 1934 epic, *Morgan Sails the Caribbean*. Harry Moore provides details and Steinbeck's response to the author in *The Novels of John Steinbeck*, p. 17.

6. Warren French, *John Steinbeck*, p. 31.

7. French, in *John Steinbeck*, sees the story of Henry Morgan and Merlin as a tension between society and art:

Despite the superficial pirate story, *Cup of Gold* really contrasts, therefore, the man who pursues the grail of power and finds he must compromise with society or be destroyed and the man who pursues the grail of art and transcends society. Although the book is not constructed in a manner to make this point satisfactorily, it is actually Steinbeck's first— but not his last—defense of the superiority of the artistic calling. One wonders to what extent the novel may have been inspired by a desire to answer the girl in New York who told Steinbeck that he should go into advertising before trying to make his living by creative writing. [p. 38]

Although not clearly articulated in *Cup of Gold*, the theme became a major one in Steinbeck's later work.

8. Peter Lisca, *The Wide World of John Steinbeck*, p. 31.

9. Nelson Valjean, *John Steinbeck, the Errant Knight: An Intimate Biography of His California Years*, p. 123.

10. Howard Levant, *The Novels of John Steinbeck: A Critical Study*, p. 25.

11. George Gordon, Lord Byron, *Don Juan*, ed. Leslie A. Marchand (Boston: Houghton Mifflin Co., 1958), p. 10.

CHAPTER 3

1. Steinbeck commented on his design and structure for *The Pastures of Heaven* in a letter to Elizabeth Otis:

The manuscript is made up of stories, each one complete in itself, having its rise, climax and ending. Each story deals with a family or an individual. They are tied together only by the common locality and by the contact with the Morans. Some of the stories are very short and some as long as fifteen thousand words. I thought of combining them with that thirty-thousand word ms. called Dissonant Symphony to make one volume. I wonder whether you think this is a good plan. I think the plan at least falls very definitely in the aspects of American life category. [*LL*, p. 43]

And to Amasa ("Ted") Miller he wrote in May, 1931:

I am doing a thing called The Pastures of Heaven which takes its name from an enclosed valley in the mountains named by the Spanish discoverers Las Pasturas del Cielo. This is a mythical place but it is only mythical in name. The place is the Corral de Tierra and I would keep that name except for the fact that I am writing about actual people who live there. Now this is a series of related stories each one dealing with a family in the Pasturas. I had intended to write a three hundred page mss but perhaps it would be better to do a two hundred page one and combine it with the other ["Dissonant Symphony"]. The stories are entities in themselves and average somewhere near fifty pages apiece.

The letter to Miller appears in Jackson J. Benson, *The True Adventures of John Steinbeck, Writer*, p. 210.

2. Benson, *The True Adventures*, pp. 210–11.

3. Steinbeck himself, it should be pointed out, had "planting hands," a lifelong love for bulbs and seedlings that he often viewed as a cathartic aside from writing but also one closely allied with writing.

4. Benson, *The True Adventures*, p. 275.

5. In a footnote to an article on Steinbeck's artistry, "Steinbeck and the Creative Process" (in Richard Astro and Tetsumaro Hayashi, eds., *Steinbeck: The Man and His Work*) Robert DeMott speculates:

I think Steinbeck's earlier short story "The Chrysanthemums" can also be read as a parable of the artist's condition in society. Elisa Allen possesses "Planter's hands," that is, a kind of creative intuition and both she and her products, the beautiful flowers, can exist only in a closed valley, a symbol of the artist's Ivory Tower. When Elisa meets the "real" world head on, represented by the tinker, she is defeated. The harsh realities of life in the 30s, Steinbeck implies, have no patience with artistic and feminine ephemera." [P. 163]

6. James Gray, *John Steinbeck*, Pamphlets on American Writers, no. 94, p. 13.

7. Benson, *The True Adventures*, p. 275.

8. A number of critical studies have focused almost exclusively on the theme of feminism as manifested in Elisa Allen. While some of Steinbeck's attitudes toward women enter the discussion of Ma Joad in chapter 4 of this book, it is a mistaken notion to pass modern liberation theories onto Steinbeck. He is concerned, of course, with Elisa as a woman—she is the protagonist of the story, and her womanhood as well as her "planting hands" forms the subject matter, but he is concerned with a feeling and genius in her that may occur in anyone, the desire to free one's personality and being in the midst of social constraints. Two such studies that focus almost exclusively on the issue of her womanhood—both rather superficially—are Mordecai Marcus, "The Lost Dream of Sex and Childbirth in 'The Chrysanthemums,'" *Modern Fiction Studies* 11 (Spring, 1965): 54–58; and Charles A. Sweet, Jr., "Ms Elisa Allen and Steinbeck's 'The Chrysanthemums,'" *Modern Fiction Studies* 20 (June, 1974): 210–14.

9. Maxwell Geismar, *Writers in Crisis: The American Novel Between Two Wars*, p. 244.

CHAPTER 4

1. Jackson J. Benson, *The True Adventures of John Steinbeck, Writer*, p. 264.

2. If the assumption were correct that an author must have first-hand, personal experience of the subject matter he deals with, one would have to say that J. R. R. Tolkien's *The Lord of the Rings* is aesthetically flawed by virtue of being fantasy, or that Tolkien is an aesthetically inferior author for having written fantasy.

3. Émile Zola, "The Experimental Novel" (1880), in *The Experimental Novel and Other Essays*.

4. Lionel Trilling, *Sincerity and Authenticity*, p. 8.

5. Thomas Kiernan, *The Intricate Music: A Biography of John Steinbeck*, pp. 62–63.

6. Benson, *The True Adventures*, p. 41.

7. For a thorough discussion of how Steinbeck treated the newspaper accounts in the fictional story, see James Delgado, "The Facts Behind John Steinbeck's 'The Lonesome Vigilante,'" *Steinbeck Quarterly* 16 (Summer–Fall, 1983): 70–79. Steinbeck's story appeared in *Esquire*, October, 1936, as "The Lonesome Vigilante," and in *The Long Valley* as "The Vigilante."

8. Jackson J. Benson and Anne Loftis, "John Steinbeck and Farm Labor Unionization: The Background of *In Dubious Battle*," *American Literature* 52 (May, 1982): 194.

9. The Communist sympathizer was declared by Harry Moore, without supporting evidence, in his *The Novels of John Steinbeck: A First Critical Study:*

Those who criticized Steinbeck's portrait of his agitator didn't know that he had made the acquaintance of a communist district organizer who gave Steinbeck his life story. Steinbeck originally began a realistic biographical sketch of him in the first person, but later transmuted this into background material for *IDB*. He was after all trying to write literature rather than a factual report. [P. 41]

Moore also suggested the Pajaro Valley as the locale of the book, a setting accepted by subsequent critics despite Steinbeck's disclaimer that

I have usually avoided using actual places to avoid hurting feelings, for, although I rarely use a person or a story as it is—neighbors love only too well to attribute them to someone. . . . As for the valley in *In Dubious Battle*—it is a composite valley as it is a composite strike. If it has the characteristics of Pajaro nevertheless there was no strike there. If it's like the cotton strike, that wasn't apples. [Ibid., p. 102]

Benson and Loftis identify the actual strike locale as the peach strike on the Tagus Ranch in Tulare County in August, 1933, with some details borrowed from the Cotton Strike of October, 1933. The Tagus Ranch, model here for the Hooper Ranch, also became the setting for *The Grapes of Wrath*.

10. Benson and Loftis, "John Steinbeck And Farm Labor Unionization," p. 199.

11. Benson, *The True Adventures*, p. 298.

12. Benson and Loftis, "John Steinbeck and Farm Labor Unionization," p. 203.

13. Ibid., p. 208.

14. Walter Ralston, *New Masses*, February 18, 1936, p. 23.

15. Fred T. Marsh, *New York Times Sunday Book Review*, February 2, 1936, sec. 6, p. 7.

16. Lincoln R. Gibbs, "John Steinbeck: Moralist," *Antioch Review*, June, 1942, reprinted in E. W. Tedlock, Jr., and C. V. Wicker, eds., *Steinbeck and His Critics*, p. 97.

17. Benson and Loftis, "John Steinbeck and Farm Labor Unionization," p. 223.

18. Kiernan, *The Intricate Music*, p. 192.

19. Joseph Fontenrose, *John Steinbeck: An Introduction and Interpretation*, p. 46.

20. Fontenrose's conception of *In Dubious Battle* as analogous to *Paradise Lost* has strong credibility but may be forced when he structures the analogy too closely, as in this passage:

Satan's role is obviously played by the Party as a collective person, although Jim or Mac or another may represent the Party in its Satanic role. In contemporary folklore the Devil's color is red. The party secretary who received Jim's application for Party membership is Harry Nilson—the Old Harry is a popular name for the Devil. Probably the detail of Mac's exhaling steam from his mouth as he ate hot stew is meant to illustrate the identity of the Party and Satan. Particular identifications suggest themselves: London is Beelzebub as Satan's right-hand man; Dakin, attached to his fine truck and equipment, is Mammon; Dick, the "bedroom radical," who employed social graces and masculine charm for the cause, is Belial; Sam, direct actionist, is Moloch calling for open war; and Burke, dissenter and stool pigeon in the strikers' camp, is Abdiel. [Ibid., p. 48]

21. To appreciate thoroughly the distinction between Doc Burton and a character like Joseph Wayne (which also is a distinction between the mystical writing of *To a God Unknown* and the concrete writing of *In Dubious Battle*), one has only to juxtapose to the descriptions of Doc a description of Joseph by his sister-in-law Rama in *To a God Unknown*. Rama says to Elizabeth:

"I do not know whether there are men born outside humanity, or whether some men are so human as to make others seem unreal. Perhaps a godling lives on earth now and then. Joseph has strength beyond vision of shattering, he has the calm of mountains, and his emotion is as wild and fierce and sharp as the lightning and just as reasonless as far as I can see or know. When you are away from him, try thinking of him and

you'll see what I mean. His figure will grow huge, until it tops the mountains, and his force will be like the irresistible plunging of the wind."
[*TGU*, p. 66]

22. F. W. Watt, *John Steinbeck*, p. 57.
23. Richard Astro, *John Steinbeck and Edward F. Ricketts: The Shaping of a Novelist*, p. 125.
24. Karl Marx and Friedrich Engels, *The Communist Manifesto*, ed. Samuel Beer, p. 19.
25. Maxwell Geismar, *Writers in Crisis: The American Novel Between Two Wars*, p. 256.
26. Ibid., p. 257.
27. One of the clearest examples of this point in American literature is that of Henry David Thoreau. When Thoreau's *A Week on the Concord and Merrimack Rivers* sold a scant 219 copies in five years of his self-paid, 1,000-copy run, the author remarked with grim humor: "I have now a library of nearly nine hundred volumes, over seven hundred of which I wrote myself." The back of that volume boldly announced that *Walden* was forthcoming. Its coming forth was belated; but it sold better—2,000 copies in the next seven years.
28. Films made from Steinbeck's novels include *Of Mice and Men* (1939), Lewis Milestone, director-producer (107 minutes); *The Grapes of Wrath* (1940), John Ford, director (129 minutes); *Tortilla Flat* (1942), Victor Fleming, director (106 minutes) (*TF* was Steinbeck's first film rights' sale for the stunning [to him] figure of $4,000); *The Moon Is Down* (1943), Nunnally Johnson, producer (90 minutes); *The Pearl* (1947), Emilio Fernández, director (77 minutes); *The Red Pony* (1949), Lewis Milestone, director-producer (89 minutes); *East of Eden* (1955), Elia Kazan, director (115 minutes); *Flight* (1950), Barnaby Conrad, producer (160 minutes) (Steinbeck makes his only appearance in any of his films); *The Wayward Bus* (1957), Victor Vicas, director (89 minutes); *The Red Pony* (1973), Robert Totten, director (95 minutes); *East of Eden* (1981), Harvey Hart, director (television miniseries adaptation); *Cannery Row* (1982), David S. Ward, producer (despite the title, based on *Sweet Thursday*); *The Winter of Our Discontent* (1984) (television movie).
Film scripts by Steinbeck include: *The Forgotten Village* (1941), Herbert Kline, director-producer (60 minutes); *Lifeboat* (1943), Alfred Hitchcock, director (96 minutes); *A Medal for Benny* (1945), Irving Pichel, director (77 minutes); *Viva Zapata!* (1952), Elia Kazan, director (113 minutes).
29. Fontenrose, *John Steinbeck*, p. 55.
30. Antonia Seixas, "John Steinbeck and the Non-Teleological Bus," in Tedlock and Wicker, eds., *Steinbeck and His Critics*, p. 277.
31. Peter Lisca, *The Wide World of John Steinbeck*, p. 135.

32. Howard Levant, *The Novels of John Steinbeck: A Critical Study*, p. 138.

33. Steinbeck presented his own theory of drama in a brief article in *Stage* (January, 1938), a theory discussed in its relation to *Of Mice and Men* by Howard Levant in *The Novels of John Steinbeck*, pp. 130–44.

CHAPTER 5

1. A dozen or more critical articles have explored, with varying degrees of success, biblical symbolism in *The Grapes of Wrath*. Among the better studies are Chris Browning, "Grape Symbolism in *The Grapes of Wrath*," *Discourse* 11 (Winter, 1968): 129–40; Gerard Cannon, "The Pauline Apostleship of Tom Joad," *College English* 24 (December, 1962): 222–24; Eric W. Carlson, "Symbolism in *The Grapes of Wrath*," *College English* 19 (January, 1958): 172–75; Charles T. Dougherty, "The Christ-Figure in *The Grapes of Wrath*," *College English* 24 (December, 1962): 224–26; Joseph Fontenrose, *John Steinbeck: An Introduction and Interpretation*, chap. 6; J. P. Hunter, "Steinbeck's Wine of Affirmation in *The Grapes of Wrath*," in Richard E. Langford, Guy Owen, and William E. Taylor, eds., *Essays in Modern American Literature*; Alan Paton and Liston Pope, "The Novelist and Christ," *Saturday Review* 37 (December 4, 1954): 15–16, 56–59; Martin S. Shockley, "Christian Symbolism in *The Grapes of Wrath*," *College English* 18 (November, 1956): 87–90. Peter Lisca has provided a fine analysis of the history of criticism on *The Grapes of Wrath* and a bibliography of such criticism in the Viking Critical Library edition of the novel.

2. Robert J. Griffin and William E. Freeman, "Machines and Animals: Pervasive Motifs in *The Grapes of Wrath*," *Journal of English and Germanic Philology* 62 (April, 1963): 569–80.

3. Mary Ellen Caldwell, "A New Consideration of the Intercalary Chapters in *The Grapes of Wrath*," *Markham Review* 3 (May, 1973): 117–18.

4. Ibid., p. 119.

5. John Steinbeck, "A Letter on Criticism," *Colorado Quarterly* 4 (1955): 218–19. Steinbeck added that "it is no more intended to be inspected than the skeletal structure of a pretty girl. Just read it, don't count it." Nevertheless, the structure does "count" and is crafted in many subtle ways. For example, in chapter 9 the Okies' old homeland ends in a fire (p. 121), and in the final chapter their new home ends in a flood. The flood, however, can bring renewal, as is symbolized in Rose of Sharon. The spiritual pilgrimage is struc-

tured geographically, the descent into hell being represented by Toprock and Needles, and the ascent into the blighted paradise by a movement in the itinerary that occurs approximately midway in the novel. Premonitory devices weld the novel's structural parts, the handbills, for example, which are first revealed as a ruse on p. 124, and proved to be a ruse during the strikes in California (see also pp. 201, 259, and 333 for development of the handbills as a plot motif). Further, the biblical symbolism that structures the novel throughout has been so carefully and thoroughly scrutinized as to need no additional comment here.

6. For discussion of Steinbeck's female characters consider also *Steinbeck's Women: Essays in Criticism*, Monograph 9, Steinbeck Monograph Series (Muncie, Ind., Ball State University, Steinbeck Society of America, 1979).

7. Richard Astro, *John Steinbeck and Edward F. Ricketts: The Shaping of A Novelist*, p. 130.

8. John Steinbeck, Foreword to "Bringing in the Sheaves," Windsor Drake [Tom Collins], *Journal of Modern Literature* special issue, (*Background of* The Grapes of Wrath) 5 (April, 1976): 213.

9. Drake, "Bringing in the Sheaves," p. 222. In his "Background of *The Grapes of Wrath*" in the same issue (see n. 8 above), Jackson J. Benson discusses at length the relation between Collins and Steinbeck and the manuscript "Bringing in the Sheaves."

10. Martin Shockley, "The Reception of *The Grapes of Wrath* in Oklahoma," *American Literature* 15 (May, 1944): 351–61; reprinted in E. W. Tedlock, Jr., and C. V. Wicker, eds., *Steinbeck and His Critics;* and in Warren French, ed., *A Companion to* The Grapes of Wrath.

11. Jackson J. Benson, *The True Adventures of John Steinbeck, Writer*, p. 418.

12. Ibid., p. 389.

13. D. H. Lawrence, "Pornography and Obscenity," in Harry T. Moore, ed., *Sex, Literature, and Censorship*, p. 69.

CHAPTER 6

1. John and Regina Hicks, *Cannery Row: A Pictorial History.* For another pictorial history of the area see Maxine Knox and Mary Rodriguez, *Steinbeck's Street: Cannery Row.*

2. Thomas Kiernan, *The Intricate Music: A Biography of John Steinbeck*, p. 201.

3. Lewis Gannett, "Steinbeck's Way of Writing," in *The Portable Steinbeck*, pp. xi–xii.

4. Steinbeck's writing life could be as orderly as his personal life was disorderly. In an interesting letter to Geroge Albee written about the time he was working on *Tortilla Flat*, Steinbeck wrote:

> Between ourselves I don't know what Miss McIntosh means by organization of myself. If she would inspect my work with care, she would see an organization that would frighten her, the slow development of thought pattern, revolutionary to the present one. I am afraid that no advice will change me much because my drive is not one I can get at. When they get tired of my consistent financial failures, they will just have to kick me out. I'm a bum, you see, and according to my sister, a fake, and my family is ashamed of me, and it doesn't seem to make any difference at all. [*LL*, p. 94]

5. Peter Lisca, *The Wide World of John Steinbeck*, p. 77. For a study arguing similarities between *Tortilla Flat* and *Morte D'Arthur*, see Arthur F. Kinney, "The Arthurian Cycle in *Tortilla Flat*," *Modern Fiction Studies* 11 (Spring, 1965): 11–20.

6. Ibid., p. 78.

7. Ibid., pp. 79–80.

8. Aristotle, *Selections*, ed. W. D. Ross, p. 328.

9. Ibid., p. 330.

10. Among Shakespeare's works *Twelfth Night, Measure for Measure*, and *As You Like It* would serve as examples of this tragicomic intermingling.

11. Lisca, *The Wide World of John Steinbeck*, p. 91.

12. Warren French, *John Steinbeck*, p. 59.

13. Wylie Sypher, "The Meanings of Comedy," in Wylie Sypher, ed., *Comedy*, p. 195.

14. George Steiner, *The Death of Tragedy*, p. 128.

15. Christopher Fry, "Comedy," in Robert W. Corrigan, ed., *Comedy: Meaning and Form*, p. 16.

16. "Interview with Peter DeVries," in Roy Newquist, ed., *Counterpoint*, (Chicago: Rand McNally, 1964), p. 153.

17. Ibid., p. 149.

18. Lisca, *The Wide World of John Steinbeck*, p. 82.

19. Howard Levant, *The Novels of John Steinbeck: A Critical Study*, p. 58.

20. Mathew Winston, "Black Humor: To Weep with Laughing," in Maurice Charney, ed., *Comedy: New Perspectives*, p. 37. A similar theme is established by Ken Kesey in his tragicomic novel *One Flew over the Cuckoo's Nest*. Confronted by the dark terror of the insane asylum, McMurphy says to Cheswick: "Maybe not you, buddy, but the rest are even scared to open up and *laugh*. You know, that's the first thing that got me about this place, that there wasn't anybody

laughing. I haven't heard a real laugh since I came through that door, do you know that? Man, when you lose your laugh you lose your *footing*" (p. 65).

21. Northrop Frye, "The Argument of Comedy," in Leonard F. Dean, ed., *Shakespeare: Modern Essays in Criticism*, p. 84.

22. Nathan Scott, "The Bias of Comedy," in Corrigan, ed., *Comedy: Meaning and Form*, p. 103.

23. Levant, *The Novels of John Steinbeck*, p. 62.

24. See Lisca, *The Wide World of John Steinbeck*, p. 78.

25. French, *John Steinbeck*, p. 125.

26. Ibid., p. 122.

27. Jackson J. Benson, "John Steinbeck's *Cannery Row*: A Reconsideration," *Western American Literature* 12, no. 1 (1977): 15–16. Benson speculates on some similarities between Twain and Steinbeck, although he carefully avoids any claim for influence:

There are, curiously enough, a number of striking parallels between Twain's and Steinbeck's careers. Both were fascinated by medieval literature, in particular, Malory's *Morte D'Arthur*, and both were fond of allegory, the tall tale, and travel literature. Both wrote a wide variety of things during their careers, moving from form to form, and both wrote a great many things of very dubious literary value. And despite a large output, both writers are known primarily for having written one major novel. However, almost everything they wrote, even their most important works, was deeply flawed in one way or another. Both in their heart of hearts were satirists—disillusioned romantic idealists. Twain and Steinbeck have been classified as "funnymen," yet each of them had at times a very black vision of man's nature. No two American writers throughout our history have had a firmer sense of the ordinary man and of ordinary life, and both maintained the common touch even after they became rich and successful. Yet, after each became rich and successful, he moved to the East, and while in the East, each became more and more pessimistic and moralistic in his work. [P. 16]

Sidney J. Krause provides another brief comparison of Twain and Steinbeck in "Steinbeck and Mark Twain," *Steinbeck Quarterly* 6 (Fall, 1973): 104–11.

28. Richard Astro, *John Steinbeck and Edward F. Ricketts: The Shaping of a Novelist*, p. 159.

29. In his "John Steinbeck's *Cannery Row*: A Reconsideration" Benson considers specific similarities between the tidal flats and life on the row:

Although the life of the Great Tide Pool is not examined in such a way as to form a systematic allegory for the human activity above it on the Row, the pool is treated with enough suggestive similarities to make it an analogue. At the Great Tide Pool, "a wave breaks over the barrier, and churns the glassy water for a moment and mixes bubbles into the pool, and then it clears and is tranquil and lovely and murderous again" (pp. 30–31). While on the Row in the morning when the sardine fleet has made a catch, the cannery whistles scream and "all over the town men and women scramble into their clothes and come running down to the Row." "The canneries rumble and rattle and squeak until the last fish is cleaned and cut and cooked and canned and the town and Cannery Row becomes itself again—quiet and magical" (pp. 1–2). In the pool, the hermit crab abandons one empty shell to take possession of another that he likes better, while on the Row, Mack and the boys abandon their discarded cannery pipes to move into Lee Chong's empty shack. In the pool, "the black eels poke their heads out of crevices and wait for prey," as above, Mack and the boys peer out at Lee Chong's and at the coming and going of Doc, waiting for the right moment to strike. While at Dora's place, her girls follow the pattern of the anemones of the pool and "expand like soft and brilliant flowers, inviting any tired and perplexed animal to lie for a moment in their arms" and "the smell of sperm and ova fill the air." In the pool, "the barnacles bubble behind their closed doors," suggesting the isolation experienced by so many on the row, by Doc, by Frankie, by William, and by the old Chinaman. [P. 27]

30. The metaphor is examined at some length by Levant, *The Novels of John Steinbeck*, pp. 169–70.

31. Sir Joshua Reynolds, *Discourses on Art*, p. 37.

32. Benson, "John Steinbeck's *Cannery Row:* A Reconsideration," p. 24.

33. Ibid., p. 30.

34. Astro, *John Steinbeck and Edward F. Ricketts*, p. 164.

35. Sypher, "The Meanings of Comedy," p. 212.

36. Henri Bergson, "Laughter," in Sypher, ed., *Comedy*, p. 62.

37. Astro, *John Steinbeck and Edward F. Ricketts*, p. 200.

38. Sypher, "The Meanings of Comedy," pp. 241–42.

39. In "Farce as Method," Robert C. Stephenson examines the history and manifold forms of farce, locating it as a kind of pregeneric comedy, an "inchoate *vis comica* in search of a body." *Tulane Drama Review* 5, No. 2 (1961): pp. 85–93.

40. Sypher, "The Meanings of Comedy," p. 239.

41. Ibid., p. 220.

42. Ibid., p. 221.

43. Benson, John Steinbeck's *Cannery Row:* A Reconsideration," p. 22.

44. Sypher, "The Meanings of Comedy," p. 245.

CHAPTER 7

1. Harry Thornton Moore, *The Novels of John Steinbeck: A First Critical Study*, p. 96.

2. Joseph Fontenrose, *John Steinbeck: An Introduction and Interpretation*, p. 99.

3. Ibid.

4. One wonders sometimes how far to extend the analogy between Ed Ricketts and the many characters in Steinbeck's novels who resemble him. Some curious points emerge that reflect Steinbeck's artistic method. For example, in *The Wayward Bus*, Steinbeck says of Mr. Pritchard: "He believed that full-lipped women were voluptuous" (p. 147), paralleling the description of Ed Ricketts Steinbeck supplied several years later in his reminiscence "About Ed Ricketts":

He hated women with thin lips. "If the lips are thin—where will there be any fullness?" he would say. His observation was certainly physical and open to verification, and he seemed to believe in its accuracy and so do I, but with less vehemence.

He loved women too much to take any nonsense from the thin-lipped ones. But if a girl with thin lips painted on fuller ones with lipstick, he was satisfied. "Her intentions are correct," he said.

While there is no resemblance between Ricketts and Pritchard, it seems, however, that Steinbeck often noted things that Ricketts said or did and, attracted to their uniqueness or peculiarity, used them in fictional characters.

5. Jackson J. Benson, *The True Adventures of John Steinbeck, Writer*, p. 643.

6. Ibid., p. 644.

7. Peter Lisca, *The Wide World of John Steinbeck*, p. 256–57.

8. Antonia Seixas, "John Steinbeck and the Non-Teleological Bus," in E. W. Tedlock, Jr., and C. V. Wicker, eds., *Steinbeck and His Critics*, pp. 277–78.

9. Warren French, *John Steinbeck*, p. 143.

10. Fontenrose, *John Steinbeck*, p. 110.

11. Thomas Aquinas, *An Aquinas Reader*, ed. Mary T. Clark, p. 352.

12. Harry Morris, "*The Pearl*: Realism and Allegory," *English Journal* 52 (October, 1963): 495.

13. *The Pearl*, trans. Sister Mary Vincent Hillmann (Notre Dame, Ind.: University of Notre Dame Press, 1967), lines 1201–1208.

14. Morris, "The Pearl," p. 487.

15. Peter Lisca has drawn fascinating analogies between *The Pearl* and Maya religion in *John Steinbeck: Nature and Myth*. He observes: "This material is so rich, and Steinbeck's utilization of it so detailed that it bulks larger than the Christian elements in the novelette as well as in the consciousness of Kino and Juana themselves" (p. 138).

CHAPTER 8

1. Jackson J. Benson, *The True Adventures of John Steinbeck, Writer*, p. 581.

2. Ibid., p. 569.

3. Ibid., p. 636.

4. Ibid., p. 674.

5. Ibid., p. 675.

6. Peter Lisca, *The Wide World of John Steinbeck*, p. 270.

7. Ibid., p. 272.

8. Ibid., p. 273.

9. Joseph Fontenrose, *John Steinbeck: An Introduction and Interpretation*, p. 124.

10. Ibid., p. 126.

11. Howard Levant, *The Novels of John Steinbeck: A Critical Study*, p. 234.

12. Ibid., p. 254.

13. Ibid., p. 241.

14. Joseph Wood Krutch, "John Steinbeck's Dramatic Tale of Three Generations," *New York Herald Tribune Weekly Book Review*, September 21, 1952, p. 1.

15. Mark Schorer, "A Dark and Violent Steinbeck Novel," *New York Times Book Review*, September 21, 1952, p. 22.

16. Lester Jay Marks, *Thematic Design in the Novels of John Steinbeck*, p. 120.

17. John Ditsky, *Essays on* East of Eden, Steinbeck Monograph Series, no. 9.

18. Warren French, Introduction to Howard Levant, *The Novels of John Steinbeck*, p. x.

19. John Cawelti, *The Six-Gun Mystique*, pp. 24–25.

20. Fontenrose, *John Steinbeck*, p. 125.

21. An excellent theological analysis of the "Cain mark" is given by Meredith Kline in Gary Tuttle, ed., *Biblical and Near Eastern Studies*, chap. 8; and also in his "Divine Kingship and Genesis 6:1–4," *Westminster Theological Journal* 24 (November, 1961): 187–204.

22. Although Steinbeck was best versed in Malory, who uses snake imagery for the Morgan figure (a passage that Steinbeck translated in his Arthurian romance), he was also an avid collector of all Arthurian editions and assuredly had read Tennyson's *The Idylls of the King*, where the most overt serpent imagery is used for the Morgan figure, here Vivien, the seducer of Merlin. (At Steinbeck's funeral, for which he left explicit instructions, Henry Fonda read lines from Tennyson's "Ulysses.") As Vivien seduces Merlin into his long sleep, Tennyson describes her in these lines:

She paused, she turn'd away, she hung her head,
The snake of gold slid from her hair, the braid
Slipt and uncoil'd itself.

The action of her hair amplifies Vivien's own actions of slinking, sliding, and slipping around Merlin in serpentine wiles to seduce him. Her final deception of Merlin, the spiritual center of Arthur's kingdom, is through sex.

23. Quotations from Keats are taken from *The Poems of John Keats*, ed. H. W. Garrod, Oxford Standard Edition.

24. One might note that one of the few childhood books that Cathy read is *Alice in Wonderland*. When her mother catches her reading it in bed one morning, she admonishes Cathy, "'You're too big for that,'" to which Cathy replies, "'I can get to be *so* little you can't even see me!'" The pattern of inwardness is thereby established early in the novel. One of Steinbeck's very earliest pieces, a satire of life at Stanford called "Adventures in Arcademy," poses a kind of *Alice in Wonderland* landscape of nonsensical activity.

25. John L. Gribben, "Steinbeck's *East of Eden* and Milton's *Paradise Lost*: A Discussion of *Timshel*," in Tetsumaro Hayashi, ed., *Steinbeck's Literary Dimension: A Guide to Comparative Studies*, pp. 94–104.

26. All quotations from *Paradise Lost* are taken from *The Complete Poetical Works of John Milton*, ed. Douglas Bush.

27. Joseph Fontenrose provides a lucid discussion of the grammatical and rhetorical significance of the actual verb form *timshol* in his *John Steinbeck*, pp. 123–24.

28. Marks, *Thematic Design in the Novels of John Steinbeck*, p. 130.

29. Ibid., p. 131.

30. All quotations from T. S. Eliot are taken from *The Complete Poems and Plays: 1909–1950*.

CHAPTER 9

1. Jackson J. Benson, *The True Adventures of John Steinbeck, Writer*, p. 870.

2. Ibid., p. 872.

3. Ibid., p. 873.

4. Ibid., p. 875.

5. The final chapter of Steinbeck's *America and Americans* (New York: Viking Press, 1966) provides an elaboration of what he packed more briefly into the Stevenson letter. Typical sentences from the chapter summarize its direction: "Mankind seems more nearly related to the predators, possessive, acquisitive, fearful, and aggressive"; "The rules were not always obeyed but they were believed in, and breaking them was savagely punished"; "Americans, very many of them, are obsessed with tensions"; "But we are also poisoned with things"; "We have the things and we have not had time to develop a way of thinking about them"; and "Ethics, morals, codes of conduct, are the stern rules which in the past we needed to survive—as individuals, as groups, as nations." In sum one can safely say that the ideas set forth in *Winter* remained steadfast in Steinbeck to his death.

6. Thomas Kiernan, *The Intricate Music: A Biography of John Steinbeck*, p. 308.

7. Warren French, "Steinbeck's Winter Tale," *Modern Fiction Studies* 11 (Spring, 1965): 66–74.

8. Peter Lisca, *John Steinbeck: Nature and Myth*, p. 182.

9. Ibid., p. 183.

10. The technical terms of C. G. Jung have so thoroughly entered the modern vernacular that much of their particular force has been lost. It is important to remember here that Jung defines "the shadow" in moral terms. In *Aion*, vol. 9, part 2, of *The Collected Works*, he writes:

The shadow is a moral problem that challenges the whole ego-personality, for no one can become conscious of the shadow without considerable moral effort. To become conscious of it involves recognizing the dark aspects of the personality as present and real. This act is the essential condition for any kind of self-knowledge, and it therefore, as a rule, meets with considerable resistance. [P. 8]

Without question, the imagery of *The Winter of Our Discontent* and the metaphorical descent of Hawley, which becomes a literal descent, is patterned on the basic premises of Jung's theory of archetypes and the unconscious.

11. In his study of archetypes published just three years (1954)

after *Aion* (1951), Jung describes the meeting with the shadow in water images similar to those we find in *Winter*. In *The Archetypes and the Collective Unconscious*, vol. 9, p. 1 of *The Collected Works*, Jung writes:

The meeting with oneself is, at first, the meeting with one's own shadow. The shadow is a tight passage, a narrow door, whose painful constriction no one is spared who goes down to the deep well. But one must learn to know oneself in order to know who one is. For what comes after the door is, surprisingly enough, a boundless expanse full of unprecedented uncertainty, with apparently no inside and no outside, no above and no below, no here and no there, no mine and no thine, no good and no bad. It is the world of water, where all life floats in suspension. [P. 21]

12. Mircea Eliade, *Myth and Reality*, p. 81.

13. Rowland A. Sherrill, *The Prophetic Melville: Experience, Transcendence, and Tragedy*, p. 225.

CHAPTER 10

1. Jackson J. Benson, *The True Adventures of John Steinbeck, Writer*, p. 1017.

2. Jackson J. Benson, "Through a Political Glass, Darkly: The Example of John Steinbeck," *Studies in American Fiction* 12 (Spring, 1984): 45.

3. Ibid.

4. Although the conception of Steinbeck as Marxist began early in his career, it persisted throughout that career despite his best efforts to dispel it. Jackson Benson details one scene drawn from Steinbeck's papers based on a State Department–sponsored trip to the USSR and East European countries:

Perhaps the true nature of the grudge held against him in his later years by the left was most nakedly revealed at a press conference held in West Berlin in 1963, at the end of a long trip the author had taken behind the Iron Curtain. A questioner, whose stridency and ideological certainty strongly suggested that he was a Party "plant," asked why Steinbeck had turned "from being a Marxist to a Puritan." The crowded auditorium was quiet as the novelist paused for a moment and then mildly replied, "I don't know what you mean. I've never been either." His novels of social reform, he said, "were stories of people, not political treatises."

The quotation is found in ibid., p. 57.

5. Mary McCarthy, "Minority Report," *Nation*, March 11, 1936, p. 327.

6. Benson, "Through a Political Glass, Darkly," p. 51.

Selected Bibliography

THE FOLLOWING bibliography contains works cited or quoted in this book and others directly related to the topics discussed. Primary works by John Steinbeck are listed at the beginning of the book. Unless directly quoted or cited in this book, essays collected in critical anthologies are not listed individually.

Any bibliographic work in Steinbeck studies must begin with Tetsumaro Hayashi's *A New Steinbeck Bibliography: 1929–1971* (Metuchen, N.J.: Scarecrow Press, 1973) and *A New Steinbeck Bibliography: 1971–1981* (Metuchen, N.J.: Scarecrow Press, 1983). Both of these works list other bibliographies and checklists of Steinbeck's primary works and Steinbeck studies.

A second essential resource is the John Steinbeck Society, which produces both a monograph series and the *Steinbeck Quarterly.* A list of available works can be obtained by writing the Steinbeck Society of America, Attention Senior Secretary, English Department, Ball State University, Muncie, Indiana 47306.

A third valuable resource is *A Catalogue of the John Steinbeck Collection at Stanford University,* compiled and concisely annotated by Susan Riggs, available by writing the Stanford University Libraries, Stanford, California   94305.

Finally, since this book focuses largely on Steinbeck's artistic aims, several rather brief works relating to Steinbeck's views but not directly cited here bear mention:

Steinbeck, John. Foreword to Fred Allen. *Much Ado About Me.*
    Boston: Little, Brown, 1956.
————. "In Awe of Words." *Exonian* 224 (March 3, 1954); reprinted in Nathaniel Benchley, Introduction to "John Steinbeck." In George Plimpton, ed. *Writers at Work: The Paris*

Review Interviews, Fourth Series. New York: Viking Press, 1976, pp. 182–83.

————. "John Steinbeck: The Art of Fiction" (interview). *Paris Review* 12 (Fall, 1969): 161–88.

————. Preface to Edith Mirrielees. *Story Writing*. New York: Viking Press, 1962.

Abrams, M. H. *Natural Supernaturalism: Tradition and Revolution in Romantic Literature*. New York: W. W. Norton & Co., 1971.

Aquinas, Thomas. *An Aquinas Reader*. Edited by Mary T. Clark. Garden City, N.Y.: Doubleday and Co., 1972.

Aristotle. *Selections*. Edited by W. D. Ross. New York: Charles Scribner's Sons, 1927.

Astro, Richard. *John Steinbeck and Edward F. Ricketts: The Shaping of a Novelist*. Minneapolis: University of Minnesota Press, 1973.

————. "Steinbeck and Ricketts: Escape or Commitment in the *Sea of Cortez?*" *Western American Literature* 6 (Summer, 1971): 109–22.

————, and Tetsumaro Hayashi, eds. *Steinbeck: The Man and His Work*. Corvallis: Oregon State University Press, 1971.

Benson, Jackson J. "Background of *The Grapes of Wrath*." *Journal of Modern Literature* 5 (April, 1976): 194–216.

————. "John Steinbeck's *Cannery Row*: A Reconsideration." *Western American Literature* 12, no. 1 (May, 1977): 11–40.

————. "Through a Political Glass, Darkly: The Example of John Steinbeck." *Studies in American Fiction* 12 (Spring, 1984): 45–58.

————. *The True Adventures of John Steinbeck, Writer*. New York: Viking Press, 1984.

————, and Anne Loftis. "John Steinbeck and Farm Labor Unionization: The Backgrounds of *In Dubious Battle*. American Literature 52 (May, 1980): 194–223.

Bergson, Henri. "Laughter." In Wylie Sypher, ed. *Comedy*. Garden City, N.Y.: Doubleday & Co., 1956.

Bodkin, Maud. *Archetypal Patterns in Poetry*. London: Oxford University Press, 1934.

Brown, Joyce Compton. "Steinbeck's *The Grapes of Wrath*." *Explicator* 41, no. 4 (Summer, 1983): 49–51.

Browning, Chris. "Grape Symbolism in *The Grapes of Wrath*." *Discourse* 11 (Winter, 1968): 129–40.

Byron, George Gordon, Lord. *Don Juan*. Edited by Leslie A. Marchand. Boston: Houghton Mifflin Co., 1958.

Caldwell, Mary Ellen. "A New Consideration of the Intercalary Chapters in *The Grapes of Wrath*." *Markham Review* 3 (May, 1974): 115–19.

Cannon, Gerard. "The Pauline Apostleship of Tom Joad." *College English* 24 (December, 1962): 222–24.

Carlson, Eric W. "Symbolism in *The Grapes of Wrath*." *College English* 19 (January, 1958): 172–75.

Carpenter, Frederic I. "The Philosophical Joads." *College English* 2 (January, 1941): 315–25.

Cather, Willa. *On Writing*. New York: Alfred A. Knopf, 1953.

Cawelti, John. *The Six-Gun Mystique*. Bowling Green, Ohio: Bowling Green State University Press, 1971.

Champney, Freeman. "John Steinbeck, Californian," *Antioch Review* 7 (Fall, 1947): 345–62; reprinted in E. W. Tedlock, Jr., and C. V. Wicker, eds. *Steinbeck and His Critics: A Record of Twenty-five Years*. Albuquerque: University of New Mexico Press, 1957, pp. 135–51.

Charney, Maurice, ed. *Comedy: New Perspectives*. New York: New York Literary Forum, 1978.

Christensen, Francis. *Notes Toward a New Rhetoric: Nine Essays for Teachers*. New York: Harper & Row, 1978.

Corrigan, Robert W., ed. *Comedy: Meaning and Form*. San Francisco: Chandler Publishing Co., 1965.

Crockett, H. Kelly. "The Bible and *The Grapes of Wrath*." *College English* 24 (December, 1962): 193–98.

Danto, Arthur C. "Naturalism." *The Encyclopedia of Philosophy*. New York: Macmillan Publishing Co., 1967, 5:448–50.

Davis, Robert Con. *Twentieth Century Interpretations: The Grapes of Wrath*. Englewood Cliffs, N.J.: Prentice-Hall, 1982.

Davis, Robert Murray. *Steinbeck: A Collection of Critical Essays*. Englewood Cliffs, N.J.: Prentice-Hall, 1972.

Delgado, James. "The Facts Behind John Steinbeck's 'The Lonesome Vigilante.'" *Steinbeck Quarterly* 16 (Summer–Fall, 1983): 70–79.

DeMott, Robert. "Cathy Ames and Lady Godiva: A Contribution to *East of Eden*'s Background." *Steinbeck Quarterly* 14 (Summer–Fall, 1981): 72–83.

————. "Steinbeck and the Creative Process: First Manifesto to End the Bringdown Against *Sweet Thursday.*" In Richard Astro and Tetsumaro Hayashi, eds. *Steinbeck: The Man and His Work.* Corvallis: Oregon State University Press, 1971, pp. 157–78.

————. "Steinbeck's *To a God Unknown.* In Tetsumaro Hayashi, ed. *A Study Guide to Steinbeck.* Metuchen, N.J.: Scarecrow Press, 1974.

DeVries, Peter. "Interview with Peter DeVries." In Roy Newquist, ed. *Counterpoint.* Chicago: Rand McNally & Co., 1964, pp. 146–54.

Ditsky, John. *Essays on East of Eden.* Steinbeck Monograph Series, no. 9. Muncie, Ind.: Ball State University, Steinbeck Society of America, 1971.

————. "*The Grapes of Wrath:* A Reconsideration." *Southern Humanities Review* 13 (Summer, 1979): 215–20.

————. "Music from a Dark Cave: Organic Form in Steinbeck's Fiction." *Journal of Narrative Technique* 1 (1970): 59–67.

————. "*The Winter of Our Discontent:* Steinbeck's Testament on Naturalism." *Research Studies* 44 (March, 1976): 42–51.

Dougherty, Charles T. "The Christ-Figure in *The Grapes of Wrath.*" *College English* 24 (December, 1962): 224–26.

Drake, Windsor [Tom Collins]. "Bringing in the Sheaves." *Journal of Modern Literature* 5 (April, 1976): 194–216.

Eliade, Mircea. *Myth and Reality.* Translated by Willard Trask. New York: Harper & Row, 1963.

Eliot, T. S. *The Complete Poems and Plays: 1909–1950.* New York: Harcourt, Brace & World, 1952.

Fensch, Thomas. *Steinbeck and Covici: The Story of a Friendship.* Middlebury, Vt.: Paul S. Eriksson, 1979.

Fontenrose, Joseph. *John Steinbeck: An Introduction and Interpretation.* New York: Barnes & Noble, 1963.

Fossey, W. Richard. "The End of the Western Dream: *The Grapes of Wrath* and Oklahoma." *Cimarron Review* 22 (1973): 25–34.

French, Warren. *John Steinbeck*. New York: Twayne Publishers, 1961; rev. ed., 1975.

———. "Steinbeck's Winter Tale." *Modern Fiction Studies* 11 (Spring, 1965): 66–74.

———, ed. *A Companion to* The Grapes of Wrath. New York: Viking Press, 1963.

Fry, Christopher. "Comedy." In Robert W. Corrigan, ed. *Comedy: Meaning and Form*. San Francisco: Chandler Publishing Co., N.J.: 1965, pp. 15–17.

Frye, Northrop. *Anatomy of Criticism*. Princeton, N.J.: Princeton University Press, 1957.

———. "The Argument of Comedy." In Leonard F. Dean, ed. *Shakespeare: Modern Essays in Criticism*. New York: Oxford University Press, 1961, pp. 79–89.

Gannett, Lewis. "Steinbeck's Way of Writing." In *The Portable Steinbeck*. New York: Viking Press, 1946.

Garcia Reloy. "The Rocky Road to Eldorado: The Journey Motif in John Steinbeck's *The Grapes of Wrath*." *Steinbeck Quarterly* 14 (Summer–Fall, 1981): 83–93.

Geismar, Maxwell. *Writers in Crisis: The American Novel Between Two Wars*. Boston: Houghton Mifflin Co., 1942.

Gibbs, Lincoln R. "John Steinbeck: Moralist." *Antioch Review*, June, 1942; reprinted in F. W. Tedlock, Jr., and C. V. Wicker, eds. *Steinbeck and His Critics: A Record of Twenty-Five Years*. Albuquerque: University of New Mexico Press, 1957, pp. 92–103.

Girard, Maureen. "Steinbeck's 'Frightful' Story: The Conception and Evolution of 'The Snake.'" *San Jose Studies* 8, no. 2 (Spring, 1982): 33–40.

Gray, James. *John Steinbeck*. Pamphlets on American Writers, no. 94. Minneapolis: University of Minnesota Press, 1971.

———. "John Steinbeck." In Charles Walcutt, ed. *Seven Novelists in the American Naturalist Tradition*. Minneapolis: University of Minnesota Press, 1974, pp. 205–44.

Gribben, John. "Steinbeck's *East of Eden* and Milton's *Paradise Lost:* A Discussion of *Timshel*." *Steinbeck Quarterly* 5

(Spring, 1972): 35–43; reprinted in Tetsumaro Hayashi, ed. *Steinbeck's Literary Dimension: A Guide to Comparative Studies*. Metuchen, N.J.: Scarecrow Press, 1973, pp. 94–104.

Griffin, Robert J., and William E. Freeman. "Machines and Animals: Pervasive Motifs in *The Grapes of Wrath*." *Journal of English and Germanic Philology* 62 (April, 1963): 569–80.

Hamby, James A. "Steinbeck's Biblical Vision: 'Breakfast' and the Nobel Acceptance Speech." *Western Review* 10 (Spring, 1973): 57–59.

Hayashi, Tetsumaro, ed. *Steinbeck's Literary Dimension: A Guide to Comparative Studies*. Metuchen, N.J.: Scarecrow Press, 1973.

———. *A Study Guide to Steinbeck*. Metuchen, N.J.: Scarecrow Press, 1974.

———. *A Study Guide to Steinbeck (Part II)*. Metuchen, N.J.: Scarecrow Press, 1979.

Hedgpeth, Joel W. "Philosophy on Cannery Row." In *Steinbeck: The Man and His Work*. Edited by Richard Astro and Tetsumaro Hayashi. Corvallis: Oregon State University Press, 1971, pp. 89–129.

Hicks, John and Regina. *Cannery Row: A Pictorial History*. Carmel, Calif.: Creative Books, 1972.

Hunter, J. P. "Steinbeck's Wine of Affirmation in *The Grapes of Wrath*." In Richard E. Langford, ed. *Essays in Modern American Literature*. DeLand, Fla.: Stetson University Press, 1963, pp. 76–89.

Jones, Lawrence W. "Poison in the Cream Puff: The Human Condition in *Cannery Row*." *Steinbeck Quarterly* 7 (Spring, 1974): 35–40.

Jung, Carl. *Aion*. Vol. 9, pt. 2 of *The Collected Works*. London: Routledge & Kegan Paul, 1969.

———. *The Archetypes and the Collective Unconscious*. Vol. 9, pt. 1 of *The Collected Works*. London: Routledge & Kegan Paul, 1969.

Kasparek, Carol A. "*The Winter of Our Discontent*: A Critical Survey." Edited by John Ditsky. *Steinbeck Quarterly* 18 (Winter–Spring, 1985): 20–34.

Keats, John. *The Poems of John Keats*. Edited by H. W. Garrod.

Oxford Standard Edition. London: Oxford University Press, 1956.

Kesey, Ken. *One Flew over the Cuckoo's Nest.* New York: Signet, 1962.

Kiernan, Thomas. *The Intricate Music: A Biography of John Steinbeck.* Boston: Little, Brown and Co., 1979.

Kinney, Arthur F. "The Arthurian Cycle in *Tortilla Flat.*" *Modern Fiction Studies* 11 (Spring, 1965): 11–20.

Klammer, Enno. "*The Grapes of Wrath*—A Modern Exodus Account," *Cresset* 25 (February, 1962): 8–11.

Kline, Meredith. "Divine Kingship and Genesis 6: 1–4." *Westminster Theological Journal* 24 (November, 1961): 187–204.

———. "Oracular Origin of the State." In Gary Tuttle, ed. *Biblical and Near Eastern Studies.* Grand Rapids, Mich.: Wm. B. Eerdmans Publishing Co., 1978, pp. 132–141.

Knox, Maxine, and Mary Rodriguez. *Steinbeck's Street: Cannery Row.* San Rafael, Calif.: Presidio Press, 1980.

Krause, Sidney J. "Steinbeck and Mark Twain." *Steinbeck Quarterly* 6 (Fall, 1973): 104–11.

Krutch, Joseph Wood. "John Steinbeck's Dramatic Tale of Three Generations." *New York Herald Tribune Weekly Book Review,* September 21, 1952, p. 1.

Labric, Rodrique E. "American Naturalism: An Appraisal." *Markham Review* 2 (February, 1971): 88–90.

Langford, Richard E., ed. *Essays in Modern American Literature.* Deland, Fla.: Stetson University Press, 1963.

Lawrence, D. H. *Sex, Literature, and Censorship.* Edited by Harry T. Moore. New York: Viking Press, 1959.

Levant, Howard. "John Steinbeck's *The Red Pony:* A Study in Narrative Technique." *Journal of Narrative Technique* 1 (1971): 77–85.

———. *The Novels of John Steinbeck: A Critical Study.* Columbia: University of Missouri Press, 1974.

———. "*Tortilla Flat:* The Shape of John Steinbeck's Career." *PMLA* 85 (October, 1970): 1087–95.

Lewis, Clifford L. "Jungian Psychology and the Artistic Design of John Steinbeck." *Steinbeck Quarterly* 10 (Summer–Fall, 1977): 89–97.

Lisca, Peter. "*The Grapes of Wrath* as Fiction." *PMLA* 72 (March, 1957): 296–309.

———. *John Steinbeck: Nature and Myth.* New York: Thomas Y. Crowell Co., 1978.

———. *The Wide World of John Steinbeck.* New Brunswick, N.J.: Rutgers University Press, 1958.

Lojek, Helen. "Jim Casy: Politico of the New Jerusalem." *Steinbeck Quarterly* 15 (Winter–Spring, 1982): 30–37.

Lowance, Mason I., Jr. *The Language of Canaan: Metaphor and Symbol in New England from the Puritans to the Transcendentalists.* Cambridge, Mass.: Harvard University Press, 1980.

McCarthy, Kevin M. "Witchcraft and Superstition in *The Winter of Our Discontent.*" *New York Folklore Quarterly* 30 (1974): 197–211.

McCarthy, Mary. "Minority Report." *Nation* (March 11, 1936.): 326–27.

McCarthy, Paul. "House and Shelter as Symbol in *The Grapes of Wrath.*" *South Dakota Review* 5 (1967–68): 48–67.

McDaniel, Barbara. "Alienation in *East of Eden:* The 'Chart of the Soul.'" *Steinbeck Quarterly* 14 (1981): 32–39.

Marcus, Mordecai. "The Lost Dream of Sex and Childbirth in 'The Chrysanthemums.'" *Modern Fiction Studies* 11 (Spring, 1965): 54–58.

Marks, Lester Jay. *Thematic Design in the Novels of John Steinbeck.* The Hague: Mouton, 1971.

Marx, Karl, and Friedrich Engels. *The Communist Manifesto.* Edited by Samuel Beer. New York: Appleton-Century-Crofts, 1955.

May, Charles E. "Myth and Mystery in Steinbeck's 'The Snake': A Jungian View." *Criticism* 15 (Fall, 1973): 322–35.

Millichap, Joseph R. *Steinbeck and Film.* New York: Frederick Ungar, 1983.

Milton, John. *The Complete Poetical Works of John Milton.* Edited by Douglas Bush. Boston: Houghton Mifflin Co., 1965.

Moore, Harry Thornton. *The Novels of John Steinbeck: A First Critical Study.* Chicago: Normandie House, 1939.

Morris, Harry. *"The Pearl:* Realism and Allegory." *English Journal* 52 (October, 1963): 487–95, 505; reprinted in Robert Murray Davis, ed. *Steinbeck: A Collection of Critical Essays.* Englewood Cliffs, N.J.: Prentice-Hall, 1972, pp. 149–62.

Motley, Warren. "From Patriarchy to Matriarchy: Ma Joad's Role in *The Grapes of Wrath." American Literature* 54 (October, 1982): 397–412.

Nagle, John M. "A View of Literature Too Ofter Neglected." *English Journal* 58 (March, 1969): 349–407.

Paton, Alan, and Liston Pope. "The Novelist and Christ." *Saturday Review* 37 (December 4, 1954): 15–16, 56–59.

Pizer, Donald. "John Steinbeck and American Naturalism." *Steinbeck Quarterly* 9 (Winter, 1976): 12–15.

Pollock, Theodore. "On the Ending of *The Grapes of Wrath." Modern Fiction Studies* 4 (Summer, 1958): 177–78.

Reitt, Barbara B. "'I Never Returned as I Went In': Steinbeck's *Travels with Charley." Southwest Review* 66 (Spring, 1981): 186–202.

Reynolds, Joshua. *Discourses on Art.* Indianapolis, Ind.: Bobbs-Merrill Co., 1967.

Ross, Woodburn O. "John Steinbeck: Naturalism's Priest." *College English* 10 (May, 1949): 432–38.

Schorer, Mark. "A Dark and Violent Steinbeck Novel." *New York Times Book Review*, September 21, 1952, p. 1.

Scott, Nathan. "The Bias of Comedy and the Narrow Escape into Faith." In Robert W. Corrigan, ed. *Comedy: Meaning and Form.* San Francisco: Chandler Publishing Co., 1965, pp. 81–115.

Seixas, Antonia. "John Steinbeck and the Non-Teleological Bus." In E. W. Tedlock, Jr., and C. V. Wicker, eds. *Steinbeck and His Critics: A Record of Twenty-five Years.* Albuquerque: University of New Mexico Press, 1957, pp. 275–80.

Sherrill, Rowland A. *The Prophetic Melville: Experience, Transcendence, and Tragedy.* Athens: University of Georgia Press, 1979.

Shockley, Martin S. "Christian Symbolism in *The Grapes of Wrath." College English* 18 (November, 1956): 87–90.

————. "The Reception of *The Grapes of Wrath* in Oklahoma."
      American Literature 15 (January, 1944): 351–61.

Slade, Leonard A., Jr. "The Use of Biblical Allusion in *The Grapes
      of Wrath.*" *CLA Journal* 11 (March, 1968): 241–47.

Steiner, George. *The Death of Tragedy.* New York: Hill and Wang,
      1969.

Stephenson, Robert C. "Farce as Method." *Tulane Drama Re-
      view* 5, no. 2 (1961): 85–93.

Stone, Donal. "Steinbeck, Jung, and *The Winter of Our Discon-
      tent.*" *Steinbeck Quarterly* 11 (Summer–Fall, 1978): 87–96.

Sweet, Charles A., Jr. "Ms Elisa Allen and Steinbeck's 'The Chry-
      santhemums.'" *Modern Fiction Studies* 20 (June, 1974):
      210–14.

Sypher, Wylie. "The Meanings of Comedy." In Wylie Sypher, ed.
      Comedy. Garden City, N.Y.: Doubleday & Co., 1956, pp.
      193–258.

Taylor, W. F. "*The Grapes of Wrath* Reconsidered." *Mississippi
      Quarterly* 12 (Summer, 1959): 136–44.

Tedlock, E. W., Jr., and C. V. Wicker, eds. *Steinbeck and His
      Critics: A Record of Twenty-five Years.* Albuquerque: Uni-
      versity of New Mexico Press, 1957.

Trilling, Lionel. *Sincerity and Authenticity.* Cambridge, Mass.:
      Harvard University Press, 1971.

Tuttle, Gary, ed. *Biblical and Near Eastern Studies.* Grand Rap-
      ids, Mich.: Wm. B. Eerdmans Publishing Co., 1978.

Valjean, Nelson. *John Steinbeck, the Errant Knight: An Intimate
      Biography of His California Years.* San Francisco: Chronicle
      Books, 1975.

Verdier, Douglas L. "Ethan Allen Hawley and the Hanged Man:
      Free Will and Fate in *The Winter of Our Discontent.*" *Stein-
      beck Quarterly* 15 (Winter–Spring, 1982): 44–50.

Watt, F. W. *John Steinbeck.* New York: Grove Press, 1969.

West, Philip J. "Steinbeck's 'The Leader of the People': A Crisis
      in Style." *Western American Literature* 5 (Summer, 1970):
      137–41.

Wilcox, Earl J. "Christian Coloring in Faulkner's *The Old Man.*"
      Christianity and Literature 28 (Winter, 1980): 63–74.

Winston, Mathew. "Black Humor; To Weep with Laughing." In
Maurice Charney, ed. *Comedy: New Perspectives*. New York:
New York Literary Forum, 1978, pp. 31–43.
Zola, Émile. "The Experimental Novel" [1880]. In *The Experimental Novel and Other Studies*. New York: Cassell, 1893.

Index

Abrams, M. H.: 29
Albee, George: 24, 63, 84, 210
Alice in Wonderland (Lewis
    Carroll): 225, 293 n.
Allegory: 189–92, 196–98; *see
    also* symbolism
Allusion: 33–40
Aquinas, Thomas: 193
Archetype: 19, 35, 261, 294 n.;
    see also typology
Aristotle: 139, 179, 241, 271
Augustine: 241

Bergson, Henri: 169
Besko, Bo: 112
Beswick, Katherine: 33, 42,
    48, 280 n.
Bible: The 30, 200, 279 n., 286;
    Steinbeck's literary use of,
    33–40, 272; biblical ana-
    logues in *The Grapes of
    Wrath*, 105–106, 119; in
    East of Eden, 22–23, 224,
    225, 233, 238; in *The Winter
    of Our Discontent*, 259–60;
    books of the Bible: Genesis,
    36, 38, 220–22, 233; Num-
    bers, 106; Deuteronomy,
    105, 106; Job, 200; Eccle-
    siastes, 116, 268; Jeremiah,
    105; Matthew, 196; Revela-
    tion, 105
Biology, marine: *see* marine
    biology
Bodkin, Maud: 35
Byron, George Gordon, Lord:
    57

Cather, Willa: 44
Cawelti, John: 217
Chaucer, Geoffrey: 141
Cinema: 95, 96, 213, 285 n.
Civilization (characters in con-
    tention with): in *Cup of
    Gold*, 50–53; in *Tortilla
    Flat*, 152; in *Cannery Row*,
    158–64, 168; in *Sweet
    Thursday*, 169, in *The Pearl*,
    198–207; in *East of Eden*,
    227–28; in *The Winter of
    Our Discontent*, 257
Collins, Tom: 104, 120–21
Comedy: *see* tragicomedy
Covici, Pascal: 6, 8, 11, 13, 15,
    16, 38, 39, 74, 85, 104, 126,
    135, 211, 213, 214, 249
Cox, Dr. Denton (Steinbeck's
    physician): 32, 268
Crane, Stephen ("The Blue
    Hotel"): 26–27

309

John Steinbeck's Fiction,

designed by Bill Cason, is set in various sizes of Caledonia by G & S Typesetters, printed on 60-pound Glatfelter Smooth Antique B-31 by Cushing-Malloy, Inc., with case binding by John H. Dekker & Sons.